$$\frac{\text{Go}}{\text{for}}$$
$$\text{it!}$$

# Go
## for
## it!

MARTYN LEWIS'S
ESSENTIAL
GUIDE TO
OPPORTUNITIES
FOR YOUNG
PEOPLE

Foreword by
HRH
The Prince of Wales

*Lennard Publishing*
produced in association with
the Prince's Trust, Drive for Youth and
the Institute for Citizenship Studies

**Go**
**for**
**it!**

First published in 1993 by
Lennard Publishing
a division of Lennard Associates Ltd
Mackerye End
Harpenden
Herts AL5 5DR

© Lennard Associates 1993

ISBN 1 85291 110 7

British Library Cataloguing in Publication
Data is available

Cover design by Cooper Wilson
Text design by Forest Publication Services
Index program by Mark Stephenson
Index by Adam Stephenson

Printed and bound in Great Britain by
Butler and Tanner Ltd, Frome and London

**CONTENTS**

For
Sylvie and Katie,
and all other youngsters
in the business of growing up,
and in memory of
Jock Barr,
who devoted his life
to helping young people.

ST. JAMES'S PALACE

For young people in Britain today the most important choices they have to make are those that shape their lives and their careers after they leave school. And those choices are often dependent on the people and organisations they approach for help and information.

Knowing who can offer the best advice – and how to get in touch with them – can be a time-consuming and difficult process for both youngsters and their parents. This comprehensive book offers a much-needed shortcut to the vast range of youth opportunities now available in Britain. The contacts on offer range from new challenges for helping character-building, to academic and other long-term career opportunities. And there is much to interest the disadvantaged and disabled too. With plans to update the book every year, it should become essential reading for Britain's young people – and all who care about them.

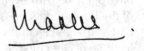

# ACKNOWLEDGEMENT

I am most grateful to the companies and Trusts listed below. Through their generous support a complimentary copy of this book will be distributed to every secondary school, college of further education and university.

The Andrew Mitchell Christian Charitable Trust
The Arrowcroft Group
The Bernard Sunley Charitable Foundation
British Rail
British Telecom
GrandMet Trust
John Laing
Johnson Fry
The Joseph Levy Charitable Foundation
Marks & Spencer
The Needham Cooper Charitable Trust
Next
Northern Foods
The Nour Foundation
The Post Office
Powergen
Reuters

I am also grateful to Burger King and WH Smith who have agreed to display the book prominently in their retail outlets, and to the following who have offerd help in developing public awareness of the book and its message: British Steel, CBI, East Midlands Electricity, Guinness, Hepworth, Institute of Directors, Next, Pizza Express, Reed Employment, Scottish Amicable and Unilever.

# PREFACE

'Is there,' I asked, 'a book that comprehensively and easily offers up a first port of call for all young people wanting to explore the huge range of opportunities available to them as they approach the end of their time at school and move on through their late teens and early twenties?'

'Yes,' came the reply, 'there must be. We'll find it for you!'

They came back days later to admit, rather sheepishly, that they were wrong.

Incredibly, no such book existed.

It does now.

That was late 1990. I had just become Chairman of a small, but innovative, charity called Drive For Youth, whose dedicated team was pioneering a new and highly successful formula for re-motivating the young, long-term unemployed, and leading them on to jobs or further education. Such young people are solidly among those in our society who need help and opportunity most – that vital life-raft which, if delivered properly and effectively, will help not just them, but, in time, society too. I have been a director of Drive for Youth since its formation in 1986, and have never ceased to be amazed at the positive way young people on the cliff-edge of desperation, often on the fringes of drugs and crime, respond when offered the right encouragement. But, of course, the opportunity to respond to the Drive for Youth course was only available to **those who knew it existed**.

It set me wondering how young people from **all** walks of life, and with all kinds of needs, set about homing in on those organisations offering the opportunities and help they needed most. So, where was the book that pulled all this advice, contacts and information together? There wasn't one. Yes, several publications did serve certain groups in special ways, but the United Kingdom as a whole had no single, all-embracing guide to opportunities for young people, no book which was an easily accessible and straightforward 'bible' of opportunity. It was clearly time that we had one, and that this unbelievable omission from the lives of youngsters and their parents and helpers was rectified.

Coincidentally, I went to a meeting around that time with Tom Shebbeare, Director of the Prince's Trust. While waiting for a colleague to join us, I aired my thoughts on what was then called simply 'The Youth Handbook'. Tom's initial reaction – like mine – was incredulity that such a book did not already exist. He rapidly, and generously, offered to fund research, first to establish whether there really was a strong market for the kind of book I had in mind and secondly to carry out the time-consuming chore of tracking down and checking the details of the hundreds of organisations and publications that would have to be pulled together.

Enter Broadcasting Support Services, with a

team led by Tom McAuliffe, whose thorough research not only uncovered an overwhelming demand for the kind of guidebook we had in mind, but carried on to gather, in the most comprehensive way, the welter of material from which the book has been compiled.

So I am deeply grateful to Tom Shebbeare and his deputy at the Prince's Trust, Jock Barr, for their rapid – indeed, splendidly unbureaucratic – response to my idea, and to Tom McAuliffe and the BSS team for their huge, invaluable, contribution to its execution. My deepest thanks go also to the book's many sponsors, recorded on page 8, whose generosity has delivered a copy free to the head of every secondary school in the country and all institutions of further and higher education, and ensured that its distribution in high street shopping places is considerably wider than would be possible through bookshops alone; to Adrian Stephenson and his team at Lennard for so readily seizing the opportunity to publish; to Bernard Donoghue, former Chairman of the British Youth Council, for casting a wise and experienced eye over the text; to careers counsellor Grenville Jenkins for allowing me to use his expert advice on job interview techniques and CVs; to Stephen O'Brien and his colleagues at Business in the Community for opening doors to potential sponsors at the highest level; to Emma Hostler at the Prince's Trust for her help in reaching those sponsors and to HRH The Prince of Wales for his interest, and words of encouragement that form the foreword.

Every effort has been made to keep the price of this book as low as possible to make it more readily accessible to the maximum number of young people. All the royalties are being divided between Drive for Youth, the Prince's Trust and the Institute for Citizenship Studies (newly formed to encourage everyone to become good citizens) – another, more indirect, way in which this book will help young people. And hopefully, it will provide a regular, on-going source of income for those three organisations, for the intention is to make this an annual publication, updating it wherever necessary.

One final word – it is possible in an undertaking of this size, that, despite the strenuous efforts of all involved, one or two organisations may inadvertently have been left out of these pages. If anyone falls into that unhappy position, may I offer my deepest apologies in advance, and assure you that a letter to me – either at the BBC Nine O'Clock News Desk or via the publishers Lennard Associates – will give me the opportunity to correct the omission in next year's edition.

Above all, to all young readers – good hunting! I hope the first signpost to the right opportunity for you is only a few pages away.

Martyn Lewis
London, March 1993

# FINDING YOUR WAY AROUND

This book is designed to give everyone quick and easy access to the particular opportunity – or range of opportunities – they are seeking. It is divided into two main sections.

### Part One: The Categories

This is the section you should turn to first if:
(a) you know the kind of opportunities you are looking for, but don't know the precise name of any organisation(s) involved;
(b) you know the name of one organisation, but would like to know what other opportunities exist in the same area;
(c) you don't have any clear idea of what you're after – but want to explore as briefly as possible the type of opportunities on offer without having to read the whole book.

There are 19 category headings:

**Volunteering**
**Community Projects**
**Working Holidays**
**Summer Vacation**
**Gap Year Challenges**
**Expeditions**
**Adventure Challenges**
**Opportunities Abroad** – a wide variety of activities in other countries including student and cultural exchanges

**Arts and Crafts** – this has three sections covering Music, Drama, and Other Activities

**Sport & Leisure**

**Careers** – this is divided into three sub-sections too:

(1) Business & Industry,

(2) Further Education, Training & Vocational Training,

(3) Higher Education and Universities

**Fund-raising** lists organisations offering financial help of various kinds

**Political** lists simply the names and addresses of the parties represented by MPs at Westminster (no more details, I'm afraid – you'll have to write for their manifestos!)

**Special Needs** deals with organisations whose sole purpose is to help people with physical or learning difficulties (as distinct from many other organisations who deal with a more general clientele, and whose ability to help people with special needs is indicated in their individual entries)

**Extra-Curricular Activities** hoovers up organisations you can join to pursue a particular interest, where the opportunity on offer combines learning with comradeship and a variety of on-going courses tailored to the particular vision and purpose of each organisation (e.g. Scouts, Girl Guides, Junior Astronomical Society)

Each of the 19 categories simply lists each relevant organisation in alphabetical order, along with the page number in Part Two where you will find its more detailed entry. If you have trouble identifying your particular interest with any of these main categories, I suggest you look for an entry in the extensive index at the back of the book.

### Part Two: The Dictionary of Opportunity

This, the main body of the book, will be the first port of call for those who already know the precise name of the organisation they are looking for. It lists by name, in alphabetical order, hundreds of organisations and publications offering advice, opportunity and help of one kind or another. Each of these entries describes briefly the work of the organisation, and lists the appropriate address, telephone and fax number from which you can obtain further details. But to save wasting your time and to avoid unnecessary telephone bills, other important information is also included, where appropriate.

Look first for the **Age Range** to see if you are eligible to apply. The **Numbers Passing Through** each year will give you some idea of the size of the organisation. The size of the **Waiting List** will tell you how much competition there might be for places. The **Costs** – if there are any – will be indicated too. **Regions Serviced** will indicate the area covered by the organisation and where there are **Regional Offices** details are supplied. Instructions on **How to Contact** each organisation should be carefully followed. The **Special Needs Provision** will, in each case, tell you whether enquiries are welcome from people with physical or learning difficulties (in most cases they are), and will give further details if these are available.

### Part Three: What to Go For and How to Apply

This section tells you how to assess your own particular skills through a questionnaire which will also help you discover what sort of activities are best for you. There is useful advice on how to complete a *Curriculum Vitae* (CV) and some examples of letters of application.

### Part Four: Help!

This is a brief section which tells you how to contact the main organisations offering help and advice with a wide range of addictions such as drugs, alcoholism, smoking and gambling. Also listed are the telephone hot-lines that offer information on all kinds of welfare benefits, legal matters, Aids and other medical problems; helping hands for those in debt, those who have left home, those who are homeless, have been raped or been victims of other kinds of crime – or simply need a shoulder to cry on.

Finally, there is an extensive **index**. I suggest you look there for any activities, organisations or publications that you may not have identified in the main category listings in Part One. There is also an order form on the very last page in case you need any more copies of this book.

**Part One**

# THE
# CATEGORIES

# NOTE

All the entries in the pages that follow are based on information from the organisations and companies concerned. Every attempt has been made to ensure that this information is accurate at the time of publication. Prices and costs listed are the latest available but are always subject to change.

# Categories

# Adventure Challenges

# Arts and Crafts – Drama

# Arts and Crafts – Music

# Arts and Crafts – Other

# Careers – Business and Industry

# Careers – Further Education, Training, Vocational Training

# Careers – Higher Education

# Community Projects

# Expeditions

# Extra Curricular Activities

# Fundraising, Sources of Money

# Opportunities Abroad

# Politics

# Special Needs

# Sport and Leisure

# Summer Vacation

# Volunteering

# Working Holidays

# Part Two

# THE DICTIONARY OF OPPORTUNITY

**ADVENTURE HOLIDAYS 1993 (publication)**
Vacation Work Publications
9 Park End Street
Oxford OX1 1HJ
Tel: 0865 241978 Fax: 0865 790885

Book listing 440 organisations offering opportunities to meet the challenge of windsurfing, canoeing, hang-gliding, sailing and climbing, mountaineering, overland expeditions, or more unusual activities from husky sledging in the Arctic to wilderness survival in Sweden, wildlife watching to volunteering on a scientific expedition in Britain or any of 100 countries abroad. The book includes information on types of accommodation, instruction provided, plus prices of the holidays and any other previous experience or equipment needed. Special chapter on young people's holidays.
ISBN 1 85458 083 3. Available through libraries, bookshops (price £5.95), or direct from the above address (price £6.95 inc p&p).

**ADVERTISING ASSOCIATION**
Abford House
15 Wilton Road
London SW1V 1NJ
Tel: 071 828 2771

Advertising is fiercely competitive and largely a young person's profession. Most jobs are in agencies but some companies have their own advertising departments and opportunities also exist in market research, sales, film production etc. Jobs in advertising are roughly split into three main areas – Account Executives, Media Planners and Creative. Account Executives are the main point of contact between clients and the agency. Media planning involves the placing of advertisements in the most effective way. Jobs in the creative department include copywriters and art directors. Contact the Advertising Association for information on careers in advertising.

**AIESEC**
26 Phipp Street
London EC2A 4NR
Tel: 071 739 9847

AIESEC is an organisation which arranges course-related paid work placements for degree level students in business studies. Each year they give 150 UK students the chance to work abroad. The idea is for the individuals to 'make a positive contribution to the participating organisation while gaining an insight into a different business environment and culture'.

### AMERICAN SCANDINAVIAN STUDENT EXCHANGE (ASSE)
PO Box 20
Harwich
Essex CO12 4DQ
Tel: 0225 506347 Fax: 0225 240952

The student exchange scheme exists to give the opportunity to young people to spend a school year abroad (current participating countries: USA, Canada, France, Germany, Iceland, New Zealand) and/or receive into their family a student of a similar age to themselves from abroad. As a participant you would live with a volunteer family and attend the local school. You would become a member of the family and community, experiencing the life of a young citizen of that country. There is a similar scheme enabling students aged 18-25 to spend up to a year studying at a college in the USA, and a scheme for students to spend a year working as an au pair in the USA.

**REGIONAL ADDRESSES:**
Scotland, Northern Ireland, South East, East and North East; PO Box 20 Harwich, Essex CO12 4DQ  Tel: 0225 506347
Fax: 0225 240952
Wales, West and South West contact:
K.M.Wright, ASSE, 4 Cunningham Close, Sketty, Swansea, SA2 8LG
Tel and Fax: 0792 205317

**AGE RANGE:**
16-18 for the North American High School
Year Programme
18-25 for the EurAupair programme and
College USA programme
**NUMBERS PASSING THROUGH:**
60 travelling abroad in 90/91
**HOW TO CONTACT:**
Telephone or letter for general information
and contact with previous participants
**REGIONS SERVICED:**
UK
**SPECIAL NEEDS PROVISION:**
Can't cater for special needs
**COSTS/WAITING LISTS:**
Costs vary depending on destination and
length of stay.  A year at a USA High
School for example will cost £2,710 plus
pocket money.  Most participants are
funded by parents but some have
successfully approached local businesses
and charities for sponsorship.  Apply as
early as possible during the school year
previous to departure and not later than
15th February

**AMNESTY INTERNATIONAL BRITISH
SECTION (AI)**
99 Roseberry Avenue
London EC1R 4RE
Tel: 071 278 6000 Fax: 071 833 1510

Amnesty International is a worldwide human
rights movement independent of any
government, political or religious ideology.
Amnesty campaigns through its membership by
the technique of letter writing. Members write
letters to the heads of governments, justice
ministers or whoever Amnesty thinks is the
appropriate person in authority requesting the
immediate and unconditional release of a
prisoner of conscience, an end to torture or a
halt to an execution. You can join AI as an
individual or as a member of a group affiliating
to Amnesty – there are over 300 youth groups in
the UK campaigning through Amnesty. Two
magazines produced by Amnesty of interest to
young people are *New Release* – the youth
magazine of AI, and *Amnesty Student.*

**REGIONAL ADDRESSES:**
AI Regional Office, St Michael's Studio,
Queen Street, Derby DE1 3DX
Tel: 0332 290852
**AGE RANGE:**
Any
**NUMBERS PASSING THROUGH:**
c 8,000

**HOW TO CONTACT:**
By letter
**REGIONS SERVICED:**
UK
**COSTS/WAITING LISTS:**
Membership costs from £6 upwards
depending on status

---

### ANGLO-AUSTRIAN SOCIETY (AAS)
46 Queen Anne's Gate
London SW1H 9AU
Tel: 071 222 0366 Fax: 071 233 0293

The AAS organises exchange holidays in Austria
for 15-17 year-olds, language courses in Austria
for young people aged 15+, German language
courses in the UK and can arrange reduced rate
air fares to Austria.

**AGE RANGE:**
15+
**NUMBERS PASSING THROUGH:**
4,000 from UK and Austria
**HOW TO CONTACT:**
Telephone, fax or letter for information
**REGIONS SERVICED:**
UK
**SPECIAL NEEDS PROVISION:**
Enquiries welcome
**COSTS/WAITING LISTS:**
Exchanges cost from £210; German courses
in Austria from £500; German courses in UK

from £60. There is a trust fund which can
help people who could not otherwise afford
to participate – details from AAS

### ANIMAL AID
7 Castle Street
Tonbridge
Kent TN9 1BH
Tel: 0732 364546  Fax: 0732 366533

The Animal Aid Youth Group is for young
people aged 11-18 who are concerned about
the plight of animals and who wish to do
something about it. They provide information,
support and campaign ideas on all aspects of
animal rights, including factory farming, animal
experiments, dissection, vegetarianism and the
fur trade and have established a network of
school groups.

**AGE RANGE:**
11-18
**NUMBERS PASSING THROUGH:**
c 4,500
**HOW TO CONTACT:**
Letter or telephone for advice and
information
**REGIONS SERVICED:**
UK and overseas
**SPECIAL NEEDS PROVISION:**
No specific provision, but enquiries welcome
**COSTS/WAITING LISTS:**
Membership of the youth group is £4 per

year. Members receive poster, stickers, badge and bi-monthly newsletter, information and magazine

### ARMY CADET FORCE ASSOCIATION (ACFA)
E Block
Duke of York's Headquarters
London SW3 4RR
Tel: 071 730 9733  Fax: 071 730 8264

A national voluntary youth organisation committed to developing confidence, self-discipline, self-respect and health in 13-18 year-olds, so that they can gain employment and take their place in society as responsible, contributing young citizens. It achieves this through a challenging, structured programme of military, adventurous, sporting and citizenship training under the guidance of youth leaders trained by the Army. It is an operating authority for the Duke of Edinburgh's Award Scheme. Training is recognised for NVQ awards. Although sponsored in part by the Army it is heavily dependent upon public financial support for the non-military side of the training.

**REGIONAL ADDRESSES:**
ACFA Scotland: Army Headquarters Scotland, PO Box 85, Edinburgh EH1 2YX
ACFA Northern Ireland: HQ N. Ireland, BFPO 825
ACFA Wales: c/o Wales TAVRA, Centre

Block, Maindy Barracks, Cardiff, CF4 3YE
Tel: 0222 220251
**AGE RANGE:**
13-18³/4
**NUMBERS PASSING THROUGH:**
40,000
**HOW TO CONTACT:**
By telephone, fax or letter for an information
booklet
**REGIONS SERVICED:**
UK
**SPECIAL NEEDS PROVISION:**
No provision
**COSTS/WAITING LISTS:**
No costs or waiting lists

---

### ARMY CAREERS

Information about careers in the army can be
obtained from the Army Careers Information
Service (ACIS) – check the telephone directory
under 'Army' for your nearest office. If you are
still at school your careers department can
arrange an interview with an Army Schools
Liaison Officer. For information about officer
careers contact – Ministry of Defence, Officer
Entry, DAR 1a, Empress State Building, Lillie
Road, London SW6 1TR. For information about
careers in the Women's Royal Army Corps
(WRAC), contact – Corps Recruiting and Liaison
Officer, WRAC Centre, Queen Elizabeth Park,
Guildford, Surrey GU2 6QH.

## ART AND DESIGN ADMISSIONS REGISTRY
Penn House
9 Broad Street
Hereford HR4 9AP
Tel: 0432 266653

Applications for university and polytechnic Art
and Design courses are processed by the Art
and Design Admissions Registry. They can
provide information about the range of courses
available, who offers them, and what you need
to get on. Write to them for further details.

**AGE RANGE:**
Any
**HOW TO CONTACT:**
Write to above address
**REGIONS SERVICED:**
UK
**COSTS/WAITING LISTS:**
£8 registration fee for EEC students; £15 for
other students

## ARTS COUNCIL
14 Great Peter Street
London SW1P 3NQ
Tel: 071 333 0100  Fax: 071 973 6590

The object of the Arts Council is to develop and
improve the knowledge, understanding and
practise of the arts, and to increase the
accessibility of the arts to the public. It achieves

this through a wide range of schemes which include providing financial support for arts organisations, artists, performers and others, and by offering subsidies to drama, opera and dance companies, orchestras and other arts organisations. The Arts Council is the umbrella organisation for arts in the UK. In the first instance you should contact your Regional Arts Board for information about assistance with your artistic venture – details from Arts Council.

**HOW TO CONTACT:**
Letter
**REGIONS SERVICED:**
UK

## ARTS DEVELOPMENT ASSOCIATION (ADA)
The Arts Centre
Vane Terrace
Darlington
Co. Durham DL3 7AX
Tel: 0325 465930

The ADA supports arts activities at a local level through a range of services including advice and information, training courses, seminars, publications and conferences and publishes a bi-monthly magazine which includes news of youth arts activities.

**AGE RANGE:**
Any

**NUMBERS PASSING THROUGH:**
Approx 500 young people
**HOW TO CONTACT:**
By letter for advice and information
**REGIONS SERVICED:**
UK
**SPECIAL NEEDS PROVISION:**
All events are held in accessible venues (often using signers) and some information is available on tape
**COSTS/WAITING LISTS:**
Details of costs available from ADA

---

**ARTSWORK LTD (Artswork)**
TVS
84 Buckingham Gate
London SW1E 6PD
Tel: 071 976 7199

Artswork is a national charity set up in 1987 to create and promote opportunities in the arts for young people (14-19 year-olds). Artswork links with regional television companies and currently operates in the North and South/South East of England with plans to move into the West Midlands. Artswork supports projects in all artforms from photography, mime, dance, drama, art and fashion to rap or rock. Activities take place in a variety of venues; in schools, colleges, youth centres, arts centres, hospitals, parks, and secure units.

**REGIONAL ADDRESSES:**
Artswork North, Tyne Tees Television, City
Road, Newcastle upon Tyne NE1 2AL
Tel: 091 261 0181 (ext 2317)
Artswork South, Meridian Broadcasting,
Television Centre, Southampton SO9 5HZ
Tel: 0703 2222555
**AGE RANGE:**
14-19
**NUMBERS PASSING THROUGH:**
c 30,000
**HOW TO CONTACT:**
Contact regional offices above
**REGIONS SERVICED:**
Meridian (South/South East), Tyne Tees
(North) – and Central TV (West Midlands)
later in 1993/94
**SPECIAL NEEDS PROVISION:**
The policy of Artswork is to include young
people with special needs, disabilities or
learning difficulties into the mainstream of its
programme and also to initiate special
programmes for these groups
**COSTS/WAITING LISTS:**
Minimal or no cost. Projects happen at
various times throughout the year

**ASSOCIATION FOR JEWISH YOUTH (AJY)**
AJY House
128 East Lane
Wembley
Middlesex HA0 3NL
Tel: 081 908 4747  Fax: 081 904 4323

The AJY mainly services youth leaders and youth workers. However, the AJY can inform young people of the services available to Jewish young people, and try to represent their interests. The AJY may have information about the availability of grants for particular purposes, and have developed an apprenticeship scheme for young people who want to become youth workers.

**REGIONAL ADDRESSES:**
Nicky Alliance Centre, Middleton Road,
Manchester M8 6JY  Tel: 061 740 6168
**AGE RANGE:**
Any
**HOW TO CONTACT:**
Letter or telephone to Head Office
**REGIONS SERVICED:**
Major Jewish communities in England
**SPECIAL NEEDS PROVISION:**
Installing loop system for people with hearing difficulties. Disabled access patchy but improving
**COSTS/WAITING LISTS:**
None

## ASSOCIATION OF BRITISH TRAVEL AGENTS (ABTA)
National Training Board
Waterloo House
11-17 Chertsey Road
Woking
Surrey GU21 5AL
Tel: 0483 727321

ABTA supplies a wide range of information on many careers in travel and tourism, both at home and abroad, what courses to take, training opportunities, ways into the industry and career development. Details of youth training, correspondence courses and other aspects of work in the tourism industry are available on request.

## ASSOCIATION OF COMMONWEALTH UNIVERSITIES (ACU)
John Foster House
36 Gordon Square
London WC1H 0PF
Tel: 071 387 8572 Fax: 071 387 2655

Provides information about Commonwealth universities – where they are; what courses are on offer; what entrance qualifications are needed; what the universities are like, and how to get in.

**REGIONAL ADDRESSES:**
All enquiries to Head Office
**AGE RANGE:**
Any
**NUMBERS PASSING THROUGH:**
c 7,000 enquiries per year
**HOW TO CONTACT:**
Letter, telephone, fax or personal visit to
Publications and Information Division.
Reference library at above address, open to
the public Mon-Fri 9.30am-1pm and 2pm-
5.30pm
**REGIONS SERVICED:**
UK
**SPECIAL NEEDS PROVISION:**
No special provision
**COSTS/WAITING LISTS:**
No cost for information services

## ASSOCIATION OF JEWISH SIXTH-FORMERS (AJ6)
1-2 Endsleigh Street
London WC1 0DS
Tel: 071 388 3776 Fax: 071 383 0390

AJ6 works to prepare Jewish students for religious
and political problems they may face on campus.
It produces the *AJ6 Guide to College Life*, runs
seminars on topics of Jewish interest, takes
school assemblies, runs local meetings and
regularly mails out the group's magazine. AJ6
runs four summer tours to Israel, organises

social events and weekends, and organises a National Conference.

**REGIONAL ADDRESSES:**
Northern Office: Mamlock House, 142 Bury Old Road, Manchester M8 6HE
Tel: 061 740 9490  Fax: 061 740 7407
**AGE RANGE:**
15-18
**NUMBERS PASSING THROUGH:**
c 1,000 members.  c 1,500 use services
**HOW TO CONTACT:**
Telephone to Head Office
**REGIONS SERVICED:**
UK
**SPECIAL NEEDS PROVISION:**
Depending on needs, AJ6 does everything possible to ensure that everyone can participate

---

**ASSOCIATION OF PHOTOGRAPHERS**
9-10 Domingo Street
London EC1Y 0TA
Tel: 071 608 0598

A trade association for freelance photographers working in fashion, advertising and magazine photography.  It runs regular careers talks in London and Manchester.  Contact above for further details (see also the British Institute of Professional Photography).

## ASTRID TRUST
9 Trinity Street
Weymouth DT4 8TW
Tel: 0305 761916  Fax: 0305 761887

The Astrid Trust was founded in 1985 to encourage through challenge and adventure, the highest qualities in youth. As well as two long trans-atlantic voyages, Astrid offers shorter voyages and the opportunity to participate in the Cutty Sark Tall Ships race. Royal Yachting Association and Duke of Edinburgh qualifications can be obtained.

**REGIONAL ADDRESSES:**
Scotland: Alan J. Miller DSC, VRD, Dollerie Lodge, by Crieff, Perthshire, PH7 3NX
**AGE RANGE:**
17-25
**NUMBERS PASSING THROUGH:**
c 180
**HOW TO CONTACT:**
Telephone, letter or fax for brochures and an application form
**REGIONS SERVICED:**
UK and rest of Europe
**SPECIAL NEEDS PROVISION:**
Enquiries welcome and each application is dealt with individually
**COSTS/WAITING LISTS:**
Three month trans-atlantic voyages cost approx £6,000 (including air fare) per head,

and participants are asked to contribute
£3,750 towards the total, through fund-
raising, sponsorship, wages, parents etc.
Additional expenses include insurance and
pocket money. Occasionally the Trust can
arrange an interest-free loan

## AU PAIR AND NANNY'S GUIDE TO WORKING ABROAD (publication)
Vacation Work Publications
9 Park End Street
Oxford OX1 1HJ
Tel: 0865 241978  Fax: 0865 790885

Guide for those who wish to work abroad as
nannies, au pairs and mothers' helps. Topics
include making the decision to go, the training
and experience that are necessary, how to find
a job, preparation, the duties and rewards of the
work, coping with problems and so on. Contains
a directory listing full details of 144 agencies
(including fees charged), and a country by
country guide giving information on visas and
other regulations, health and insurance, and the
advantages and disadvantages of working in 20
different countries from Europe to North
America. Includes some basic advice on how to
make looking after children easier – cooking for
children, first aid and children's ailments,
recommended games etc.
ISBN 1 85458 087 6. Available through libraries,
bookshops (price £8.95), or direct from the
above address (price £9.95 inc p&p).

## AU PAIR IN AMERICA
Department YIH
37 Queens Gate
London SW7 5HR
Tel: 071 581 2730 Fax: 071 589 4469

Au Pair in America provides opportunities for young people aged 18-25 with some childcare experience and able to drive, to spend 12 months living and working with an American host family as an au pair exchange visitor. A 13th month is allowed for independent travel.

**REGIONAL ADDRESSES:**
All contact is through the London office
**AGE RANGE:**
18-25
**NUMBERS PASSING THROUGH:**
c 3,000 participants each year
**HOW TO CONTACT:**
Telephone or fax with name and address for a brochure and application form quoting department code as per address
**REGIONS SERVICED:**
Western Europe
**SPECIAL NEEDS PROVISION:**
All enquiries considered individually
**COSTS/WAITING LISTS:**
Participants must leave a $500 deposit which is refunded on successful completion.
Applications should be made several months in advance

**AUPAIRCARE**
44 Cromwell Road
Hove
Sussex BN3 3ER
Tel: 0273 220261  Fax: 0273 220376

Aupaircare gives young British people, aged 18-25 with some child care experience and able to drive, the opportunity to work as an au pair for a year in the USA with an American family. Aupaircare provides return flights, visas, board and lodging plus $100 per week pocket money as well as the opportunity to experience the American way of life.

**AGE RANGE:**
18-25
**HOW TO CONTACT:**
Telephone, letter or fax for brochure, information sheet and application form
**REGIONS SERVICED:**
UK and Republic of Ireland
**SPECIAL NEEDS PROVISION:**
No provision
**COSTS/WAITING LISTS:**
Prior to departure, applicants must leave a goodwill deposit of $500 which will be refunded upon completion of their 12-month stay in the USA.  Apply 3 months in advance

## AU PAIRS – ITALY
46 The Rise
Sevenoaks
Kent TN13 1RJ
Tel: 0732 451522  Fax: 0732 451522

Au Pairs – Italy places au pairs, mother's helps, nannies and governesses with families in Italy and Sicily. Monthly salaries up to approx £800 with board and lodging provided. The usual length of stay is 6-12 months but summer jobs are available from June until September mainly for 3 months and occasionally for 1-2 months. Italian is not essential, but some experience with children, patience, cheerfulness, adaptability and a willingness to help where needed is essential.

**AGE RANGE:**
18+
**NUMBERS PASSING THROUGH:**
240
**HOW TO CONTACT:**
SAE for information sheet, an application form and recent job list
**REGIONS SERVICED:**
UK
**SPECIAL NEEDS PROVISION:**
No provision
**COSTS/WAITING LISTS:**
There is an optional services charge covering translation into Italian if required, advice

regarding passports, immigration
requirements and travel arrangements,
insurance, addresses of other au pairs in the
area and follow-up service. It is best to apply
1-2 months in advance

## AVRIL DANKWORTH NATIONAL
## CHILDREN'S MUSIC CAMPS (NCMC)
56 Station Road
Long Marston
Tring
Herts HP23 4QS
Tel: 0296 668485

NCMC aims to bring together young people of
all musical ability levels to share their enjoyment
of music in a social environment. There are four
one-week camps under canvas in the July/
August period. The first two are for young
people aged 13 to 17, the others for 8-12 year-
olds. A wide range of musical interests,
experiences and activities is offered including
vocal and instrumental sessions. The only
criterion is a love of music and the timetable is
tailored according to ability and interests.

**AGE RANGE:**
8-17
**NUMBERS PASSING THROUGH:**
Nearly 300 (140 aged 13-17 and 16 helpers
aged 18-22)

**HOW TO CONTACT:**
By telephone, letter or in person
**REGIONS SERVICED:**
UK
**SPECIAL NEEDS PROVISION:**
No provision
**COSTS/WAITING LISTS:**
Course fee for 13-17 year-olds is £150
inclusive of tuition, food, loan of tent etc.
Brochures go out in December for the
following summer; applications must be
made by mid-February. The camps are very
popular and many applications have to be
refused

---

**AYUSA INTERNATIONAL**
44 Cromwell Road
Hove
Sussex BN3 3ER
Tel: 0273 220261 Fax: 0273 220376

AYUSA International offers students between
16 and 18 years old with at least four GCSEs
(grade C or above), the opportunity of studying
at an American High School for an academic
year or semester (6 months). Students live with
an American family during their stay and have
the opportunity of experiencing the American
way of life and culture.

**AGE RANGE:**
16-18

**HOW TO CONTACT:**
Telephone, fax or letter for brochure and
registration form
**REGIONS SERVICED:**
UK and Republic of Ireland
**SPECIAL NEEDS PROVISION:**
No provision
**COSTS/WAITING LISTS:**
Programme fees are approximately £2,500.
Students should apply 6-9 months in advance

---

**BACKPACKERS CLUB**
PO Box 381
Reading
Berkshire RG3 4RL
Tel: 0491 628739
(24-hour telephone service)

The Backpackers Club is an organisation which
supports and promotes backpacking, whether
you are a walker, cyclist, canoeist, or just
interested in this way of life. Membership of the
club offers access to an Overseas Backpacking
Travel Information Service, a Postal Lending
Library, a Farm Pitch Directory, a Long Distance
Path Site and Pitch Directory, the club magazine,
a special Camping Equipment and Personal
Effects Insurance Scheme, the Backpacking
Advisory Service, and the opportunity to take
part in regular backpacking weekends in various
parts of the UK.

**AGE RANGE:**
Any
**HOW TO CONTACT:**
Letter to above address
**REGIONS SERVICED:**
UK/International
**SPECIAL NEEDS PROVISION:**
Enquiries welcome
**COSTS/WAITING LISTS:**
Membership up to 18yrs – £7 per year.
18+ – £12 per year.

## BANKING INFORMATION SERVICE
Careers Department
6th Floor
10 Lombard Street
London EC3V 9AT
Tel: 071 626 9386

The Banking Information Service is the central source of help, advice and information about a career in high street banking. It produces information packages covering the wide variety of careers available including advice about gaining entry, getting employment and subsequent training and career development. It is also worthwhile writing to the banks themselves for information about their own recruitment drives and career opportunities.

**BARCLAYS YOUTH ACTION AWARDS**
(in association with Youth Clubs UK)
11 St Bride Street
London EC4A 4AS
Tel: 071 353 2366  Fax: 071 353 2369

Although individuals cannot apply to the Barclays Youth Action Scheme, it is worth mentioning for the help it can provide. Groups of young people, up to the age of 24, can apply for grants of between £500 and £2000 for projects which benefit their local community. Funds are for 12 months only and projects with short-term targets are therefore favoured. There are awards in each of the following categories:
Promoting health and fitness
Fostering creativity
Coping with change
Helping young people in trouble or at risk
Community participation
International awareness
Integrating people with a disability
Environmental youth work

**AGE RANGE:**
Up to 24
**HOW TO CONTACT:**
All applications must be made on the required form through Youth Clubs UK at the above address. Applicants must be voluntary groups and will be required to supply the name and address of an independent person

in their community, as a referee
**REGIONS SERVICED:**
England, Wales, Scotland and Northern
Ireland
**SPECIAL NEEDS PROVISION:**
Any eligible group can apply
**COSTS/WAITING LISTS:**
None
**CLOSING DATE FOR APPLICATIONS:**
 31st March.  Successful applicants should be
informed about mid-June

---

### BLACK ENVIRONMENT NETWORK (BEN)
26 Bedford Square
London WC1B 3HU
Tel: 071 636 4066  Fax: 071 436 3188

Young people who belong to an ethnic minority
group and want to do an environmental project
can join BEN and receive advice and information
on the environment and apply for grants to carry
out projects, for example, the Ethnic Minorities
Award Scheme (EMAS).  The leader of the
project should wherever possible be from an
ethnic minority as should as some of the
participants of the scheme.

**AGE RANGE:**
Any
**HOW TO CONTACT:**
Letter to Head Office for advice and contacts

**REGIONS SERVICED:**
UK
**SPECIAL NEEDS PROVISION:**
Enquiries welcome
**COSTS/WAITING LISTS:**
The service is free and applications for
funding should ideally be made 3-6 months
in advance

## BOYS' BRIGADE
Felden Lodge
Felden
Hemel Hempstead
Herts HP3 0BL
Tel: 0442 231681  Fax: 0442 235391

The Boys' Brigade offers a wide range of social
and sporting activities. It offers opportunities for
year-round activities, including helping the
elderly or the disabled in the community, or
participating in award schemes, such as the
Duke of Edinburgh's Award, through activities
such as camping, canoeing, life-saving, arts and
crafts.  Camp sites, mountaineering clubs and
outdoor centres throughout the UK provide a
wealth of exciting opportunities.  The Boys'
Brigade is a Christian, uniformed association.

**REGIONAL ADDRESSES:**
Scotland: Carronvale House, Carronvale,
Larbert, Stirlingshire FK5 3LH
Tel: 0324 562008

Northern Ireland: Rathmore House, 126
Glenarm Road, Larne, Co Antrim BT40 1DZ
Tel: 0574 272794
Wales: 80 Woodville Road, Cathays, Cardiff
CF2 4ED  Tel: 0222 232052
**AGE RANGE:**
6-18
**NUMBERS PASSING THROUGH:**
100,000 members
**HOW TO CONTACT:**
By letter or telephone to regional office
**REGIONS SERVICED:**
UK
**SPECIAL NEEDS PROVISION:**
Enquiries welcome
**COSTS/WAITING LISTS:**
Subscriptions vary but average 30p a week.
There is a charge for uniform and for
additional activities such as camping/
expeditions etc.

### BP PORTRAIT AWARD
National Portrait Gallery
St Martin's Place
London WC2H 0HE
Tel: 071 306 0055  Fax: 071 306 0056

The BP Portrait Award is an annual competition
aimed at encouraging young artists to take up
portraiture.  The competition is judged from
original paintings with a first prize of £10,000,
a second prize of £4,000 and third prize of

£2,000. An exhibition of works selected from the entries is held at the National Portrait Gallery and in the past many artists who have had their work shown have gained commissions as a result.

**AGE RANGE:**
18-40
**NUMBERS PASSING THROUGH:**
Over 600 entries in 1991
**HOW TO CONTACT:**
Write or telephone for an application form
**REGIONS SERVICED:**
UK
**SPECIAL NEEDS PROVISION:**
Anyone can enter the competition
**COSTS/WAITING LISTS:**
£5 registration fee
**CLOSING DATE FOR APPLICATIONS:**
Early April

## BRATHAY EXPLORATION GROUP
Brathay Hall
Ambleside
Cumbria LA22 0HP
Tel: 05394 33942

Brathay Exploration Group is a non-profit, voluntary organisation and has been running expeditions, training courses and other events for over 40 years. The group can give you the chance to explore areas of the UK and far-flung places like China and South America in a way which will increase your awareness and understanding of the natural environment and the people and cultures visited. You can become a member of the group without joining an expedition and the benefits include; the opportunity to plan and run your own expedition using the group's expertise, equipment and facilities for a small fee; copies of the group's own magazine; a copy of the annual account of expeditions; the opportunity to stay in the members' hut on the Brathay Estate in the heart of the Lake District; join in a range of members' events including the annual members' reunion at Brathay in October.

**AGE RANGE:**
15-27
**NUMBERS PASSING THROUGH:**
300 members.  100 took part in expeditions/ courses
**HOW TO CONTACT:**
By letter, telephone (24 hours) or in person for information and application form
**REGIONS SERVICED:**
UK
**SPECIAL NEEDS PROVISION:**
No specific provision.  Each application dealt with individually
**COSTS/WAITING LISTS:**
Membership costs £13  and associate membership is £10.  Individual expedition/ course fees vary depending on destination

Direct bursary grants are available to help
with expedition/course fees, as well as advice
on fund-raising

---

**BREAKS FOR YOUNG BANDS (publication)**
Omnibus Press
c/o Book Sales/Music Sales Ltd
8-9 Frith Street
London W1V 5TZ
Tel: 071 434 0066  Fax: 071 439 2848

*Breaks for Young Bands: the step-by-step guide
to success in the music business* is a practical
self-help guide for young hopeful bands wanting
to progress in the music industry.  ISBN 0 711
90978 4.  Price £5.95.  Available from
booksellers, through your local library or direct
from the above address.

---

**BREMEX TRAINING SCHEME (Bremex)**
London Information Centre
18 Westbourne Park Villas
London W2 5EA
Tel: 071 229 9251

Through a range of action-packed training
courses Bremex enables young men and women
to develop their full potential, and to aim for
high standards of achievement.  They offer
opportunities to enjoy and gain competence in
expedition, mountaineering and outdoor pursuit

techniques under tough conditions in the
mountains of the UK. Instruction is given by
experts on courses lasting either three months or
nine months part-time. Absolute beginners are
welcomed, and will be given special help. In
addition there are opportunities to develop
leadership and group management skills, and
members are encouraged to give voluntary
service to the community where their expertise
can be of value. Enquiries welcomed from
anybody prepared to work hard, show
enthusiasm, co-operate positively within a team,
and display stamina.

**AGE RANGE:**
16+
**NUMBERS PASSING THROUGH:**
c 100
**HOW TO CONTACT:**
Telephone or letter to above address for
information and/or leaflets
**REGIONS SERVICED:**
UK
**SPECIAL NEEDS PROVISION:**
Bremex courses make heavy demands on the
physical and mental qualities of members,
but Bremex will endeavour to accommodate
anybody prepared to pull their weight
**COSTS/WAITING LISTS:**
Initial course fees – £36.00 per month if in
work, £26.00 per month if in education, out
of work etc. No waiting lists for enrolment at
present

**BRITISH FEDERATION OF YOUNG CHOIRS
(BFYC)**
37 Frederick Street
Loughborough
Leics LE11 3BH
Tel: 0509 211664  Fax: 0509 233749

The work of the BFYC is concerned with encouraging young people to sing by organising local, regional, national and international choral events for young singers, supporting member choirs with advice, information and grant-aid and encouraging links between young choirs in Britain and their counterparts overseas. They can help you find out about local activities, keep you informed about events in this country and abroad and provide exciting opportunities to sing at large-scale choral events with orchestras and leading conductors.

**AGE RANGE:**
Any
**NUMBERS PASSING THROUGH:**
3,000 directly in 1991 – more indirectly through their teacher or choir leader
**HOW TO CONTACT:**
By telephone or letter to above address (BFYC request that your teacher, youth worker or conductor does the same) for more information including details of local and international choral activities available
**REGIONS SERVICED:**
UK

**SPECIAL NEEDS PROVISION:**
All BYFC events are held in fully accessible
venues
**COSTS/WAITING LISTS:**
Individual membership is £15; Choir – £30.
Participation fees at choral events range from
£5 per choir to £3 per head

---

### BRITISH FILM INSTITUTE (BFI)
21 Stephen Street
London W1P 1PL
Tel: 071 255 1444  Fax: 071 436 7950

The British Film Institute exists to stimulate a
wider public interest in the arts of film, video
and television – all the techniques by which
images are made to move. The BFI Library and
Information Services Department houses the
world's largest collection of information on film
and television. BFI runs The Museum of The
Moving Image (MOMI), and The National Film
Theatre (NFT). Membership of the BFI is open
to anyone over 16, and offers a range of special
offers: free subscription to *Sight and Sound*
magazine; access to BFI Library Reading Room;
reduced rates for *Monthly Film Bulletin*
magazine; free copy of *BFI Film and Television
Handbook*; and concessions on NFT tickets.

**AGE RANGE:**
Any.  16+ for membership
**HOW TO CONTACT:**
Telephone, letter or fax to above address for

general information about BFI
**REGIONS SERVICED:**
UK
**SPECIAL NEEDS PROVISION:**
BFI is working on special needs provision in all areas of its work. Enquiries welcome
**COSTS/WAITING LISTS:**
Annual membership: £15.75. Other types of membership are also available. Contact BFI for more information

---

### BRITISH INSTITUTE OF PROFESSIONAL PHOTOGRAPHY
2 Amwell End
Ware
Hertfordshire SG12 9HN
Tel: 0920 464011

Professional photographers work in one or more specialist field. Regarded by some as the most glamorous of these are fashion, advertising and press photography which are usually the hardest to break into but the majority of professionals work in social photography which includes portraiture (usually in a studio) and weddings etc. There are also opportunities to work in fields such as industrial and commercial, scientific, medical or forensic photography some of which involve using advanced techniques. For more information about a career in photography contact the above address.

## BRITISH RED CROSS YOUTH
British Red Cross National HQ
9 Grosvenor Crescent
London SW1X 7EJ
Tel: 071 235 5454  Fax: 071 235 7447

As a member of the British Red Cross you can receive free training in areas such as first aid, survival skills, health and hygiene, child care or learn the skills needed to care for a sick or handicapped relative at home or to provide service to the local community. Red Cross Youth often work alongside adult members helping with rescue operations, manning first aid posts and looking after disabled youngsters on specially arranged holidays, as well as being involved with fund-raising ventures. There are also opportunities for leadership and development training, various leisure activities and the chance to make new friends through the large Red Cross network.

**REGIONAL ADDRESSES:**
91 regional associations – details from HQ
**AGE RANGE:**
5-25
**NUMBERS PASSING THROUGH:**
c 25,000 members
**HOW TO CONTACT:**
By letter to above address for information and a local contact.  Or check the telephone directory for your nearest branch

**REGIONS SERVICED:**
UK
**SPECIAL NEEDS PROVISION:**
Enquiries welcome
**COSTS/WAITING LISTS:**
Some clubs have a small weekly subscription

---

## BRITISH SCHOOLS EXPLORING SOCIETY (BSES)

c/o Royal Geographical Society
1 Kensington Gore
London SW7 2AR
Tel: 071 584 0710  Fax: 071 581 7995

BSES was founded in 1932 by Commander George Murray Levick, a member of Captain Scott's last expedition and exists to provide an opportunity for self development and self awareness for young people through meeting the challenges of a scientifically based expedition in harsh and hostile environments overseas. The expeditions have been to arctic and sub-arctic regions (eg Greenland, Iceland, Alaska) but the Society is experimenting with warmer climes. Each year expeditions are mounted for 6 weeks during the summer holidays, and 3 or 4 month long 'gap' year expeditions are also undertaken.

**AGE RANGE:**
$16^1/2$ – 20 on 1st July of year of participation
**NUMBERS PASSING THROUGH:**
c 200

**HOW TO CONTACT:**
By letter with SAE for information, leaflets
and application form
**REGIONS SERVICED:**
UK
**SPECIAL NEEDS PROVISION:**
Some provision but limited by the nature of
the expeditions
**COSTS/WAITING LISTS:**
Cost of expeditions varies depending on the
location.  For example in 1992, a 6-week
expedition to Iceland or Greenland cost
approximately £1,800-£2,100, which
covered travel, food, major equipment, share
of sea-freight, briefing weekend in UK,
insurance and administration.  Expedition
cost also gives entitlement to 5-year society
membership.  There are various ways of
raising the money such as business
sponsorship, from Trusts and charities, part-
time working etc.  The Society can help with
advice and information on how to go about
fund-raising

## BRITISH SPORTS ASSOCIATION FOR THE DISABLED (BSAD)
The Mary Glen Haig Suite
34 Osnaburgh Street
London NW1 3ND
Tel: 071 383 7277 Fax: 071 383 7332

BSAD provides opportunities for young people
with disabilities in a vast range of sports at all

levels as well as advice on vacation employment, especially volunteer work, and information for school projects, exams etc.

**REGIONAL ADDRESSES:**
About 15 regional offices – addresses available from Head Office

**AGE RANGE:**
Any (Junior championships in swimming, athletics and basketball for under 18s)

**HOW TO CONTACT:**
Telephone the Regional Development Officer at your local office (address available from above) for advice, information and names of other relevant contacts if required

**REGIONS SERVICED:**
UK

**SPECIAL NEEDS PROVISION:**
BSAD deals mainly with individuals with any type of disability but is willing to provide information and advice etc. to anyone irrespective of ability

**COSTS/WAITING LISTS:**
No costs or waiting lists

## BRITISH TRUST FOR CONSERVATION
## VOLUNTEERS (BTCV)
36 St Mary's Street
Wallingford
Oxon OX10 0EU
Tel: 0491 39766  Fax: 0941 39646

BTCV provides numerous opportunities for young people to become involved with conservation in a practical way.  Nearly 600 conservation working holidays, 'Natural Breaks', are run throughout the year.  These offer the opportunity to meet new people, learn skills such as drystone walling. dune restoration, footpath work and much more.

**REGIONAL ADDRESSES:**
North: Conservation Volunteers Training Centre, Balby Road, Doncaster DN4 0RH
Tel: 0302 859522
West: Conservation Centre, Firsby Road, Quinton, Birmingham B32 2QT
Tel: 021 426 5588
South East: Southwater Country Park, Cripplegate Lane, Southwater, W. Sussex RH13 7UN  Tel: 0403 730572
Wales: Frolic House, Frolic Street, Newtown, Powys, SY16 1AP  Tel: 0686 628600
Northern Ireland: Conservation Office, 137 University Street, Belfast  Tel: 0232 322862
**AGE RANGE:**
16+

**NUMBERS PASSING THROUGH:**
700 under 18
**HOW TO CONTACT:**
Telephone or SAE to Information Officer at
Head Office for local BTCV offices and
conservation groups
**REGIONS SERVICED:**
England, Wales and Northern Ireland. For
Scotland see Scottish Conservation Projects
Trust
**SPECIAL NEEDS PROVISION:**
Projects for young people with learning
disabilities are run by most BTCV area offices
**COSTS/WAITING LISTS:**
Student membership is £6 and is necessary
for participation in working holidays. The
average price of a 'Natural Breaks' is £29 for
one week, inclusive of food and
accommodation. One month advance
booking is recommended

---

### BRITISH UNIVERSITIES NORTH AMERICA
### CLUB (BUNAC)
16 Bowling Green Lane
London EC1R 0BD
Tel: 071 251 3472  Fax: 071 251 0251

BUNAC is a non-profit making organisation
which enables students and young people to
travel and work in America, Canada and
Australia through various programmes. The
largest of these is 'BUNACAMP' which places

people aged 19¹/₂-35 as counsellors on American
children's summer camps to teach a wide variety
of activities from mid June to mid/end August
and allows time to travel for up to six weeks
afterwards.  There are also general work and
travel programmes mainly for students and 'gap-
year' students in America, Canada and Australia.

**REGIONAL ADDRESSES:**
There are voluntary representatives at most
university campuses
**AGE RANGE:**
Programmes are mainly aimed at university
students.  However BUNACAMP is open to
anyone aged 19¹/₂ -35
**NUMBERS PASSING THROUGH:**
9,000
**HOW TO CONTACT:**
Send your name and address on a postcard to
the London address requesting a 'Working
Adventures Abroad' brochure or telephone
with any enquiries
**REGIONS SERVICED:**
UK
**SPECIAL NEEDS PROVISION:**
Enquiries welcome
**COSTS/WAITING LISTS:**
Costs of the schemes vary but all programmes
are designed to be self-financing so
participants can recover the costs of travelling
abroad by working once they arrive

## BRITISH YOUTH COUNCIL (BYC)
57 Chalton Street
London NW1 1HU
Tel: 071 387 7559  Fax: 071 383 3545

The British Youth Council is the umbrella body for people aged 16-25 working to increase the participation of young people at all levels of political and public decision-making. With an affiliated membership of more than six million young people, it represents youth nationally and internationally. BYC's primary aim is to advance the interests and views of young people and to enable young people to play a more active part in decisions that affect your lives. BYC is run by young people. They come together at council meetings to debate and discuss ideas and they elect an executive to carry out policy decisions. All the main voluntary youth organisations are a part of BYC, as are many local youth councils and political youth groups. Membership offers subscription to a bi-monthly *Youth Bulletin*, containing news and information concerning young people, articles by a range of people from politics and the youth service, and information on the activities of BYC. It also offers access to BYC's advice and information service and, above all, it offers the opportunity for you and your group to have a say in the major decisions that affect your lives.

## BRITISH YOUTH OPERA (BYO)
58 Clapham Common Northside
London SW4 9RZ
Tel: 071 738 2725/9351  Fax: 071 924 3725

Every summer BYO provide specialist training opportunities for musicians, conductors, assistant designers/directors, stage crew etc. Under expert professional tuition, they rehearse two operas which are performed in London and on tour.  Young people who apply should already be trained up to a reasonably high standard (especially singers).

**AGE RANGE:**
Singers 22-30, instrumentalists 18-30
**NUMBERS PASSING THROUGH:**
Over 200
**HOW TO CONTACT:**
SAE with covering letter, or telephone for advice, information and leaflets
**REGIONS SERVICED:**
UK
**SPECIAL NEEDS PROVISION:**
Enquiries welcome
**COSTS/WAITING LISTS:**
Training courses are free of charge and students receive subsistence whilst they are on tour.  For rehearsals in London students are expected to pay for their own accommodation/travel/living expenses etc.

## BUSINESS AND TECHNICIAN EDUCATION
## COUNCIL (BTEC)
Central House
Upper Woburn Place
London WC1H 0HH
Tel: 071 413 8400  Fax: 071 387 6068

BTEC offers work-related qualifications delivered by schools, colleges and universities in a wide range of subject areas, including agriculture, business and finance, caring, computing, construction, design, engineering, hotel and catering, leisure and sciences. You may study full-time or part-time. BTEC qualifications are recognised by employers and professional bodies. They also enable students to progress to degree courses. BTEC is working closely with the National Council for Vocational Qualifications (NCVQ) to help develop the national framework of vocational qualifications through NVQs and GNVQs.

**AGE RANGE:**
16+
**NUMBERS PASSING THROUGH:**
There are currently more than 600,000 students working full- or part-time towards BTEC First, National and Higher National qualifications and the new BTEC GNVQs. New registrations in 1992 exceeded 280,000
**HOW TO CONTACT:**
Telephone or letter to BTEC Information Services (address and phone number above)

**REGIONS SERVICED:**
England, Wales and Northern Ireland
**SPECIAL NEEDS PROVISION:**
May be arranged with the college where you
wish to study
**COSTS/WAITING LISTS:**
BTEC information and leaflets are free.
Programmes are usually free to full-time
students under 18. Some full-time students
over 18 have their fees paid by their Local
Education Authorities and receive a grant.
Part-time students may have their fees paid by
their employers. Many courses are over-
subscribed, you will need to apply for a place
as early as possible

---

## BUSINESS IN THE COMMUNITY (BITC)
227A City Road
London EC1V 1LX
Tel: 071 253 3716  Fax: 071 253 2309

BITC is the umbrella organisation for the Local
Enterprise Agency network and can direct young
people to one of 300 agencies around the
country who deal with youth enterprise. BITC
can also advise and assist with the setting up and
development of small businesses.

**REGIONAL ADDRESSES:**
Details from above
**AGE RANGE:**
Any

**HOW TO CONTACT:**
Telephone or letter to the Information Officer
at the above address
**REGIONS SERVICED:**
UK
**SPECIAL NEEDS PROVISION:**
Each case dealt with individually
**COSTS/WAITING LISTS:**
No costs

## CAMBRIDGE OCCUPATIONAL ANALYSTS
The Old Rectory
Sparham
Norwich NR9 5AQ
Tel: 036 288722  Fax: 036 288733

Cambridge Occupational Analysts offer a range
of self-assessment questionnaires for young
people in the 5th and 6th form. The programmes
are geared towards helping you make the best,
and most carefully researched, decisions about
what career to work towards, or what course to
go for in higher or further education.  Should
you go on to do 'A' levels or a BTEC/SCOTVEC?
How about a GNVQ or Access course?  Should
you be looking to further or higher education, or
should you look at in-house training within a
particular career?  The print-outs do not make
decisions for you.  They will not give you easy
answers.  But they will help you make a sound
choice.  The tests aim to match your main
interests, abilities and personal qualities with

the ranges of careers or courses that are available to you. They are available on computer or on paper. Essentially they ask you to respond to a range of questions about whether you like maths, English, sciences, arts etc., whether you can work well under pressure, are a good communicator, a poor motivator, what interests you, what doesn't, what you are good at, what you are not, academic abilities, practical skills and so on to build up a detailed 'personal profile'. Your personal profile is then used to provide you with a detailed summary of your options for careers or courses. It will outline why a particular option might be right for you, and will explain why another preferred option may not be right. You are not bound by the findings of the test – the intention is to provide you with a clear picture of your skills, aptitudes and abilities, and to match and link these to suggested options for your future.

**AGE RANGE:**
5th and 6th form pupils and students at colleges of further education
**HOW TO CONTACT:**
Through careers teachers, Careers Offices or contact the above address
**REGIONS SERVICED:**
UK

## CAMP AMERICA
37a Queen's Gate
London SW7 5HR
Tel: 071 589 3223/4  Fax: 071 581 3258

Camp America is looking for young people to work as Youth Leaders at American children's summer camps. Preferably you will have skills to teach activities such as sports, arts and crafts, drama etc. You don't need to be an expert to apply. Camp America provides free London – New York return flight; pocket money; board and lodging at camp; J1 cultural exchange visa and time for independent travel after your nine-week placement.

**AGE RANGE:**
18-35
**NUMBERS PASSING THROUGH:**
Approx 6,500 placements from 10,500 applications
**HOW TO CONTACT:**
By letter to Dept: ANRZIC for advice, information and application form
**REGIONS SERVICED:**
UK
**SPECIAL NEEDS PROVISION:**
No information available
**COSTS/WAITING LISTS:**
First deposit – £25, second deposit/insurance – £130

## CAMPHILL VILLAGE TRUST
Delrow House
Hillfield Lane
Aldenham
Watford
Herts WD2 8DJ
Tel: 0923 856006  Fax: 0923 858035

The Camphill Village Trust runs eight communities where adults with mental handicaps can achieve richer, more meaningful lives. Young people who would like to assist in the running, upkeep, and development of these communities should contact head office for more information about where the communities are, and what you can do to help.

**REGIONAL ADDRESSES:**
The Trust runs village communities in Aberdeen, North Yorkshire, Hertfordshire, Gloucestershire, West Midlands, Cleveland, and Dumfries.  Full details from head office.
**AGE RANGE:**
Any
**HOW TO CONTACT:**
Letter, telephone to Head Office
**REGIONS SERVICED:**
UK
**SPECIAL NEEDS PROVISION:**
The village communities operate for the benefit of people with special needs
**COSTS/WAITING LISTS:**
None for advice and information

### CAMPING CLUB YOUTH (CCY)
Greenfields House
Westwood Way
Coventry CV4 8JH
Tel: 0203 694995  Fax: 0203 694886

Camping Club Youth aims to help and encourage young people to camp in the correct and safest way through instructional weekends as well as 'Fun and Adventure Weekends' enabling them to pass the CCY test. Each member receives *The Fundamentals of Good Camping* handbook written and published by the club.

**REGIONAL ADDRESSES:**
Contact through Head Office
**AGE RANGE:**
12-21
**NUMBERS PASSING THROUGH:**
2,000 members
**HOW TO CONTACT:**
Telephone, letter or fax to the membership department at HQ for leaflets and an application form
**REGIONS SERVICED:**
UK
**SPECIAL NEEDS PROVISION:**
Each case dealt with individually
**COSTS/WAITING LISTS:**
£3 annual subscription

## CAMPING FOR THE DISABLED (CFD)
20 Burton Close
Telford
Shropshire TF4 2BX
Tel: 0743 761889/0952 507653/
0909 562430

CFD can give advice and information about equipment, camping sites in the UK and abroad with special facilities and other sources of help for individuals and groups.

**AGE RANGE:**
Any
**NUMBERS PASSING THROUGH:**
200
**HOW TO CONTACT:**
Telephone or letter
**REGIONS SERVICED:**
UK
**SPECIAL NEEDS PROVISION:**
Mainly deals with disabled people
**COSTS/WAITING LISTS:**
Subscription is £2 per year for individuals and £5 for a group

## CAMPUS TRAVEL
52 Grosvenor Gardens
London SW1W 0AG
Tel: 071 730 3402 – European enquiries
071 730 8111 – Worldwide enquiries

Campus Travel specialises in student and youth travel worldwide. They can offer students and young people under 26 discount fares on scheduled flights worldwide, low-cost flexible charter flights to popular destinations, and discount rail fares in Europe. They can provide help and advice on a wide range of travel ideas.

**REGIONAL ADDRESSES:**
Outlets Birmingham, Bradford, Brighton, Bristol, Cambridge, Cardiff, Dundee, Edinburgh, Glasgow, Leeds, Liverpool, London, Manchester, Newcastle, Nottingham, Oxford and Sheffield. Contact Head Office for addresses.
**AGE RANGE:**
Under 26
**HOW TO CONTACT:**
Telephone, or in person to nearest branch
**REGIONS SERVICED:**
UK and worldwide
**COSTS/WAITING LISTS:**
No costs for information and advice

## CANAL CAMPS
see WATERWAY RECOVERY GROUP

## CAREER DEVELOPMENT LOANS (CDLs)

Career Development Loans are available throughout Great Britain to help individuals aged 18+ pay for vocational training to improve their job prospects. You can apply for a loan of between £300 and £5,000 to cover up to 80% of fees, plus other course support expenses – whether full-time, part-time or distance learning – lasting between one week and a year. The Employment Department, which runs CDLs, in conjunction with Barclays, the Co-operative and Clydesdale Banks, offer successful applicants a 'repayment holiday': no repayments are required during training and for up to three months afterwards, during which time the Department pays the interest on the loan. It's then up to you to repay the loan, plus any interest.

For further details and an application form call 0800 585 505 free of charge.

## CAREERS, EDUCATION AND TRAINING FOR AGRICULTURE AND THE COUNTRYSIDE (CETAC)
c/o Warwickshire Careers Service
10 Northgate Street
Warwick CV34 4SR

Contact CETAC for advice and information on education, training, voluntary work, careers for people with disabilities, careers in agriculture, horticulture, landscaping, forestry, veterinary work, gamekeeping, fish farming, organic farming, rural crafts, and other land-related industries. A wide range of free literature is available on receipt of a written request sent with a stamped addressed envelope.

## CAREERS OFFICES

Careers Offices have details of local vacancies and training places for younger people. Careers Offices have specialist knowledge about all sorts of jobs, courses and training, as well as knowing the local job market. They also have access to computer-based lists of vacancies. One way they can guide you is by compiling profiles to pinpoint your strengths and weaknesses – you may even find you have a hidden talent! For your nearest Careers Office, look in the telephone directory either under 'Careers Office' or under the local authority; alternatively ask at your local library.

## CAREERS RESEARCH AND ADVISORY CENTRE (CRAC)

Sheraton House
Castle Park
Cambridge CB3 0AX
Tel: 0223 460277  Fax: 0223 311708

CRAC offers 'Insight into Management' courses to 16-19 year-old students and undergraduates.

Students from a range of disciplines and individuals working in a wide variety of different organisations can gain experience of teamwork, analysing problems and decision-making under pressure. You will be encouraged to examine a wide range of career possibilities, discover what it is really like working in different management areas and gain a general understanding of business priorities and the world of work.

CRAC also offers a five-day 'Insight into Management in Europe' course, designed to help you make career decisions as well as acquire some vital business skills. It will bring together students from other EC countries and involve managers from multi-national companies and EC institutions. This course aims to give you an insight into different management careers. In addition the course helps you to relate your own qualifications, strengths and experience to opportunities in a variety of companies and organisations.

CRAC/SERC Graduate Schools are organised to give you a taste of the challenges, issues and problems you will face in a career outside academia. The courses are designed for penultimate and final year PhD students and run by managers from a wide range of jobs and environments.

**AGE RANGE:**
16-19 year-old students, undergraduates, European higher education students, PhD scientists and technologists

**HOW TO CONTACT:**
For information about 'Insight into
Management' courses contact address above.
CRAC mainly provides information through
its publications, not through individual
advice.  For details of the range of careers
books/publications contact: Hobsons
Publishing, Bateman Street, Cambridge CB2
1LZ   Tel: 0223 354551
**REGIONS SERVICED:**
UK and Europe
**SPECIAL NEEDS PROVISION:**
Insight courses cost £35-£75; travel costs only
for Graduate Schools

**CARRY THE CAN (CTC)**
16 Woodrush Close
London SE14 6DJ
Tel: 081 692 0013

A new organisation set up for graffiti artists who
would like to channel their skills for the benefit
of the community around them.  CTC aims to
make spaces available where graffiti artists can
perform and practice their art without causing
danger to themselves or offence to public and/
or property.

**AGE RANGE:**
Any
**HOW TO CONTACT:**
Letter, telephone for further information

**REGIONS SERVICED:**
UK
**SPECIAL NEEDS PROVISION:**
Enquiries welcome

---

## CATHEDRAL CAMPS
Manor House
High Birstwith
Harrogate
HG3 2LG
Tel: 0423 770385

Volunteers do routine maintenance and simple conservation work on cathedrals and Christian buildings of architectural significance, carrying out both routine and sometimes more spectacular tasks under the guidance of craftsmen. Camps take place at different cathedrals between mid July and early September and last for one week with volunteers working approximately 36 hours a week, 8.30am to 5.00pm each day. Food and accommodation are provided and volunteers sleep in the Cathedral hall or similar building. Each camp is run by a leader and two assistant leaders, and volunteers are asked to contribute to the social life of the camp and help with domestic duties on a rota basis. Projects qualify under the Duke of Edinburgh's Award Scheme.

**REGIONAL ADDRESSES:**
Booking Secretary/ Administrator:
Shelley Bent, 16 Glebe Avenue, Flitwick,

Bedfordshire, MK45 1HS
**AGE RANGE:**
16-30
**NUMBERS PASSING THROUGH:**
700
**HOW TO CONTACT:**
By letter to Booking Secretary – at Flitwick
address above – for brochures and bookings
**REGIONS SERVICED:**
UK
**SPECIAL NEEDS PROVISION:**
People with special needs welcome on
camps; bursaries available
**COSTS/WAITING LISTS:**
The Camp fee is £33.  Local Education
Authorities occasionally give grants but this is
rare.  Some bursaries are available from
Cathedral Camps in cases of hardship/
unemployment.  Camps are usually over-
subscribed and you are advised to apply
early.  Brochures for each year are available
in February

---

**CATHOLIC YOUTH SERVICE (CYS)**
39 Fitzjohn's Avenue
London NW3 5JT
Tel: 071 435 3596  Fax: 071 435 3596

CYS exists within the total Youth Service of
England and Wales to provide a distinctive
contribution to the growth and development of
young people based on the principles and

practice of the faith of the Catholic Church. CYS relies heavily on volunteers for support for the work that it does.

**AGE RANGE:**
Any
**HOW TO CONTACT:**
Letter, telephone to above address
**REGIONS SERVICED:**
England and Wales

---

## CENTRAL BUREAU FOR EDUCATIONAL VISITS AND EXCHANGES
Seymour Mews House
Seymour Mews
London W1H 9PE
Tel: 071 486 5101  Fax: 071 935 5741

The Central Bureau is the UK national office responsible for information and advice on all forms of educational visits and exchanges; the development and administration of a wide range of curriculum-related pre-service and in-service exchange programmes; the linking of educational establishments and local education authorities with counterparts abroad; and the organisation of meetings, workshops and conferences related to professional international experience. Its information and advisory services extend throughout the educational field.

**REGIONAL ADDRESSES:**
Scotland: 3 Bruntsfield Crescent, Edinburgh

EH10 4HD  Tel: 031 447 8024
Fax: 031 452 8569.
Northern Ireland: 16 Malone Road, Belfast
BT9 5BN  Tel: 0232 664418
Fax: 0232 661275.

**AGE RANGE:**
No specific age

**HOW TO CONTACT:**
By letter, telephone, fax or in person to your
nearest office for advice, information, leaflets,
reference books etc.

**REGIONS SERVICED:**
UK

**SPECIAL NEEDS PROVISION:**
The service can be used by anyone

**COSTS/WAITING LISTS:**
Costs include registration fees for some
schemes and travel costs depending on the
programme.  Prices of publications vary.
Some funding is available from the
Department of Education and Science, the
Scottish Office Education Department and the
Department of Education for Northern Ireland

---

**CENTRE FOR INFORMATION ON
LANGUAGE TEACHING AND RESEARCH
(CILT)**
Regent's College
Inner Circle
Regent's Park
London NW1 4NS
Tel: 071 486 8221  Fax: 071 224 3518

Careers in languages cover specialist fields such as interpreting, translating and teaching. A wide range of career opportunities also exists in international trade, banking, business, the Civil Service, local government, information and library work, insurance, work in international organisations, journalism, the media, secretarial work, tourism and other areas, both for language specialists and for those with a language linked to the career of their choice. The range of languages in demand is ever-increasing, and includes European languages., Chinese and Japanese, the languages of South America (Spanish and Brazilian Portuguese), Arabic, and Community Languages such as Urdu. There is a variety of information available on careers. Some of this may be held in school and college libraries and at local Careers Offices and public libraries. Most booklets are inexpensive and easily obtainable. CILT does not provide an advisory service on careers with languages, but publishes some relevant titles. For details of the titles available contact the above address.

---

**CHALLENGE TO YOUTH**
BP Oil UK Ltd
Community and Educational Affairs
Department
BP House
Breakspear Way
Hemel Hempstead
Herts HP2 4UL
Tel: 0442 225446  Fax: 0442 225919

The BP Challenge to Youth programme comprises a number of schemes and competitions which give you and your friends the opportunity to work as a team to come up with designs and to build practical objects to the benefit of the community or the environment. The purpose of the Challenges is 'to bridge the gap between the theory of the classroom and the practicality of the adult world'. Cash prizes are awarded to teams for working well as a team, for innovation and for the success of their designs. Current challenges include the 'Buildacar' competition which has proved such a success that it now takes place every two years. Other projects have involved using technology to solve the problems faced by the elderly in their homes, or to design and produce aids for the disabled. Starter packs, advice and other needs are provided throughout the duration of all projects. 'Challenges' change from year to year but they always involve design, technology, making decisions, achieving results and teamwork.

**AGE RANGE:**
5-19
**HOW TO CONTACT:**
Write to above address, through your school or youth group, for information and entry forms
**REGIONS SERVICED:**
UK
**COSTS/WAITING LISTS:**

Write to above address, through your school
or youth group, for details of current
competitions

## CHARTERED ASSOCIATION OF CERTIFIED
## ACCOUNTANTS (ACCA)
England, Wales and Northern Ireland:
Student Services Department
29 Lincoln's Inn Fields
London WC2A 3EE.
Tel: 071 242 6855.

Certified accountants may work in any of the
three main fields of accountancy – public
practice (accounting firms offering a range of
accounting services), industry and commerce
or the public sector (local or central government,
or in publicly owned industries). Contact above
for careers and courses information and advice.

## CHARTERED INSTITUTE OF MARKETING
Education Department
Moor Hall
Cookham
Maidenhead
Berks SL6 9QH

Marketing covers a wide range of occupations
such as market research, communications, sales,
brand management, distribution, product
development, sales promotion to name but a
few. The Chartered Institute of Marketing offers

professional courses, i.e. the Certificate in Marketing, Certificate in Sales Mangement, and the Diploma in Marketing, leading to membership of the Institute.

### CHARTERED INSURANCE INSTITUTE (CII)
Careers Department
7th Floor
Aldermary House
10-15 Queen Street
London EC4N 1TX
Tel: 071 248 3925

A wide range of professional, administrative and clerical careers are available in insurance – as underwriter, broker, salesperson, claims official, clerk, surveyor and loss adjuster. For more information about starting out in or developing your career in insurance contact the CII. They produce a range of factsheets, leaflets and booklets covering all aspects of the insurance industry – entry requirements, courses and training opportunities, career development etc. – and will also deal with telephone enquiries. For details of your nearest branch contact the above address.

**REGIONAL ADDRESSES:**
Scotland: 2 Woodside Place, Glasgow G3 7QF  Tel: 041 331 1046

## CHURCH OF ENGLAND YOUTH SERVICES
Board of Education
Church House
Great Smith Street
London SW1P 3NZ
Tel: 071 222 9011  Fax: 071 799 2714

Church of England Youth Services addresses the spiritual, educational and social needs of young people irrespective of their religious affiliation or organisational membership. The Church's youth work is delivered mainly through volunteer youth workers. Support, advice consultancy and training is offered through the network of Diocesan Youth Officers of whom there are approximately 60 in 43 dioceses. Diocesan Youth Workers can provide information about youth groups and events and activities around the country. In addition to the Diocesan Youth network, training opportunities and resource production are provided by the four main Church of England agencies:

Church Youth Fellowship Association (CYFA)
Church Lads and Church Girls Brigade (CLCGB)
Girls Friendly Society (GFS)
Anglican Youth People's Association (AYPA)
The National Youth Officers at the above address can put you in touch with Diocesan Youth Officers and/or any of the agencies.

## CHURCH ORGAN SCHOOL
Scottish Amateur Music Association
7 Randolph Crescent
Edinburgh EH3 7TH
Tel: 0738 71574

Young organists are invited to apply for the 1993 course which will be held at St Salvator's Hall, St Andrews from 2-6 August. No standard of playing is required.

**AGE RANGE:**
Any

**NUMBERS PASSING THROUGH:**
30

**HOW TO CONTACT:**
By telephone or letter for further information

**REGIONS SERVICED:**
UK but mainly Scotland

**SPECIAL NEEDS PROVISION:**
Special tuition at an advanced level available

**COSTS/WAITING LISTS:**
There is a course fee of £205 which includes tuition, accommodation and the services of professional musicians. Some local authority grants may be available. Waiting lists can be up to six months preceeding the next year's course

## CITIES IN SCHOOLS (CiS)
60/61 Trafalgar Square
London WC2N 5DS
Tel: 071 839 2899  Fax: 071 839 6186

If you have been turned off school you can get some education and develop other skills by joining a CiS project. We also aim to help you build confidence and improve your image of yourself. If you are interested in volunteering to help other young people in a local project you might be eligible for free training.

**REGIONAL ADDRESSES:**
CiS – Tower Hamlets: 91 Brick Lane, London E1 6QN  Tel: 071 247 9489
CiS – Gwent: c/o K Block, British Steel, Strip Products, Llanwern Works, Newport, Gwent NP9 0XN  Tel: 0633 290011 (ext 4441)

**AGE RANGE:**
Varies according to the project

**NUMBERS PASSING THROUGH:**
CiS projects are generally small, with larger vacation programmes.  More than 300 people have been involved so far

**HOW TO CONTACT:**
Referrals normally come from school teachers and youth agencies but it is possible for young people to refer themselves onto a CiS project.  Contact numbers are above

**COSTS/WAITING LISTS:**
No costs.  There are waiting lists in local CiS areas.  If there are places you will be invited to join a project

**CITY AND GUILDS (C&G)**
326 City Road
London EC1V 2PT
Tel: 071 728 2468  Fax: 071 753 5280

City and Guilds of London Institute, to give it it's full name, does not run courses itself.  The courses are offered in approved centres, such as colleges of further education, training centres, by companies etc. Most C&G courses run on a part-time day-release basis, but full-time and evening courses are also available.  In general, there are no specified lengths of study nor minimum age or educational requirements for candidates. Courses are available in subjects as diverse as gamekeeping, floristry and tree surgery through to electrical and electronic engineering, and computer-aided draughting and design. You may take C&G courses in photography, fashion, languages, furniture craft, animal care, or in any one of hundreds of subjects offered. You might take a City and Guilds as you gain experience at work, and as part of learning your job and developing a career, or you might take one in the hope of gaining employment in the future.  Holders of C&G Certificates have evidence that they have achieved a nationally recognised standard – a bonus when meeting new employers.  City and Guilds Certificates can also help towards gaining National Vocational Qualifications (NVQs) – see separate entry. Most C&G examinations and tests which are available in the UK are also available to candidates in about 70 countries around the world. For information about examinations available world-wide, contact Division 25, City and Guilds of London Institute, 46 Brittania Street, London WC1X 9RG. For information about C&G courses in your local area contact your nearest college of further education, your Local Education Authority or Careers Office. For a free City and Guilds 'List of Publications' or 'List of Subjects' write to Sales Section, City and Guilds of London Institute, 76 Portland Place, London W1N 4AA.

**AGE RANGE:**
14+
**NUMBERS PASSING THROUGH:**
1.3 million entrants for C&G awards every year
**HOW TO CONTACT:**
Letter, telephone, fax
**REGIONS SERVICED:**
UK

---

**CITY TECHNOLOGY COLLEGES (CTCs)**
The CTC Trust
15 Young Street
London W8 5EH
Tel: 071 376 2511  Fax: 071 938 1961

City Technology Colleges (CTCs) are sponsored by industry and maintain close links with local employers. They are secondary schools, normally catering for 11-18 year-olds, but they are particularly geared to helping young people continue their education by offering a variety of subjects at a variety of levels in preparation for the world of work. They offer a wide variety of course options at 16+ including 'A' and 'AS' levels, International Baccalaureate, BTEC National and First Diplomas, and other vocational certificates such as City and Guilds, Institute of Linguists, RSA and National Vocational Qualifications.

**REGIONAL ADDRESSES:**
CTCs are presently open, or preparing to open in London (5), Derby, Corby, Nottingham, Birmingham, Telford, Dartford, Bristol, Middlesborough, Bradford and Gateshead. There are plans for CTCs to be set up in Preston and Lincoln.

**AGE RANGE:**
11-18 usually

**NUMBERS PASSING THROUGH:**
c 8,000 in 1991

**HOW TO CONTACT:**
Letter, telephone, fax to CTC Trust for details of your local CTC

**REGIONS SERVICED:**
See above

## CIVIL SERVICE COMMISSION
Alencon Link
Basingstoke
Hampshire RG21 1JB
Tel: 0256 846560

The Civil Service comprises over 60 departments and their executive agencies and is one of Britain's largest employers with opportunities in a very wide range of occupations. There are opportunities for administrators (both in the UK and Europe), scientists, engineers and other professionals such as accountants, diplomatic service officers, tax inspectors, actuaries, economists, customs officers, government communication trainees, health and safety inspectors, press and publicity specialists, prison service staff, psychologists, legal trainees, museum and gallery curators, factory and agricultural inspectors, librarians, immigration officers, IT specialists, research officers, linguists and statisticians.

The entry level is dependent upon a combination of qualifications, age and experience. Vacancies will be advertised in jobcentres and via other media such as national, local and specialist press and to careers services, as appropriate. For more information on the work and opportunities available in individual government departments and agencies, please see your careers service.

**COMETT
(Community Action Programme for
Education and Training in Technology)**
COMETT Liaison Office
Room IF.14
Department for Education
Sanctuary Buildings, Great Smith Street
London SW1P 3BT
Tel: 071 925 5254  Fax: 071 925 5379

The objectives of the EC COMETT Programme
are to stimulate and develop co-operation
between higher ecducation institutions and
industry in the field of education and training for
technology. Initiatives include financial support
for work placement of undergraduate and
postgraduate students to industrial enterprises
in other EC or EFTA countries for periods ranging
from 3-12 months.

**REGIONAL ADDRESSES:**
Details available from above
**AGE RANGE:**
No strict limits other than normal university
age range
**NUMBERS PASSING THROUGH:**
c 1,000
**HOW TO CONTACT:**
Telephone for advice and an information
pack on the programme.  Students must be
registered with a UK university and
undertaking a technology-related degree
course

**REGIONS SERVICED:**
UK
**COSTS/WAITING LISTS:**
Applications are only accepted once a year so there could be a long wait between initial contact and receiving any grant

## COMMISSION OF THE EUROPEAN COMMUNITIES

The Commission of the European Communities can give information on all aspects of what it means to live in a Member State of the EC. They produce a range of literature – including information about the right to work in Member States, Young People and Europe, Disabled People in the Community, mutual recognition of Diplomas and other Professional qualifications, freedom of movement, and education and training initiatives and opportunities.

**REGIONAL ADDRESSES:**
England: 8 Storey's Gate, London SW1P 3AT
Tel: 071 973 1992
Scotland: 9 Alva Street, Edinburgh EH2 4PH
Tel: 031 225 2058
Wales: 4 Cathedral Street, Cardiff CF1 1SG
Tel: 0222 395489
Northern Ireland: 9/15 Bedford Street, Belfast BT2 7EG  Tel: 0232 240708

## COMMITTEE OF SCOTTISH CLEARING BANKERS
19 Rutland Square
Edinburgh EH1 2DD
Tel: 031 229 1326

Can provide advice and information on all aspects of careers in high street banking in Scotland, from gaining entry to getting employment and developing your career.

## COMMONWEALTH YOUTH EXCHANGE COUNCIL (CYEC)
7 Lion Yard
Tremadoc Road
London SW4 7NQ
Tel: 071 498 6151  Fax: 071 720 5403

CYEC can assist, through advice, information, publications and grant aid, the planning and financing of a youth exchange link between your group and partner groups overseas. Commonwealth Youth Exchange projects are a challenging and exciting way of sharing and learning about young people in the 50 member countries of the Commonwealth.

**AGE RANGE:**
16-25
**NUMBERS PASSING THROUGH:**
In 1991 CYEC gave financial support to 1,040 young people from 82 groups and advice and information to many more

**HOW TO CONTACT:**
Letter or telephone. Open to contact by
either young people or youth organisations
**REGIONS SERVICED:**
UK
**SPECIAL NEEDS PROVISION:**
CYEC are open to all and they encourage
participation of special needs groups in
exchanges
**COSTS/WAITING LISTS:**
CYEC do not charge for services. Grants
cover 20-25% of the total cost of an
exchange. The remaining costs are raised by
the individual group by sponsorship, fund-
raising etc. Applications for financial support
should be made about 12 months before the
project takes place

---

**COMMUNITY CIRCUS**
14 Gotham Street
Leicester LE2 0NA
Tel: 0533 854059  Fax: 0533 544248

Community Circus is essentially a travelling
circus school working mainly in inner cities
offering training in street theatre skills and
workshops in circus skills, clowning, face
painting, stilt walking, juggling and much more.
The main difference compared to traditional
circus is that the skills learned are for personal
confidence, shared pleasure and shared events.

**AGE RANGE:**
Any
**NUMBERS PASSING THROUGH:**
c 6,000
**HOW TO CONTACT:**
By telephone for further information, as well
as contacts with courses run by Fool Time –
Britain's only circus school (see separate
entry)
**REGIONS SERVICED:**
UK
**SPECIAL NEEDS PROVISION:**
Workshops dealing specifically with special
needs
**COSTS/WAITING LISTS:**
Individual organisations usually pay for
workshops

---

**COMMUNITY LINKS**
Canning Town Public Hall
105 Barking Road
London E16 4HQ
Tel: 071 473 2270  Fax: 071 473 6671

Community Links is a multi-purpose social action
centre based in East London. which encourages
and enables goups and individuals to understand
and tackle their own problems. Their Children's
and Youth Work Programme includes a huge
variety of activities – some specifically targeting
young people with special needs, but all open
to everyone.  Young people are involved in

running all that is done by Community Links and the organisation is entirely dependent upon the active involvement of more than 300 trained volunteers. The 1993 activity programme will include 120 holiday playschemes, 56 camping holidays, 16 regular after-school clubs (6 providing full care), 10 weekly groups working with 120 young people at risk of going into care, 12 children's Fun Days attracting over 60,000 children, information and advice services for over 750 young people, 16 weekly youth groups and an extensive range of seasonal activities. Community Links is constantly seeking new volunteers and participants.

**AGE RANGE:**
No limits
**NUMBERS PASSING THROUGH:**
7,000+ per year
**HOW TO CONTACT:**
Write to the above address

---

**COMMUNITY SERVICE VOLUNTEERS (CSV)**
237 Pentonville Road
London N1 9NJ
Tel: 071 278 6601  Fax: 071 837 9621

Community Service Volunteers invites all young people to experience the challenge, excitement and reward of helping people in need. Every year 2,500 volunteers work throughout the UK with elderly people, adults with disabilities, children who are handicapped, in care or in trouble, and homeless people. Volunteers work hard, have fun, and gain valuable experience. Volunteers work away from home, full time, from four to twelve months. In return you will receive full board, lodging, and a weekly allowance. Applications are welcome throughout the year, and no previous experience or qualifications are needed.

**AGE RANGE:**
16-35
**NUMBERS PASSING THROUGH:**
2,500 each year
**HOW TO CONTACT:**
By phone or letter to address above
**REGIONS SERVICED:**
UK
**COSTS/WAITING LISTS:**
No costs involved for information or to take up placements. Usually takes six to eight weeks to place volunteers after application

---

**COMPUTER PALS ACROSS THE WORLD
(CPAW)**
c/o Swinnerton Middle School
Nuneaton
Warwickshire
Tel: 0203 382 961

CPAW is a worldwide organisation which promotes links and friendships between individuals of all nations by using the latest technology to put you in touch.

---

**CONCORDIA (YSV) LTD**
8 Brunswick Place
Hove BN3 1ET
Tel: 0273 772086  Fax: 0273 27284

Concordia offers volunteering opportunities in Europe on short term community or environmental work projects involving young people from other countries.

**AGE RANGE:**
18-30
**NUMBERS PASSING THROUGH:**
250
**HOW TO CONTACT:**
Telephone or letter for leaflets and information
**REGIONS SERVICED:**
UK
**SPECIAL NEEDS PROVISION:**
No provision
**COSTS/WAITING LISTS:**
Enrolment fees are £16-£35, depending on the country involved.  Volunteers are expected to pay their own travel costs.
Contact in spring when project details become available

**CONSERVATION VOLUNTEERS –
NORTHERN IRELAND (CVNI)**
The Pavilion
Cherryvale Playing Fields
Ravenhill Road
Belfast BT6 0BZ
Tel: 0232 645169

An opportunity to be involved in practical conservation and do something that makes a difference such as tree-planting, creating habitats for wildlife, helping to save wildlife in rural areas etc., by taking part in a working holiday or weekend break with CVNI. There are also training courses available and you can become a member of CVNI either through school or as an individual.

**AGE RANGE:**
Any
**NUMBERS PASSING THROUGH:**
c 350
**HOW TO CONTACT:**
Contact individual area offices (addresses available from main office) by SAE preferably or by telephone
**REGIONS SERVICED:**
UK
**SPECIAL NEEDS PROVISION:**
Access to certain sites
**COSTS/WAITING LISTS:**
Annual membership is £10. No charge for any volunteering work

**CONSERVATIVE PARTY**
32 Smith Square
London SW1P 3HH
Tel: 071 222 9000

**CONSTRUCTION INDUSTRY TRAINING
BOARD (CITB)**
Careers Advisory Service
Bircham Newton
King's Lynn
Norfolk PE31 6RH
Tel: 0553 776677

The CITB can give advice and information on all
aspects of the construction industry from
traditional trades used in house building and
renovation such as bricklaying, scaffolding,
plumbing, roofing, joinery, painting and
decorating and plastering to the skills required
on large construction projects.

**CONTEMPORARY ART SOCIETY (CAS)**
20 John Islip Street
London SW1P 4LL
Tel: 071 821 5323  Fax: 071 834 0228

Membership society which promotes
contemporary art and helps acquire work by
living artists for gift to public galleries.

## CONTINENTAL CONNECTIONS
Cranford
Church End
Albury
Near Ware,
Herts SG11 2JG
Tel: 0279 771541  Fax: 0279 755778

Continental Connections is an organisation which arranges holiday exchanges between young people aged 13 to 18 who wish to improve their language ability in French, German or Spanish.  Young people are matched with others of similar age and interests for a period of up to two weeks in each country.  The agency can also send young people as paying guests to families with or without tuition during their stay.

**AGE RANGE:**
13-18
**NUMBERS PASSING THROUGH:**
c 100
**HOW TO CONTACT:**
Telephone, SAE or fax for further information
**REGIONS SERVICED:**
UK
**SPECIAL NEEDS PROVISION:**
No specific provision
**COSTS/WAITING LISTS:**
The agency fee for 1992 was £100 which included telephone and postage costs and the introduction to the foreign family.  Contact

from September onwards for the following year. There are no waiting lists as such but early contact is advised to leave time for the right family to be found.

## CO-OP YOUNG PEOPLE'S FILM AND VIDEO FESTIVAL
Member Relations Department
Co-operative Retail Services Ltd
29 Dantzic Street
Manchester M4 4BA
Tel: 061 832 8152  Fax: 061 832 7355

Entries for the film and video festival are invited from schools, colleges, youth groups etc. The emphasis is on groups of young people working together to produce an entry. The festival is held each year with national screenings taking place alternately at the National Film Theatre in London and the National Museum of Film, Photography and Television in Bradford.

**AGE RANGE:**
Up to 21 (flexible if some members of the group are over 21)
**HOW TO CONTACT:**
Telephone or letter to above address
**REGIONS SERVICED:**
UK
**COSTS/WAITING LISTS:**
None

**COOPERATION PROJECT**
PO Box 28183
Washington
DC 20038-8183
USA
Tel: 010 202 857 8037
Fax: 010 202 861 0621

The Cooperation Project is the joint work of non-governmental organisations dedicated to promoting multicultural perspectives on ecological and social issues. The three branches of the project, in Russia, Japan and the USA collaborate in organising international citizen exchange programmes, including voluntary service work camps and nature expeditions, language exchange programmes and educational tours. The purpose of these exchanges is to introduce people from a wide variety of countries to the host country and its people, as well as to the positive and negative aspects of its social and economic systems, particularly their effects on ecology and human life.

**AGE RANGE:**
18+
**NUMBERS PASSING THROUGH:**
150
**HOW TO CONTACT:**
The best contact address for Great Britain is in Holland : The Cooperation Project,

Foundation for Ecological Cooperation,
Postbus 13844, 2501 EV Den Haag, The
Netherlands. The main office in the west is
the Washington address above and you can
write to either for further information

**REGIONS SERVICED:**
Worldwide

**SPECIAL NEEDS PROVISION:**
No specific provision, but individuals are
encouraged to contact the project to see what
can be arranged

**COSTS/WAITING LISTS:**
Participants are responsible for their own
travel costs and there are participation and
membership fees – contact The Cooperation
Project for full details. Some help is available
for those unable to pay the full fees but funds
are currently quite limited

---

## CO-OPERATIVE DEVELOPMENT AGENCIES

Co-operative Development Agencies can offer
free help and advice on setting up in business as
a co-operative covering all stages of development
from an initial idea through to viability testing,
raising capital and business planning. Details of
local offices are listed in the yellow pages under
'Local or Business Enterprise Agencies', or
contact the Industrial Common Ownership
Movement (see separate entry) who can advise
you of your nearest agency.

## COUNCIL FOR BRITISH ARCHAEOLOGY (CBA)
112 Kennington Road
London SE11 6RE
Tel: 071 582 0494

The CBA is a registered charity dedicated to advancing the study and practice of archaeology and can provide information and advice on where to study and careers in archaeology. They also produce relevant publications e.g. *A Job in Archaeology* (careers booklet) and *Guide to University Courses in Archaeology*. Many county, regional and local archaeological societies are affiliated to the CBA – contact the CBA at the above address for further details.

## COUNCIL FOR ENVIRONMENTAL EDUCATION (CEE)
University of Reading
London Road
Reading RG1 5AQ
Tel: 0734 756061   Fax: 0734 756264

The CEE acts as a national focus, in England, Wales and Northern Ireland, encouraging and promoting an environmental approach to education. The CEE Youth Unit works directly with the youth service and environmental organisations, providing advice and training on the development of environmental youth work. The CEE Information Unit responds to requests for environmental information from young people, often by referring them to other appropriate organisations.

**AGE RANGE:**
Any
**NUMBERS PASSING THROUGH:**
c 500 requests for information from young people each year
**HOW TO CONTACT:**
Send SAE for information and leaflets
**REGIONS SERVICED:**
UK
**SPECIAL NEEDS PROVISION:**
Information service is open to anyone
**COSTS/WAITING LISTS:**
None

## COUNCIL FOR NATIONAL ACADEMIC AWARDS (CNAA)
344-354 Gray's Inn Road
London WC1X 8PB
Tel: 071 278 4411 Fax: 071 833 1012

The CNAA is the degree awarding body for UK polytechnics and colleges. They produce a handbook, available from their Publications Department, which lists the 2,600+ CNAA undergraduate and postgraduate courses which are available throughout the UK.

**AGE RANGE:**
Any

**NUMBERS PASSING THROUGH:**
Over a quarter of a million students register
on a CNAA course each year
**HOW TO CONTACT:**
Contact Publications Department at the
above address for handbook of courses.
Thereafter you should deal with polytechnics/
colleges directly
**REGIONS SERVICED:**
UK
**COSTS/WAITING LISTS:**
No costs

## COUNCIL FOR THE PROTECTION OF RURAL ENGLAND (CPRE)
25 Buckingham Palace Road
London SW1W 0PP
Tel: 071 976 6433  Fax: 071 976 6373

CPRE can provide free advice, information and
leaflets about the protection of the countryside.
If you want to become practically involved in
local conservation campaigns you can become
a member of CPRE and they will keep you
informed of all that is going on in your area.

**REGIONAL ADDRESSES:**
Approx 44 regional offices.  Contact address
above for details of your nearest branch
**AGE RANGE:**
Any
**HOW TO CONTACT:**
By letter to local branch.  Information about

your nearest branch from address above –
phone, letter, fax
**REGIONS SERVICED:**
England only
**SPECIAL NEEDS PROVISION:**
Enquiries welcomed
**COSTS/WAITING LISTS:**
No costs for general information.
Membership costs £10 per year.  No waiting
lists

---

### COUNCIL ON INTERNATIONAL
### EDUCATIONAL EXCHANGE (CIEE)
33 Seymour Place
London W1H 6AT
Tel: 071 706 3008  Fax: 071 724 8468

CIEE's University Enrolment Service offers young
people, educated to at least 'A' level standard,
the opportunity to take degree-level courses in
many different subjects at US universities, and
language and culture courses at European
universities.  All courses run during the summer
and are an excellent way of learning about and
experiencing the US education system and
culture, improving your language skills and
adding to your CV.  For an administrative fee
CIEE will provide academic advice, process
your enrolment and make accommodation and
visa arrangements.

**AGE RANGE:**
Any

**NUMBERS PASSING THROUGH:**
18
**HOW TO CONTACT:**
By letter addressed to the particular
programme you are interested in
**REGIONS SERVICED:**
UK
**SPECIAL NEEDS PROVISION:**
CIEE aim to make their programmes as
accessible as possible
**COSTS/WAITING LISTS:**
USA administration fee – £80; France – £70.
Tuition and accommodation for two courses
costs £600-£900, plus flight. Apply from
April and no later than 4 weeks before the
start of the course

---

## CULTURAL AND EDUCATIONAL SERVICES ABROAD (CESA)
44 Sydney Street
Brighton BN1 4EP
Tel: 0273 683304 Fax: 0273 683954

CESA offers an information and advice service
on language courses abroad, mainly within the
European Community, but they also have
contacts in China, Mexico and Japan. You can
choose between taking a very intensive language
course, or more of a 'holiday' course with
lessons in the morning and plenty of free time to
add to the enjoyment of your stay. Once you
have decided on a course, CESA can make all

the necessary arrangements from reserving your place in the language school to arranging whichever type of accommodation you need for your stay.

**AGE RANGE:**
12+ – French and German courses only (all linguistic levels).  16+ – all languages (all linguistic levels)

**NUMBERS PASSING THROUGH:**
500 in 1992

**HOW TO CONTACT:**
By telephone or letter for details of courses available

**REGIONS SERVICED:**
UK (CESA also advise and book courses for students from USA, Europe and Hong Kong)

**COSTS/WAITING LISTS:**
Costs vary depending on country, length of stay, time of the year and type of course, e.g. two weeks in France, 20 hours of tuition and half board family accommodation costs approx £600.  Travel costs are not included in the course fees and most students make their own arrangements.

---

**CYCLISTS' TOURING CLUB (CTC)**
Cotterell House
69 Meadrow
Godalming
Surrey GU7 3HS
Tel: 0483 417217  Fax: 0483 426994

The CTC is the governing body for recreational and utility cycling. It is the largest (and oldest est. 1878) association for cyclists in the UK. Although primarily a membership organisation, the CTC does much work for all cyclists, whatever their age or ability. Cycling is an economical form of transport, it's healthy and it's fun. The CTC organises various events and operates through a large network of local groups with various special interest sections (young people, disabled etc.). There are local volunteering opportunities setting up and running CTC clubs.

**REGIONAL ADDRESSES:**
70 regional district associations – details from HQ
**AGE RANGE:**
Any
**HOW TO CONTACT:**
Telephone, letter or fax for further information about membership
**REGIONS SERVICED:**
UK and overseas
**SPECIAL NEEDS PROVISION:**
CTC can provide facilities, e.g. blind and disabled tandems, ideas and information
**COSTS/WAITING LISTS:**
Under 18 annual membership – £12; Full – £24; Unemployed – £12; Household groups – £40

## DEMOCRATIC UNIONIST PARTY
296 Albertsbridge Road
Belfast BT5 4GX
Tel: 0232 458597

## DEPARTMENT FOR EDUCATION
Sanctuary Buildings
Great Smith Street
Westminster
London SW1P 3BT
Tel: 071 925 5000  Fax: 071 925 6000

The DE can provide information and leaflets on many aspects of education eg grants and loans for further education, options at 16 etc. as well as on the many European Community programmes available such as ERASMUS, TEMPUS, COMETT etc. (see individual entries)

**REGIONAL ADDRESSES:**
Scottish Office Education Department, New St Andrew's House, Edinburgh EH1 3SY
Tel: 031 556 8400.
Department of Education – Northern Ireland, Rathgael House, Balloo Road, Bangor, County Down BT19 2PR  Tel: 0247 270077.
**AGE RANGE:**
Any
**HOW TO CONTACT:**
Telephone or letter for further information or leaflets depending on the nature of the enquiry

**REGIONS SERVICED:**
England and Wales – see above for Scotland
and Northern Ireland
**SPECIAL NEEDS PROVISION:**
Information is available to everyone
**COSTS/WAITING LISTS:**
Most leaflets are free

## THE DESIGN COUNCIL
28 Haymarket
London SW1Y 4SU
Tel: 071 839 8000.

The Design Council can provide comprehensive
information about all aspects of the design
industry and can offer detailed information about
ways of getting in and developing your career as
a designer. They have a very large design
bookshop and produce a range of booklets and
factsheets covering courses and career
development in design.

**REGIONAL OFFICES:**
Northern Ireland: Business Design Centre,
39 Corporation Street, Belfast BT1 3BA
Tel: 0232 238452
Scotland: Ca'd'Oro Building, 45 Gordon
Street, Glasgow G1 3LZ  Tel: 041 221 6121
Wales: QED Centre, Main Avenue, Treforest
Estate, Treforest CF37 5YR  Tel: 0443 841888

### DEUTSCHER AKADEMISCHER AUSTAUSCHDIENST (DAAD)
#### (German Academic Exchange Service)
Kennedyallee 50
W-5300 Bonn 2
Germany
Tel: 010-49/228-882 1
Fax: 010-49/228-882 444

Applicants must be academic students enroled at institutions of higher education or research institutes with a good basic knowledge of the German language. The three main schemes run by DAAD are; scholarships for university summer courses in Germany for undergraduate students; annual scholarships for postgraduate students for study in Germany; group study visits for undergraduate or postgraduate visits to Germany. DAAD also produce many leaflets and booklets on the German educational system including scholarships, funding, exchanges programmes etc.

**REGIONAL ADDRESSES:**
London Branch: 17 Bloomsbury Square, London WC1A 2LP Tel: 071 404 4065 Fax: 071 430 2634
**AGE RANGE:**
Any
**NUMBERS PASSING THROUGH:**
In 1990 the DAAD provided funding for over 16,500 people worldwide for study research and training in Germany

**HOW TO CONTACT:**
Telephone, letter, fax or in person to the
London office for information and an
application form for funding schemes if
eligible
**REGIONS SERVICED:**
UK (the service operates worldwide)
**SPECIAL NEEDS PROVISION:**
Enquiries welcome – the same provisions
apply to all applicants
**COSTS/WAITING LISTS:**
Applications for funding should be made a
year in advance

## DIRECTIONS (publication)
British Film Institute
21 Stephen Street
London W1P 1PL
Tel: 071 255 1444

A guide to practical training courses run by and
for the independent film and video sector. As
well as a regional guide to training courses, it
features articles providing sound advice on
diverse topics and a noticeboard of changes and
developments affecting training. Published twice
each year. Available from British Film Institute
(price £3.50 inc p&p).

## DIRECTORY OF COLLEGE
## ACCOMMODATIONS USA AND CANADA
### (publication)
Vacation Work Publications
9 Park End Street
Oxford OX1 1HJ
Tel: 0865 241978 Fax: 0865 790885

Some 175 colleges and universities in the USA and Canada offer inexpensive (from $5 per night) but clean and comfortable accommodation to travellers. This directory gives all the information travellers need to stay on a campus, including the dates the accommodation is available, rates, facilities, restrictions and telephone numbers to contact. ISBN 0 87866 869 1. Available through libraries, bookshops (price £5.95), or direct from the above address (price £6.95 inc p&p).

## DIRECTORY OF JOBS AND CAREERS
## ABROAD (publication)
Vacation Work Publications
9 Park End Street
Oxford OX1 1HJ
Tel: 0865 241978  Fax: 0865 790885

A guide to permanent career opportunities abroad. Explains the most successful methods of finding work abroad for people of all walks of life, from the school leaver to the fully qualified professional. Gives facts on careers abroad for teachers, doctors, fitters, policemen, secretaries, printers, engineers, accountants, nurses, lawyers, computer operators, journalists and more. Lists the trades and professions most in demand in Europe, Australia, New Zealand, USA, Canada, and China giving details of the qualifications required and addresses to contact.

ISBN 85458 025 6. Available through libraries, bookshops (price £9.95), or direct from the above address (price £10.95 inc p&p).

### DIRECTORY OF SUMMER JOBS ABROAD
### 1993 (publication)
Vacation Work Publications
9 Park End Street
Oxford OX1 1HJ
Tel: 0865 241978  Fax: 0865 790885

30,000 varied vacancies listed at employers' request in over 40 different countries, including Germany, France, Spain, Switzerland, Scandinavia, Italy, Israel, Morocco, Greece etc. Jobs for couriers, sailing and scuba diving instructors, voluntary workers, overland expedition leaders, English teachers, secretaries, hiking tour managers, hotel workers, fruit pickers, villa staff etc. Full details of jobs offered, the period of work and wages are given, together with names and addresses of employers. Wages up to £1000 per month. Special supplements on working with families and cheap travel. Facts about visas and work permits plus a section

on health insurance. Plus a chapter on winter
jobs abroad.
ISBN 1 85458 079 5. Available through libraries,
bookshops (price £7.95) or direct from the
above address (price £8.95 inc p&p).

## DIRECTORY OF SUMMER JOBS IN BRITAIN 1993 (publication)

Vacation Work Publications
9 Park End Street
Oxford OX1 1HJ
Tel: 0865 241978  Fax: 0865 790885

30,000 vacancies listed at employers' request
in England, Scotland and Wales. Fruit and hop
picking, hotels, sports instruction, farming, child
care, office work, holiday camps, archaeological
digs, riding centres, voluntary work etc. The
jobs vary in location from offices in London, to
fairgrounds, to remote Scottish castles, and can
pay as much as £220 per week. Details of
wages and hours, general conditions of work,
and qualifications required are given, together
with names and addresses of whom to contact
when applying. Also includes advice on
approaching an employer, and how to create
your own job.
ISBN 1 85458 081 7. Available through libraries,
bookshops (price £7.95) or direct from the
above address (price £8.95 inc p&p).

### DIRECTORY OF WORK AND STUDY IN DEVELOPING COUNTRIES (publication)
Vacation Work Publications
9 Park End Street
Oxford OX1 1HJ
Tel: 0865 241978  Fax: 0865 790885

A guide to employment, voluntary work, and academic opportunities in the Third World for those who wish to experience life there as more than a tourist. It lists thousands of opportunities for work or study with over 400 organisations in over 100 countries throughout the developing world as well as sources of further information. Both short and long term openings are covered in Africa, the Middle East, Asia, the Far East, the Pacific, Latin America, and the Caribbean.
ISBN 1 85458 029 9  Available in bookshops (price £7.95), through libraries or direct from the above address (price £8.95 inc p&p).

### DRAGONS INTERNATIONAL
The Old Vicarage
South Newington
Banbury
Oxon OX15 4JN
Tel: 0295 721717  Fax: 0295 721991

Dragons International is a commercial company specialising in exchange holidays to France, Germany and Spain and paying guest visits to France.  They can also offer escorted travel to

France for those who already have an exchange partner or host family and simply need to travel there and back. Applicants for exchanges are matched with a partner of similar age, interests and background and the exchanges take place at various times between April and September. Supervised travel is provided throughout the journey to France and passengers are collected from 16 different meeting points in the UK.

**AGE RANGE:**
11-19
**HOW TO CONTACT:**
Write to the above address for further information
**REGIONS SERVICED:**
UK
**COSTS/WAITING LISTS:**
The cost depends on the UK point of departure and varies from about £150 to £200. This includes the return fare, supervised travel, matching of partners and insurance. Early application is recommended as applications are dealt with as received

---

**DRIVE FOR YOUTH (DFY)**
Celmi Centre
Llanegryn
Tywyn
Gwynedd LL36 9SA
Tel: 0654 710454 Fax: 0654 712326

Drive For Youth specialises in 22-week courses

for motivating the young, long-term unemployed, and placing them in jobs or further education. The success rate is among the highest in the country. To qualify for acceptance as a DFY Trainee, you need to have been out of work for at least one year, and have a genuine desire (however small!) to escape from the mess which you feel your life has become. Our intense career and development programme, based at our own residential centre in the Snowdonia National Park, includes: outdoor pursuits with the emphasis on working as a team, personal counselling, community projects in Britain and abroad where you help others, and in-depth careers help and guidance. Completion of the course earns you a DFY Graduate's Diploma and a City and Guilds Certificate.

**REGIONAL ADDRESSES:**
London Office: 39 Portman Square, London W1H 9HB  Tel: 071 487 2748
Fax: 071 935 0806
**AGE RANGE:**
18-24
**NUMBERS PASSING THROUGH:**
240 a year
**HOW TO CONTACT:**
For information, advice, brochure and regular newsletter, telephone Celmi Training Centre or write (no stamp necessary) to:
Drive For Youth, FREEPOST, Celmi Training

Centre, Llanegryn, Nr Tywyn, Gwynedd,
Wales  LL36 9SA

**REGIONS SERVICED:**
England, Scotland and Wales

**SPECIAL NEEDS PROVISION:**
Limited because of the nature of the course,
but has proved possible in the past under
some circumstances – please enquire

**COSTS/WAITING LISTS:**
There is no cost for the course, which is
funded by business, charitable trusts and the
government (through TECs and LECs).
Courses (6 a year) start from April to October.
Apply January through September

---

## DUKE OF EDINBURGH'S AWARD SCHEME
Gulliver House
Madeira Walk
Windsor
Berks SL4 1EU
Tel: 0753 810753  Fax: 0753 810666

This award scheme offers you the chance to
make new friends, develop new skills and
challenge yourself by taking part in a wide
programme of adventurous, artistic, practical
and sporting activities that you choose. The
scheme is open to any young person aged 14-
25, provided participation will not cause a
deterioration in health, who is capable of making
a commitment, understands the nature of that

commitment, is capable of choosing their own programme and has the will to take part rather than just the willingness to be led through it.

**REGIONAL ADDRESSES:**
Scotland: 69 Dublin Street, Edinburgh EH3 6NS  Tel: 031 556 9097
Wales: Oak House, 12 The Bulwark, Brecon, Powys LD3 7AD  Tel: 0874 3086
Northern Ireland: Northern Bank House, 109 Royal Avenue, Belfast BT1 1EW
Tel: 0232 232253
Local contacts available from Head Office
**AGE RANGE:**
14-25
**NUMBERS PASSING THROUGH:**
85,000
**HOW TO CONTACT:**
By letter to Head Office or Regional Office for leaflets, information and a local contact
**REGIONS SERVICED:**
UK
**SPECIAL NEEDS PROVISION:**
Programmes are usually sufficiently flexible to require no special provision
**COSTS/WAITING LISTS:**
Membership fee is £7.30 for Bronze/Silver level and £9.40 for Gold level.  Other costs will vary according to local circumstances and activities chosen.  Some funding may be available from various sources such as Local Education Authorities, Rotary Clubs etc. as well as from individual fund-raising ventures.

Some local groups may occasionally have
waiting lists

---

### DULUX COMMUNITY PROJECTS (DCP)
PO Box 343
London WC2E 3RJ

Each year ICI Paints, as sponsor of the Dulux
Community Projects Scheme, invites
applications for free supplies of paint for use
with worthwhile community projects. An
independent panel decides which of the projects
merits donations of paint and allocates supplies
accordingly. Applications are accepted from
voluntary groups or registered charities whose
work benefits the community.

**AGE RANGE:**
Any
**NUMBERS PASSING THROUGH:**
About 250 out of 300 groups awarded paint
**HOW TO CONTACT:**
The dates of the scheme vary from year to
year. However applications are generally
processed between Easter and mid June of
each year. For an application form send a
large SAE to the above address, but only
during the application period
**REGIONS SERVICED:**
UK
**SPECIAL NEEDS PROVISION:**
Any eligible group can apply

**COSTS/WAITING LISTS:**
None

## EARTH ACTION (FRIENDS OF THE EARTH
## YOUTH SECTION)
26-28 Underwood Street
London N1 7JQ
Tel: 071 490 1555  Fax: 071 490 0881

Earth Action is the youth section of Friends of the Earth and enables young people to become actively involved in campaigning on environmental issues.  Local groups are based in schools and colleges, or in a local area, town or village, and together form a large network supported and co-ordinated nationally by the Earth Action Office.  Local group activities could include anything from presenting a talk in school on tropical rainforests, writing to your MP, initiating a recycling scheme in your school, to getting out on the streets to inform the public on what is happening.  Help for each campaign is provided by the Earth Action Office.

**REGIONAL ADDRESSES:**
Network of local groups
**AGE RANGE:**
14-18
**NUMBERS PASSING THROUGH:**
50 local groups, but increasing
**HOW TO CONTACT:**
Send large SAE to above address for letter and

leaflet in response to initial enquiry. An Earth
Action Starter Pack will be sent out to those
interested in more information

**REGIONS SERVICED:**
England, Wales and Northern Ireland

**SPECIAL NEEDS PROVISION:**
No special provision but all young people are
encouraged to become involved

**COSTS/WAITING LISTS:**
A group licensing fee is about £10 (1992).
Groups receive six newsletters each year –
*Earth Action Report* and several action
guides. Groups raise money through their
own fund-raising activities

---

### EARTHWATCH
Belsyre Court
57 Woodstock Road
Oxford OX2 6HU
Tel: 0865 311600  Fax: 0865 311383

Earthwatch raises funds from the business
community, trusts and individuals to enable
them to give awards of financial aid to students
over 16 and to teachers to participate on many
of the environmental expeditions it sponsors.
Further information on criteria, eligibility, how
to apply etc. is available from Earthwatch
Education Awards at the above address.

**AGE RANGE:**
16+

**HOW TO CONTACT:**
SAE to above address for an information
packet
**REGIONS SERVICED:**
UK
**SPECIAL NEEDS PROVISION:**
Enquiries welcome
**COSTS/WAITING LISTS:**
Membership is £22. Some projects require
participants to raise some funds for
themselves and Earthwatch can give some
advice on sponsorship and fund-raising

---

**ECCTIS 2000**
Fulton House
Jessop Avenue
Cheltenham
Gloucester GL50 3SH
Tel: 0242 518724  Fax: 0242 225914

ECCTIS is a government-owned, computerised
course information service covering over 80,000
courses in all universities and colleges of further
education. ECCTIS is available at nearly 3,500
access points in the UK, in schools, further and
higher education colleges, Careers Offices and
through TECs and LECs. ECCTIS is available at
these centres either on personal computers using
compact disc or as an on-line service. You will
find ECCTIS quick and easy to use. ECCTIS can
also be found at higher education and careers
fairs.

In considering your choice of college or university course you may use the service directly or with the help of an adviser. ECCTIS gives you information on who offers courses on your chosen subject areas and location, the entry requirements and a description of what the course involves – whether it is a university degree or vocational course at a further education college – full-time or part-time. Whatever your starting point and interest there will be information on a course for you. ECCTIS gives you information on how to contact universities and colleges and how to apply for courses. The vocational qualifications which are accredited by NCVQ and awarded by BTEC, City and Guilds and RSA are explained together with their links to careers. During late August and throughout September ECCTIS 2000 provides information on vacancies on degree and HND courses. ECCTIS carries information on access courses to higher education for students without 'A' levels or equivalent qualifications.

**AGE RANGE:**
Courses for 16+ but you can start looking at 14

**HOW TO CONTACT:**
At your school, Careers Office, further education college, university, TEC/LEC or careers and higher education fairs

**REGIONS SERVICED:**
UK and overseas

**SPECIAL NEEDS PROVISION:**
Information available on college courses for
students with special needs and facilities for
the disabled at universities
**COSTS/WAITING LISTS:**
Free (institutions subscribe to the system)

---

**EDUCATION YEARBOOK 1993
(publication)**
Longman Group UK Ltd
6th Floor
Westgate House
The High
Harlow
Essex CM20 1YR
Tel: 0279 442601  Fax: 0279 444501

The Education Yearbook, published annually,
is a comprehensive guide to all aspects of
education and training.  It contains several
chapters of particular interest to young people
such as information on higher, further and
vocational education including universities and
colleges, business, technical and management
education, art and design, music, dance and
drama colleges, and independent further
education establishments.  The Employment
and Careers section contains details of Industrial
Training Boards, the careers services,
professional bodies and sponsored training and
apprenticeships. Studying and travelling abroad
are widely covered from details of exchange

visits, voluntary service and working holidays to European organisations, European schools, the British Council and embassies and institutes providing further information on education and travel abroad. Copies are usually available for reference in public libraries, Careers Offices and schools. ISBN 0 582 07871 7.

---

## EDUCATIONAL GRANTS ADVISORY SERVICE (EGAS)
Family Welfare Association
501-505 Kingsland Road
Dalston
London E8 4AU

EGAS advises students about non-statutory sources of financial help, specialising in advice about educational trust funds. They hold details about educational charities on a computerised database as well as information on Government departments, educational and professional institutes and student welfare services, enabling them to provide an expert and up to date advice service on the complex world of educational funding.

**AGE RANGE:**
16+
**NUMBERS PASSING THROUGH:**
6,000+
**HOW TO CONTACT:**
By letter for advice and information

**REGIONS SERVICED:**
UK
**SPECIAL NEEDS PROVISION:**
EGAS tries to give priority to people from
disadvantaged groups which includes people
with disabilities
**COSTS/WAITING LISTS:**
Enquiries should be made as far in advance of
the course starting as possible

---

**EMPLOIS D'ETE EN FRANCE 1993
(publication)**
Vacation Work Publications
9 Park End Street
Oxford OX1 1HJ
Tel: 0865 241978  Fax: 0865 790885

Book listing thousands of vacancies in France.
Jobs include all the usual holiday resort
opportunities from Brittany to the Cote d'Azure,
for waiters and bar staff, sports instructors,
receptionists, helpers in childrens' summer
camps etc.  The book includes special
information for foreign students, with details of
documents necessary to work in France – social
security etc.  Full details of wages and hours,
qualifications needed and general conditions of
work are given, plus names and addresses of
companies, and who to contact.
ISBN 2 9504172 2 1 Available through libraries,
bookshops (price £7.95), or direct from the
above address (price £8.95 inc p&p)

**EN FAMILLE OVERSEAS (EFO)**
The Old Stables
60b Maltravers Street
Arundel
West Sussex BN18 9BG
Tel: 0903 883266  Fax: 0903 883582

EFO offers you the chance to get to know a foreign country and its people, to speak the language, and experience family life by arranging for you to stay with a host-family, mainly in France but also in Germany, Italy and Spain. You will be treated as one of the family, taking part in all the family activities and meet their friends and relations, making it an ideal way to improve your spoken language and make new friends. Special language holidays are also available which provide some form of tuition, ranging from classes at a language school through to intensive language practice whilst staying with a teacher's family.

**AGE RANGE:**
Any
**NUMBERS PASSING THROUGH:**
1,000
**HOW TO CONTACT:**
Telephone or SAE for advice and information
**REGIONS SERVICED:**
UK
**SPECIAL NEEDS PROVISION:**
No provision

**COSTS/WAITING LISTS:**
Fees are approx £40. Host-family weekly
charges in European countries approximately
£165-£230. Language courses cost from
£452 for two weeks including accommodation and lessons. No waiting lists but
two months notice of stay is preferred.

### ENDEAVOUR TRAINING LTD (Endeavour)
17a Glumangate
Chesterfield
Derbyshire S40 1TX
Tel: 0246 237201 Fax: 0246 203828

Young people can join a local group, take part
in follow up and activity weekends, undertake
community work, help staff summer camps for
underprivileged children, hold local social
events and competitions. There are also
opportunities to take part in expeditions and
work projects both at home and overseas.

**AGE RANGE:**
16+
**NUMBERS PASSING THROUGH:**
500+ staff and volunteers working with
2,000-3,000 people every year
**HOW TO CONTACT:**
The Endeavour Association office, in
whatever manner is convenient – letter, fax,
phone etc – for information and leaflets
**REGIONS SERVICED:**
UK

**SPECIAL NEEDS PROVISION:**
Enquiries welcome
**COSTS/WAITING LISTS:**
Membership fees; £3.50 unwaged, £7.50
employed, £10 family membership. All
courses are subsidised to take into account
personal circumstances. Most of the work
undertaken is funded by the Endeavour
Association

---

## ENGINEERING CAREERS INFORMATION
## SERVICE (ECIS)
Vector House
41 Clarendon Road
Watford
Herts WD1 1HS
Tel: 0923 238441  Fax: 0923 256086

Engineering covers such a vast range it is
impossible to describe all the different fields in
any detail here. Any form of manufacturing or
production requires engineers from the design
stage right through to the final product, whether
it is an aeroplane, a washing machine, a
computer or motorway. The list is endless and
engineers usually specialise in one particular
branch. ECIS can provide information on careers
in the manufacturing branches of engineering.
For more general information on the whole
range of engineering careers write to ECIS at the
above address or telephone free of charge on
0800 282167.

### ENGLISH SPEAKING UNION (ESU)
Dartmouth House
37 Charles Street
London W1X 8AB
Tel: 071 493 3328  Fax: 071 495 6108

If you are an undergraduate or have just completed your 'A' levels you could spend your gap year at an independent school in Canada, USA or South America or work for a US Senator on Capitol Hill during your university vacation.

**AGE RANGE:**
No specific age range
**NUMBERS PASSING THROUGH:**
80
**HOW TO CONTACT:**
Send SAE to Education Dept
**REGIONS SERVICED:**
UK
**SPECIAL NEEDS PROVISION:**
No special provision – enquiries welcome
**COSTS/WAITING LISTS:**
Costs will include flight and insurance expenses plus some pocket money

## ENVIRONMENT COUNCIL
80 York Way
London N1 9AG
Tel: 071 278 4736  Fax: 071 837 9688

The Environment Council is a forum for organisations and individuals working towards a sustainable future. It is an independent charity, made up of individuals from all walks of life, all of whom have a common interest in environmental issues, and a desire to make progress happen. Membership brings a number of benefits, including regular news of the latest developments through periodical newsletters. The EC's Information Programme produces a range of directories such as *Who's Who in the Environment*, *Directory of Environmental Courses*, and a leaflet entitled *Careers in the Environment*.

**AGE RANGE:**
Any
**HOW TO CONTACT:**
Telephone, letter, fax to above address for general information.  SAE required for leaflets
**REGIONS SERVICED:**
UK
**SPECIAL NEEDS PROVISION:**
Enquiries welcome
**COSTS/WAITING LISTS:**
None for general information

**ERASMUS**
**(European Community Action Scheme for**
**the Mobility of University Students)**
Erasmus UK Student Grants Council
University of Kent
Canterbury CT2 7PD
Tel: 0227 762712  Fax: 0227 762711

The ERASMUS scheme encourages the exchange of students in higher education and offers them the opportunity to study in another EC member state, or EFTA territory, as part of their course. Grants are available, via your university, as a 'top-up' to other funding received. These are not intended to cover the full costs of studying abroad.

**AGE RANGE:**
From second year of higher education
**HOW TO CONTACT:**
Write to above address for further general information, or contact your higher education institution about their involvement in particular subject areas. For information on ERASMUS programmes offered by UK higher education institutions please see *The UK Guide*, available from ISCO Publications, 12a-18a Princess Way Camberley, Surrey GU15 3SP
**REGIONS SERVICED:**
UK

## EURO-ACADEMY
77A George Street
Croydon
Surrey CR0 1LD
Tel: 081 686 2363  Fax: 081 681 8850

Homestays and language courses in France, Germany, Spain, Italy and Portugal all year round for all levels and ages, providing a focus for those studying European languages, literature, art, history etc. Ideal for those about to take GCSEs or 'A' levels, gap year students and undergraduates. Also available are vacation courses with leisure activities and sports options (tennis, riding, windsurfing etc.)

**AGE RANGE:**
16-27
**NUMBERS PASSING THROUGH:**
c 500 individuals and 300 travelling in groups
**HOW TO CONTACT:**
Telephone, letter, fax or in person for advice, information and brochures
**REGIONS SERVICED:**
UK
**SPECIAL NEEDS PROVISION:**
Enquiries welcome
**COSTS/WAITING LISTS:**
Homestays cost from £170 (1 week) to £340 (2 weeks). Vacation courses from £450 to £520 (2 weeks). French University summer schools from £520 (3 weeks) to £790. Full

details in Euro-Academy brochure. Travel
grants for approved study visits are available
from Local Education Authorities – apply
through school or college. Information on
scholarships for long term study abroad can
be obtained from the cultural section of the
relevant embassy. Bookings should ideally
be made two to three months in advance but
can be accepted later.

## EUROPE – A MANUAL FOR HITCH-HIKERS
### (publication)
Vacation Work Publications
9 Park End Street
Oxford OX1 1HJ
Tel: 0865 241978  Fax: 0865 790885

This manual covers the whole of Europe and
gives country by country information on hitching
techniques, route planning, sources of free maps
and attitudes towards hitch-hikers. It includes a
town guide of Europe's largest cities and maps
of the principal motorways which reveal the
best hitching points as well as cheap and free
ways of crossing the channel; reading foreign
number plates; hitch-hiking agencies; the law;
a hitch-hiking vocabulary in ten languages and
the best and worst places to hitch in Europe.
ISBN 0 907638  28 7.   Available through
libraries, bookshops (price £3.95), or direct
from the above address (price £4.95 inc p&p).

## EUROPEAN COMMUNITY YOUTH ORCHESTRA (ECYO)

6a Pont Street
London SW1X 9EL
Tel: 071 235 7671 or 071 235 6641
Fax: 071 235 7370

The Youth Orchestra meets twice annually for a course of approximately two weeks, followed by a tour of 8-10 concerts either within Europe or elsewhere in the world. This is an opportunity to work with world leading conductors and to meet young people of all 12 EC countries. Applications are invited from orchestral musicians, post grade 8.

**AGE RANGE:**
14-23
**NUMBERS PASSING THROUGH:**
c 180
**HOW TO CONTACT:**
Telephone, letter or fax to Head Office for an application form
**REGIONS SERVICED:**
UK
**SPECIAL NEEDS PROVISION:**
No special provision but every effort would be made to include someone if possible
**COSTS/WAITING LISTS:**
Audition deadline is normally in October for the following year. Once the orchestra is chosen there is also a reserve list

## EUROPEAN LANGUAGE PROGRAMMES
44 Cromwell Road
Hove
Sussex BN3 3ER
Tel: 0273 220261  Fax: 0273 220376

Challenge Educational Services organise European Language Programmes offering tuition in French, Spanish and German, based in the relevant countries. Courses in France and Spain are offered in various universities including the Sorbonne in Paris and Madrid University. Courses in German are at a well-established language school. Courses are available for all ages and at all levels, and short term as well as semester and academic year courses are offered. Programmes are comprehensive, including board and lodging plus other services, ideal as a gap-year opportunity or purely to improve knowledge of a European language for career development.

**AGE RANGE:**
Any
**HOW TO CONTACT:**
Telephone, letter or fax for brochure and booking form
**REGIONS SERVICED:**
UK and Republic of Ireland
**COSTS/WAITING LISTS:**
Cost dependent on length of course.
Application preferably three months in

advance, though late bookings accepted dependent on availability

## EUROPEAN WORK EXPERIENCE
Kipling House
43 Villiers Street
London WC2N 6NE

EWE is funded by the European Commission, the UK Government and industry. It offers work experience exchange schemes for 16-19 year-old students between the UK and other EC member states. The object is to develop awareness in industrial, economic, language, European and social aspects. For further details contact the EWE Project Co-ordinator at the above address.

## EXPEDITION ADVISORY CENTRE
Royal Geographical Society
1 Kensington Gore
London SW7 2AR
Tel: 071 581 2057  Fax: 071 584 4447

The Expedition Advisory Centre can provide information, advice, training and publications for anyone planning or wishing to join a scientific or adventurous expedition overseas. This includes annual seminars in November on 'Planning a Small Expedition' and in May on 'Independent Travel'. The EAC at the Royal

Geographical Society publishes various books of interest to young people thinking of becoming involved in an expedition or travel, either through a structured organisation such as Operation Raleigh, or independently:

*Fund-raising for Expeditions*: this booklet advises on budgetting, cost-cutting, the expedition image and fund-raising, and details over 70 expedition grant-giving organisations (price £2.50),

*Fund-raising to Join an Expedition*: a guide for those raising funds required to join ventures such as Operation Raleigh (price £1.50),

*Bicycle Expeditions*: planning, equipping and undertaking long-distance bicycle journeys (price £6.50),

*Joining an Expedition*: how to take advantage of the expedition opportunities offered by over 50 UK-based organisations, with fund-raising advice (price £4.00),

*Sources of Information for Independent Travellers*: where to get the best information on health, equipment, visas, insurance, maps etc (price £3.00).

**AGE RANGE:**
Any
**NUMBERS PASSING THROUGH:**
10,000+ enquiries per year
**HOW TO CONTACT:**
By letter, telephone or fax for advice, information and publications
**REGIONS SERVICED:**
UK

**SPECIAL NEEDS PROVISION:**
No specific provision
**COSTS/WAITING LISTS:**
Details of costs of publications, courses and
seminars available from above. Replies
usually within 21 days

---

## EXPERIMENT IN INTERNATIONAL LIVING
### (EIL)
'Otesaga'
West Malvern Road
Malvern
Worcestershire WR14 4EN
Tel: 0684 562577  Fax: 0684 562212

EIL is a non-profit, non-political and non-
religious organisation, existing to promote
international understanding and has been
involved in international education and
exchange since 1932, working mainly through
the 'homestay' principle, sending and receiving
people to and from more than 50 countries
worldwide, either in groups or as individuals.
As well as its main programme of individual
homestays, EIL can arrange youth exchanges,
including Young Worker and Disabled and
Disadvantaged programmes with EEC and East
European countries, Language Acquisition
programmes in many countries and much more.
They can also arrange a one year Au Pair
Homestay programme to the USA.

**AGE RANGE:**
18+
**NUMBERS PASSING THROUGH:**
2,800
**HOW TO CONTACT:**
For Homestays, contact main office above by letter or telephone. For Au Pair programme contact CBR Au Pair, 63 Foregate Street, Worcester WR1 1DX Tel: 0905 26671
**REGIONS SERVICED:**
UK
**SPECIAL NEEDS PROVISION:**
Specific programmes available
**COSTS/WAITING LISTS:**
Costs vary enormously depending on the type of programme, the country visited and the length of stay. Language courses tend to cost more. Eight weeks notice before departure is required. Write or telephone for a comprehensive brochure with full information

## FAIRBRIDGE
5 Westminster Bridge Road
London SE1 7XW
Tel: 071 928 1704  Fax: 071 928 6016

Fairbridge offers support with a taste of adventure through outdoor activities (such as climbing, abseiling, camping etc.), conservation and community projects, sail training on a tall ship and basic training in various job skills. You'll be able to make new friends, do something different and stretch yourself. Fairbridge Drake will open up new interests and give you constructive help in finding a job. All training is under the supervision of qualified instructors.

**REGIONAL ADDRESSES:**
14 Team Centres around the UK. Details available from Main Office
**AGE RANGE:**
14-25
**NUMBERS PASSING THROUGH:**
c 7,300
**HOW TO CONTACT:**
Telephone, write or call in person to the nearest Team Centre
**REGIONS SERVICED:**
UK
**SPECIAL NEEDS PROVISION:**
Courses and activities are altered to cater for group and individual needs
**COSTS/WAITING LISTS:**
Course participants are asked to contribute £15 towards the running costs if they can afford it. Basic courses usually last 7-10 days. Waiting lists vary. Ideally, give as much notice as possible

**FESTIVAL WELFARE SERVICES (FWS)**
61b Hornsey Road
London N7 6DG
Tel: 071 700 5754

FWS is a small charity whose main concern is to encourage festival organisers to make provisions for appropriate welfare services to be available on site. As a service to festival-goers, FWS produces a free, regularly updated list of festivals, starting in early April until early September, which they send out together with a copy of their free *Survival Guide*, full of advice and information on attending a festival. They also produce a range of publications on a variety of related subjects from organising a festival to advice on drugs and alcohol. For further information send a stamped addressed envelope (approx 9" x 6.5") to the above address.

### FILM AND TELEVISION LIGHTING APPRENTICE PROGRAMME FOR SCHOOL LEAVERS
c/o Training Services
City of Westminster College
Lancaster Road
London W11 1QT
Tel: 071 258 2888  Fax: 071 229 1025

A 4-year apprenticeship designed to equip young people with the knowledge and skills needed to become competent and qualified lighting technicians in the film and television industry. It is run in conjunction with companies within the film and television industry, and successful completion of the apprenticeship leads to a Diploma from the British Kinematograph, Sound and Television Society (BKSTS). Other youth training courses offered by City of Westminster College include Stage Electrics, Sound Engineering, Video, Photography, Graphics etc.

**AGE RANGE:**
16-18 only
**HOW TO CONTACT:**
Letter, telephone, fax to above address
**REGIONS SERVICED:**
UK
**SPECIAL NEEDS PROVISION:**
Enquiries welcome

---

### FILM AND TELEVISION TRAINING
### (publication)
British Film Institute
21 Stephen Street
London W1P 1PL
Tel: 071 636 3289

A comprehensive guide to colleges and workshops offering practical courses in film and video production. Updated annually.
Available from the above address (price £4.75 inc p&p).

---

### FILM AND TV: THE WAY IN (publication)
British Film Institute
21 Stephen Street
London W1P 1PL
Tel: 071 636 3289

Film and television offer a wide variety of career opportunities for young people. *Film And TV: The Way In – A Guide To Careers* by Robert Angell is a clear and concise guide, full of useful information and helpful advice, describes the best routes to secure employment.

ISBN 0 85170 218 X. Available through public libraries, bookshops (price £5.50), or direct from the above address (price £6.00 inc p&p).

## FOOL TIME: CENTRE FOR CIRCUS SKILLS AND PERFORMING ARTS
Britannia Road
Kingswood
Bristol BS15  2DA
Tel: 0272 478788  Fax: 0272 476354

Fool Time is Britain's leading training centre for circus skills. Our curriculum is designed to integrate the traditional physical skills of circus with the dramatic quality and emotional interplay of dance, movement and theatre. For further details and our current prospectus please contact the above address.

**AGE RANGE:**
Minimum 18
**HOW TO CONTACT:**
Telephone, letter, fax or in person for further information
**REGIONS SERVICED:**
UK and international

**COSTS/WAITING LISTS:**
Please write for information on course fees
and audition dates.  Ideally, apply six months
in advance

---

**FORD CONSERVATION AWARDS**
The Conservation Foundation
1 Kensington Gore
London SW7 2AR
Tel: 071 823 8842  Fax: 071 823 8791

The Ford Conservation Awards are organised
each year by the Conservation Foundation and
entries are invited from individuals, community
groups and organisations involved in almost
any type of conservation project.  There are
several categories including a Young People's
section and the winner of each category receives
a cash prize.  The overall national winner is also
invited to represent their country at the Ford
European Conservation Awards Final.

**AGE RANGE:**
Any (there is an award for young people's
projects up to and including 18 years)
**HOW TO CONTACT:**
Send SAE for further information
**REGIONS SERVICED:**
UK
**SPECIAL NEEDS PROVISION:**
No special provision but anyone can enter a
project

**COSTS/WAITING LISTS:**
The closing date is usually around the
beginning of September each year

---

## FOREST SCHOOL CAMPS (FSC)
110 Burbage Road
London SE24 9HD

An FSC camp is an adventure about a group of
young people going to live in a remote place for
a week or two, learning to live in harmony with
themselves, with others and with their
surroundings. A typical standing camp has
about 65 young people and 20 leaders and lasts
2 weeks. Mobile camps (travelling on foot,
cycle and canoe) are smaller. At 18, young
people can train as leaders – apply to Head
Ofice.

**AGE RANGE:**
6-17 (first time camp members are not
accepted after 15th birthday)
**NUMBERS PASSING THROUGH:**
1,300
**HOW TO CONTACT:**
By letter to: New Enquiries, Elaine Morton,
7 Park Crescent, London N3 2NL for a
programme of camps
**REGIONS SERVICED:**
UK
**SPECIAL NEEDS PROVISION:**
10% of places are kept for young people with

special needs. One camp is run for those with severe learning difficulties and a weekend for active young people with physical disabilities

**COSTS/WAITING LISTS:**

A two-week camp (including escorted travel from London main-line station) costs approx £170. Waiting list for some age-groups. Programme is published in January and prompt booking is recommended

---

### FORTE COMMUNITY CHEST
The Conservation Foundation
1 Kensington Gore
London SW7 2AR
Tel: 071 823 8842  Fax: 071 823 8791

The Forte Community Chest is available to support community projects aimed at conserving the environment. £200 - £1,000 is available each quarter or £2,000 is available once a year. Any community-based environmental project may be considered for grant aid, such as the restoration of historic buildings, planting trees, restoring ponds, school nature gardens and other projects. An independent panel meets to allocate £3,750 each quarter. Applications are invited from anyone with a specific scheme with an aim to conserve the environment.

## FOYER FOUNDATION FOR YOUTH
91 Brick Lane
London E1 6QN
Tel: 071 377 9789  Fax: 071 247 1633

Young people caught in the 'no job – no home' trap in the UK can get help from Foyers, a new scheme based on a very successful French concept. Foyers are special hostels that provide a secure home, together with advice about job hunting or skills training. Because the planned network of Foyers is still in its early stages, the Foyer Foundation (spearheaded by GrandMet and Shelter) has been set up to act as a central information source. The length of stay provided by the hostels is dependent on need, but will not be longer than two years.

**AGE RANGE:**
16-25
**HOW TO CONTACT:**
Contact the above address by letter or phone to find out about your nearest Foyer

## FREEFONE ENTERPRISE
Tel: Freefone 0800 222999

Call the freefone number for details of your local Small Firms Centre. Small Firms Centres can provide free information and advice about business problems, and they can point you in the direction of other sources of help to help you get your business idea off the ground.

---

### FRIENDS FOR THE YOUNG DEAF (FYD)
East Court Mansion Council Offices
College Lane
East Grinstead
West Sussex RH19 3LT
Tel: 0342 323444  Fax: 0342 410232

FYD organise an annual programme of projects and courses for deaf, hard of hearing and hearing young people. The intention is to encourage the personal development of individuals, to create opportunities for deaf children and young people to have fun and try out new experiences, and to help integrate deaf and hearing children and young people. Recent projects include conservation holidays, activity weekends, yachting fortnights, participating in sports festivals, and adventure weeks. FYD also offer training in leadership skills, fund-raising, many types of work experience, and in a number of other areas. Volunteers are always welcome to help out with the work of FYD.

**REGIONAL ADDRESSES:**
FYD Midland Office, Rooms 16 & 17, Ladywood Arts and Leisure Centre, Freeth Street, Ladywood, Birmingham
Tel: 021 454 4423  Fax: 021 454 4375
**AGE RANGE:**
7 – 25

**NUMBERS PASSING THROUGH:**
4,000 approx
**HOW TO CONTACT:**
Letter, telephone, in person, for advice,
information, leaflets and a list of forthcoming
projects
**REGIONS SERVICED:**
UK
**SPECIAL NEEDS PROVISION:**
Communication facilitators/interpreters
available for the deaf/ hard of hearing
**COSTS/WAITING LISTS:**
Costs for courses/projects/training vary.  Some
help may be available (further details from
FYD)

---

## FRIENDS OF THE EARTH (SCOTLAND)
## (FOE)
Bonnington Mill
72 Newhaven Road
Edinburgh EH6 5QG
Tel: 031 554 9977  Fax: 031 554 8656

FOE Scotland is independent of FOE (England
and Wales) and works on the full range of
environmental issues. Campaign topics include
the ozone layer, tropical deforestation, recycling
and waste disposal and countryside issues.  If
you wish to find out more about, or become
involved in environmental issues, contact FOE
for further information.

**REGIONAL ADDRESSES:**
Several local, independent groups throughout
Scotland
**AGE RANGE:**
Any
**HOW TO CONTACT:**
By letter (with SAE) for information and
leaflets
**REGIONS SERVICED:**
Mainly Scotland
**SPECIAL NEEDS PROVISION:**
No special provision
**COSTS/WAITING LISTS:**
None

---

## FRONTIER – THE SOCIETY FOR
## ENVIRONMENTAL EXPLORATION
77 Leonard Street
London EC2A 4QS
Tel: 071 613 2422  Fax: 071 613 2992

The Society is a non-profit making company,
established in 1989. Its objective is to provide
an effective channel through which individuals
can make a potent personal contribution to
urgent research and conservation issues in
developing countries. Anyone committed to
taking an active part in environmental protection
can join a Frontier project. Specific skills, such
as scientific, mechanical or administrative, are
useful but not essential as all work is supervised
by qualified research scientists and Frontier

staff. Great value is placed during selection on genuine enthusiasm for environmental issues and the capacity to tolerate a degree of hardship.

**AGE RANGE:**
Over 17 years
**NUMBERS PASSING THROUGH:**
150-200 per year
**HOW TO CONTACT:**
Send an SAE for information pack on projects and an application form
**REGIONS SERVICED:**
UK and worldwide
**SPECIAL NEEDS PROVISION:**
No special provision. Each case dealt with individually
**COSTS/WAITING LISTS:**
Participation in a 10-week expedition to Africa would cost candidates approximately £2,400 which covers all expenses such as air fare, camp equipment, insurance, food, transportation etc. Some examples of sources of funds are; Trusts; sponsorship from local companies; places of higher education or Local Education Authorities; personal fund-raising projects. Candidates should preferably apply 6 months in advance

---

**FULBRIGHT COMMISSION (US-UK EDUCATIONAL COMMISSION)**
62 Doughty Street
London WC1N 2LQ
Tel: 071 486 7697  Fax: 071 244 4567

The Fulbright Commission runs a programme of educational and cultural exchanges with the USA. A range of awards is available to fund study at postgraduate level in the US in any field. The Commission's Educational Advisory Service deals with enquiries on all aspects of US education and advises students wishing to pursue their further education in the United States.

**AGE RANGE:**
Any
**HOW TO CONTACT:**
Telephone or write with A4 size SAE for further information
**REGIONS SERVICED:**
UK
**SPECIAL NEEDS PROVISION:**
No special provision

### FULLEMPLOY TRAINING
County House
190 Great Dover Street
London SE1 4YB
Tel: 071 378 1774  Fax: 071 407 6178

A training organisation helping young people, mainly from minority ethnic communities, into work. Training is provided in many areas, and particularly in office skills and self-employment. May also be able to provide advice and access to equipment, and can provide on-going training and counselling for new businesses.

**REGIONAL ADDRESSES:**
Fullemploy Birmingham: 7th Floor, Bridge
House, 63 Smallbrook, Queensway,
Birmingham B5 4JP  Tel: 021 643 1282
Fax: 021 616 1052
Fullemploy Gloucester: Fullemploy House,
33 St Michael's Square, Gloucester GL1 1HX
Tel: 0452 310004  Fax: 0452 424435
Fullemploy Leeds: Unit 30, Chel Building,
26 Roundhay Road, Leeds LS7 1AB
Tel: 0532 440602  Fax: 0532 446792
Fullemploy Sandwell: 43 High Street, West
Bromwich, B70 6PB  Tel: 021 525 3464
Fullemploy Manchester: 3rd-5th Floor Basil
House, 105-107 Portland Street, Manchester
M1 6DF  Tel: 061 228 7481
Fax: 061 236 5450
Fullemploy Wales: Coptic House, 4/5 Mount
Stuart Square, Cardiff CF1 6EE
Tel: 0222 464445  Fax: 0222 484751
Contact Head Office for list of London
addresses

**AGE RANGE:**
18+

**HOW TO CONTACT:**
Letter, telephone, fax, or in person for more
information

**REGIONS SERVICED:**
England and Wales

**SPECIAL NEEDS PROVISION:**
Enquiries welcome

**COSTS/WAITING LISTS:**
None for information

## GAP ACTIVITY PROJECTS LTD (GAP)
44 Queen's Road
Reading
Berkshire RG1 4BB
Tel: 0734 594914  Fax: 0734 576634

GAP offers work opportunities overseas for young people aged 18-19 in their gap year between school and higher education or training. Placements are usually for 6-9 months, thereby leaving time for travel.  GAP operates in 29 different countries and the type of work varies from teaching English as a foreign language, through to conservation work and social/community work.

**AGE RANGE:**
School leavers aged 18-19
**NUMBERS PASSING THROUGH:**
800 placements out of 1,800 applications
**HOW TO CONTACT:**
Telephone, letter or fax for advice, information and an application form
**REGIONS SERVICED:**
UK
**SPECIAL NEEDS PROVISION:**
No provision
**COSTS/WAITING LISTS:**
£15 registration fee on application to cover administrative costs.  On selection volunteers pay a GAP fee which is currently £350, and additional costs for insurance and medical

requirements. A one or two week TEFL course (approx £100-£150) is required for English teaching. Once at the placement, volunteers receive free board and lodging and, in most cases, pocket money. Students need to apply as early as possible, during their last year at school, preferably in September or October. The closing date for applications is 1st February each year

---

**GIRL GUIDES ASSOCIATION (GGA)**
17-19 Buckingham Palace Road
London SW1W 0PT
Tel: 071 834 6242  Fax: 071 828 8317

The aim of guiding is to help girls and young women to develop emotionally, mentally, physically and spiritually so that they can make a positive contribution to their community and to the wider world. Guiding offers friendship and fun with a wide range of indoor and outdoor activities.

**REGIONAL ADDRESSES:**
Contact through Head Office
**AGE RANGE:**
Brownie Guides 7-10yrs; Guides 10-14yrs; Ranger Guides 14-18yrs; Young Leaders 15-18yrs
**NUMBERS PASSING THROUGH:**
c 730,000 members
**HOW TO CONTACT:**
Letter to HQ in London for further

information
**REGIONS SERVICED:**
UK
**SPECIAL NEEDS PROVISION:**
Enquiries welcome
**COSTS/WAITING LISTS:**
Small annual subscription

## A GIRL'S GUIDE TO EUROPE (publication)
Livewire Books For Teenagers
c/o The Women's Press
34 Great Sutton Street
London EC1V 0DX
Tel: 071 251 3007

A guide for the school leaver heading for work in Europe in 1993. It offers practical information on a range of areas including accommodation, employment and health services. Available through libraries, bookshops, or direct from the above address (price £4.50).

## GIRLS VENTURE CORPS AIR CADETS (GVAC)
Redhill Aerodrome
Kings Mill Lane
South Nutfield
Redhill
Surrey RH1 5JY
Tel: 0737 823345

The GVAC offers a wide and challenging range

of activities aimed at giving its members a broader outlook and greater sense of purpose. Activities include, camping, canoeing, skiing, rifle shooting, gliding, drill, drama and handicrafts as well as more unusual pursuits such as theory of aviation and air experience flights in small aircraft. Leadership and initiative training plays a major role and every aspect of the Duke of Edinburgh's Award Scheme is covered.

**REGIONAL ADDRESSES:**
Details from Head Office
**AGE RANGE:**
11-20
**NUMBERS PASSING THROUGH:**
2,000-3,000
**HOW TO CONTACT:**
Write or phone Head Office for details of nearest unit
**REGIONS SERVICED:**
There are regional offices covering the majority of England
**SPECIAL NEEDS PROVISION:**
Enquiries welcome
**COSTS/WAITING LISTS:**
Costs include subscriptions, course and camp fees and uniform

## GRANDMET TRUST
64/65 North Road
Brighton
East Sussex BN1 1YD
Tel: 0273 570170  Fax: 0273 682086

Grand Metropolitan is one of the UK's most successful national companies. GrandMet Trust is the part of the company that gives all kinds of help to people in need.  Its special concern is with deprived inner-city areas where young people in particular want jobs and homes.  The Trust can boost your job chances at one of its nationwide network of training centres where you can get the very best training in a huge range of skills.  But the Trust doesn't stop at occupational training.  The training teams offer moral support, expert advice on the sort of job you should be trying for and all the encouragement and help you need when you are applying for jobs.

**REGIONAL ADDRESSES:**
London, Midlands and North: 91 Brick Lane, London E1 6QN  Tel: 071 247 5884  Fax: 071 377 8477
South: Suite 4, Thrift House, 12/15 Wellington Place, Hastings, East Sussex TN34 1NY  Tel: 0424 718491  Fax: 0424 718519
Scotland: Olympic House, 142 Queen Street, Glasgow G1 3BU  Tel: 041 204 4090  Fax: 041 204 2576

**HOW TO CONTACT:**
For the address and phone number of your nearest GrandMet training centre ask your Jobcentre, contact the Trust's Head Office (address above) or your nearest regional office

---

**GRANTS TO STUDENTS: A BRIEF GUIDE**
**(publication)**
DFE Publications Despatch Centre
PO Box 2193
London E15 2EU

Once you know where you want to study, you have to work out how you're going to pay for it! This book will tell you how to apply for a grant. As long as you haven't had a grant before (in which case you are unlikely to get another one) and you are offered a place on a course at college or university, you are eligible for a grant from the LEA where you live.

In Scotland you get grants from the Scottish Education Department. Tuition fees are paid in full for UK students and the amount you get for living expenses usually depends on your parents' income.

However if you are a married woman your grant will be assessed on your husband's income and if you have been working for at least three years you will be classed a mature student and you will probably be entitled to the full grant.

Should you decide to go for Further Eductaion (instead of Higher Education), you should contact your LEA to find out what they can offer you. This is because grants for FE courses are discretionary and different LEAs have different policies. This information and much more is given in *Grants to Students: a brief guide* which is available from school, college and LEA careers libraries or free of charge from the above address.

---

**GREENPEACE**
Canonbury Villas
London N1 2PN
Tel: 071 354 5100  Fax: 071 696 0014/0012

Greenpeace is an international, independent environmental pressure group which acts against abuse to the natural world. Local support groups organise fund-raising activities, such as street collections and sponsored events. Occasionally they help with campaigns by lobbying MPs, organising petitions and generally publicising campaign issues. If you want to become involved write to the Public Information Office at the above address for details of your nearest area co-ordinator.

**REGIONAL ADDRESSES:**
200 local support groups – contact main office for details

**AGE RANGE:**
Any
**HOW TO CONTACT:**
Write to the Public Information Unit at the
above address
**REGIONS SERVICED:**
UK
**SPECIAL NEEDS PROVISION:**
Enquiries welcome

---

### GROUNDWORK FOUNDATION
Bennetts Court
6 Bennetts Hill
Birmingham B2 5ST
Tel: 021 236 8565  Fax: 021 236 7356

Groundwork is a fast-growing national network
working towards the restoration of landscapes
and wildlife habitats, and towards the positive
use of derelict and disused wasteland in and
around Britain's towns and cities. Groundwork's
'Countryside Initiative', is helping to make the
countryside more accessible and aims to develop
a better understanding between town and
country dwellers. If you want the opportunity to
improve the environment in your area, contact
the address above for more information.

**REGIONAL ADDRESSES:**
There are about 30 Groundwork Trust
locations around the country – details from
above address

**AGE RANGE:**
Any
**HOW TO CONTACT:**
Telephone or letter to above address for
details of Groundwork Trust locations
**REGIONS SERVICED:**
Areas where Trusts operate
**SPECIAL NEEDS PROVISION:**
Provision varies between Trusts
**COSTS/WAITING LISTS:**
None

---

### HAIRDRESSING TRAINING BOARD
3 Chequer Road
Doncaster DN1 2AA
Tel: 0302 342837  Fax: 0302 323381

The Hairdressing Training Board is the best first
point of contact for information about careers in
hairdressing.  They produce a comprehensive
career leaflet which outlines career opportunities
within hairdressing.

---

### HEALTH PROJECTS ABROAD (HPA)
HMS President
Victoria Embankment
London EC4Y 0HJ
Tel: 071 583 5725  Fax: 071 583 2840

HPA works in developing countries and offers a
year long programme which includes a selection

weekend, two training/briefing weekends, 3 months abroad and a follow-up weekend. Volunteers face the challenge of raising money to help support the projects and will then spend 3 months working alongside the local people to help complete the projects, being involved in simple tasks such as assisting with construction and renovation work. There are two weeks at the end of each project for the volunteer to spend time travelling. HPA provides a support structure to help volunteers in their fund-raising, in preparing for their time abroad and to give support when they return.

**AGE RANGE:**
18-28

**NUMBERS PASSING THROUGH:**
24 in 1991, 36 in 1992 and over 50 planned for 1993

**HOW TO CONTACT:**
Send SAE to above address or telephone for further information

**REGIONS SERVICED:**
UK

**SPECIAL NEEDS PROVISION:**
Generally many of the projects are not suitable, but each application is dealt with individually

**COSTS/WAITING LISTS:**
Each volunteer must raise £2,250 as a contribution to their air fares, food, accommodation and travel and to the cost of running the projects. Volunteers are asked to

cover food and accommodation expenses for
the HPA weekends (typically £22-£25).
Examples of sources of funding are the
Prince's Trust, Rotary Clubs, Local Councils,
local businesses, various trusts and grant-
making bodies as well as individual activities
such as parachute jumps, raffles, sponsored
events etc.

---

**HELP US HELP YOU (publication)**
Duke of Edinburgh's Award
69 Dublin Street
Edinburgh EH3 6NS
Tel: 031 556 9097

Available from the Duke of Edinburgh's Award
scheme, *Help Us Help You* contains information
on voluntary work opportunities for young
people. The directory is aimed specifically at
Award participants but is also a useful source of
information on organisations for any young
person interested in volunteer work. Details are
given of the type of work of each organisation
and how to contact them.

---

**HISPANIC AND LUSO BRAZILIAN
COUNCIL**
Canning House
2 Belgrave Square
London SW1X 8PJ
Tel: 071 235 2303  Fax: 071 235 3587

Canning House is a centre for information and contact on Spain, Portugal and Latin America in the UK. It promotes the teaching of Spanish & Portuguese, organises cultural events, runs a lending library (50,000 books), and offers an information service on classes, courses, and opportunities in Britain and abroad.

**AGE RANGE:**
Any
**NUMBERS PASSING THROUGH:**
Several thousand
**HOW TO CONTACT:**
Telephone, letter or in person to Education Department for information and leaflets, advice and contacts. Contact Library for books
**REGIONS SERVICED:**
UK
**SPECIAL NEEDS PROVISION:**
Enquiries welcome
**COSTS/WAITING LISTS:**
Annual subscription for students – £8.00. Information leaflets – £2.00-£3.00. Course fees around £50.00. No waiting lists

## HITCH-HIKERS' MANUAL – BRITAIN
### (publication)
Vacation Work Publications
9 Park End Street
Oxford OX1 1HJ
Tel: 0865 241978  Fax: 0865 790885

This guide provides information on hitching techniques, route planning, the law, which lifts to turn down and hitch-cycling. The Town Guide covers 200 British towns and pinpoints the best places to stand when trying to hitch out and explains how to reach these positions on foot or by public transport. It also includes 38 pages of motorway maps showing where you would be unwise to hitch, be breaking the law and where you are most likely to have the shortest wait.

ISBN 0 907638 26 0 Available through libraries, bookshops (price £3.95), or direct from the above address (price £4.95 inc p&p).

---

**HOLIDAY CARE SERVICE**
2 Old Bank Chambers
Station Road
Horley
Surrey RH6 9HW
Tel: 0293 774535  Fax: 0293 784647
Minicom: 0293 776943

A national charity that advises on holidays for people who are elderly, disabled, single parents, on low income or anyone who has difficulty in finding a suitable holiday. Also provides competitive travel insurance designed for people with a pre-existing medical condition, their friends and family, and runs Tourism for All Holidays, a low-cost holiday scheme. The Holiday Care Awards recognise excellent service

in the Tourism Industry for people with
disabilities.

**AGE RANGE:**
Any (18+ for volunteer helpers)
**HOW TO CONTACT:**
Telephone, SAE, fax or minicom for
information sheets listing holiday ideas or
information about volunteering
**REGIONS SERVICED:**
UK
**SPECIAL NEEDS PROVISION:**
Service for people with special needs
**COSTS/WAITING LISTS:**
All information is free

---

**HOME FROM HOME (publication)**
Central Bureau for Educational Visits and
Exchanges
Seymour Mews
London W1H 9PE
Tel: 071 725 9402 (credit card orders)

Have you ever wanted to find out what it is like
to live in another country? Do you want to
improve your language skills and make lasting
friendships internationally? *Home from Home*
has all the answers. It is an authoritative guide
to over 120 bona fide organisations arranging
homestays, exchanges, home exchanges, farm
stays and term stays in more than 50 countries.
You could stay with a French family in Paris,

sample dhal with a Nepalese family, exchange hospitality with an Italian partner, study for a term in a Bavarian school, discover Ashanti traditions in Ghana, teach English to a family in Japan or swap your home for one in the USA. ISBN 0 900087 85 4. Price £6.99. Available from bookshops or direct from the above address (price £8.49 inc p&p).

### HORTICULTURAL VOLUNTEERS IN SCOTLAND (HVS)
c/o Horticultural Therapy Scotland
4 Drum Street
Edinburgh
EH17 8QG
Tel: 031 658 1096

If you have experience and/or basic qualifications in horticulture, have worked in some capacity with people with special needs, and are looking for a way to use your skills Horticultural Volunteers in Scotland will help. They help projects use horticulture as therapy for people with disabilities, by providing a volunteer with horticultural skills. You may help in preparing a new site for a horticultural therapy unit, or train clients and care staff in basic horticultural tasks. Horticultural Volunteers in Scotland will place you in a project that reflects your own particular skills and interests. Minimum period of service is six months, the maximum one year. Board, lodging

and pocket money provided throughout your
stay.

**AGE RANGE:**
18+
**HOW TO CONTACT:**
Letter, telephone to above address
**REGIONS SERVICED:**
Scotland, see entry for LAND USE VOLUNTEERS
for rest of UK

---

**HOTEL AND CATERING TRAINING
COMPANY (HCTC)**
Careers Department
International House
High Street
Ealing
London W5 5DB
Tel: 081 579 2400

The HCTC supplies a wide range of advice and
information on all aspects of careers in the hotel
and catering industry – what courses to take,
training opportunities, ways into the industry
etc. It also provides training programmes for
young people leading to National and Scottish
Vocational Qualifications. Free literature and
information packages available on request.

## INDEPENDENT RADIO DRAMA
## PRODUCTIONS LTD (IRDP)

PO Box 518
Manningtree
Essex CO11 1XD
Tel: 0206 395795/081 521 7384  Fax: 0206
395795

IRDP is dedicated to encouraging young people to write for radio. They run free radio writing and acting workshops as well as supplying a free radio writing kit with cassettes. They are also responsible for the Woolwich Young Radio Playwrights' Festival which provides free writing and performing workshops at regional centres including BBC Wiltshire Sound and Downtown Radio (Northern Ireland). Workshops can be organised on request. Each year the festival runs a competition. There are ten winners and their plays are broadcast on regional radio stations and on LBC Radio in London.

**AGE RANGE:**
Up to 21
**NUMBERS PASSING THROUGH:**
250
**HOW TO CONTACT:**
Telephone 081 521 7384 for leaflets and further information
**REGIONS SERVICED:**
UK
**SPECIAL NEEDS PROVISION:**
Workshops for special needs groups available

**COSTS/WAITING LISTS:**
No costs or waiting lists.  Contact IRDP at
least a month before a workshop.  Workshops
are advertised by leaflet in schools and
colleges

## INDEPENDENT SCHOOLS CAREERS
## ORGANISATION (ISCO)
12A-18A Princess Way
Camberley
Surrey GU15 3SP
Tel: 0276 21188

ISCO produces a range of publications of interest
to young people including; over 100 information
sheets on individual careers; guidelines on
interview techniques, writing applications and
choosing a university or polytechnic;
opportunities in the gap year; directory of
independent colleges offering courses in typing,
computer work, beauty therapy, cookery, drama,
dance etc.  Write to ISCO at the above address
for a full list.

## INDIAN VOLUNTEERS FOR COMMUNITY
## SERVICE (IVCS)
12 Eastleigh Avenue
Harrow
Middlesex HA2 0UF
Tel: 081 864 4740

Applicants are placed initially in a selected rural

development project in north India for two weeks as observers and paying guests. After this period of adjustment and orientation they are given a choice of other projects to move on to. Some of these projects will accept applicants in some sort of volunteering capacity for longer periods and many will provide board and lodging free if the applicant is able to make him/herself useful. Length of stay is flexible. No placements are possible between April and September.

**AGE RANGE:**
18+
**NUMBERS PASSING THROUGH:**
32
**HOW TO CONTACT:**
Telephone or SAE
**REGIONS SERVICED:**
UK
**SPECIAL NEEDS PROVISION:**
No provision
**COSTS/WAITING LISTS:**
Annual membership fee of £10 to IVCS. If selected, a payment of £48 which includes two weeks' board and lodging at the initial project, an orientation day and printed material. Individuals are responsible for their own air fares, travel in India and pocket money. Past applicants have raised money through local appeals and sponsored events

## INDUSTRIAL COMMON OWNERSHIP
## MOVEMENT (ICOM)
Vassalli House
20 Central Road
Leeds LS1 6DE
Tel: 0532 461738  Fax: 0532 440002

ICOM can provide help and advice to anyone involved in setting up or running a workers' co-operative. A co-operative is a system where all the people working in a business or enterprise own and control the business. ICOM produce various factsheets and publications and can advise on legal issues affecting co-ops and sources of finance as well as putting you in touch with other co-ops. ICOM can also provide details of local Co-operative Development Agencies.

**AGE RANGE:**
Any
**HOW TO CONTACT:**
Letter, phone or fax for leaflets and information
**REGIONS SERVICED:**
UK
**SPECIAL NEEDS PROVISION:**
No special provision but anyone can use the services of ICOM
**COSTS/WAITING LISTS:**
Cost of membership depends on the size of co-op. Courses cost from £75. Various books and publications for sale

## INSIGHT INTO MANAGEMENT COURSES
### (Careers Research and Advisory Centre)
Sheraton House
Castle Park
Cambridge
CB3 0AX
Tel: 0223 460277 Fax: 0223 311708

Insight Courses give sixth-formers and undergraduates an insight into management. Students from a range of disciplines can meet individuals working in a wide variety of different organisations and gain experience of teamwork, analysing problems and making decisions under pressure. You will be encouraged to examine a wide range of career possibilities, discover what it is really like working in particular management areas and gain a general understanding of business priorities and the world of work.

**AGE RANGE:**
Sixth-formers and Undergraduates
**NUMBERS PASSING THROUGH:**
3,700 in 1990
**HOW TO CONTACT:**
CRAC mainly provide careers information through their publications, not through individual contact. For details of the range of careers books/publications contact; Hobsons Publishing, Bateman Street, Cambridge. Tel: 0223 354551. For information about 'Insight into Management' courses contact address above

**REGIONS SERVICED:**
UK
**COSTS/WAITING LISTS:**
Courses cost £35-£75

---

## INSTANT MUSCLE LTD (IM)
Springside House
84 North End Road
London W14 9ES
Tel: 071 603 2604  Fax: 071 603 7346

Instant Muscle provides a free, intensive, one-to-one business counselling and enterprise training, particularly for unemployed and disadvantaged people. IM will guide you through all the skills you need, such as taxation, marketing, accounting, book-keeping, and market research until your business is fit to be up and running.  It also offers a free 24-month aftercare service to all new businesses started at its Centres or on board its innovative Mobile Training Units.

**REGIONAL ADDRESSES:**
East Anglia: 7 Tey Road, Earls Colne,
Colchester CO6 2LG  Tel: 0787 222027
Humberside: Ground Floor, Carmelite House,
Posterngate, Hull HU1 2JN
Tel: 0482 588202
London: same as Head Office
North West: Lakeside Opportunities Centre,
Bowness Road, Middleton, Manchester

M24 4NU  Tel: 061 654 6874
South Wales: 13 Market Street, Pontypridd,
Mid Glamorgan CF37 2ST  Tel: 0443 486200
Yorkshire: 24b Hallgate, Doncaster
DN1 3NG Tel: 0302 364956

**AGE RANGE:**
18-59

**NUMBERS PASSING THROUGH:**
Nearly 500 in 1991 between 18 and 24 (46%
of total clients)

**HOW TO CONTACT:**
Telephone for an appointment or write to the
nearest Regional Office

**REGIONS SERVICED:**
See above

**SPECIAL NEEDS PROVISION:**
Enquiries welcome

**COSTS/WAITING LISTS:**
All services are free.  Waiting lists vary
between regions – in some, opportunities are
almost immediately available

---

**INSTITUTE FOR CITIZENSHIP STUDIES**
Queen Mary and Westfield College
University of London
Mile End Road
London E1 4NS
Tel: 071 975 5539  Fax: 071 607 7067

The purpose of this Institute, which was founded
by the then Speaker of the House of Commons
Bernard Weatherill, is to encourage citizenship,

in particular amongst young people. It runs competitions to offer opportunities to practice citizenship skills like letter writing and debating, as well as preparing materials to enable young people and their teachers to consider how democracy developed and how it works today.

### INSTITUTE FOR COMPLEMENTARY MEDICINE
21 Portland Place
London W1N 3AF

Alternative medicine covers a wide range of practices such as homoeopathy, where the whole person is taken into account in treatment rather than just individual symptoms, herbal medicine, acupuncture, reflexology and osteopathy to name just a few. Some training courses in alternative medicine require previous conventional medical training while others do not (homoeopathic doctors are medically qualified – although you can train and practice as a homoeopath without training as a doctor first). For more information on training available in alternative medicine send an SAE to the above address.

## INSTITUTE OF CHARTERED ACCOUNTANTS IN ENGLAND AND WALES
Chartered Accountants' Hall
PO Box 433
Moorgate Place
London EC2P 2BJ
Tel: 071 628 7060

The Institute of Chartered Accountants in England and Wales is the largest professional accountancy body in Europe with some 100,000 members. Its role is to educate and train members, to undertake technical work, to preserve the professional independence of chartered accountants and to maintain high standards of professional conduct. Members of the Institute work in a wide range of fields including public practice (i.e. for accountancy firms), in industry and commerce and the public sector. For further information on how to become a chartered accountant please contact, by letter or phone, the Institute's Student Recruitment Section at the above address.

## INSTITUTE OF PUBLIC RELATIONS
The Old Trading House
15 Northburgh Street
London EC1V 0PR
Tel: 071 253 5151

Public Relations Officers work towards

promoting the image of organisations in either the private or public sector. Private industry, central and local government, public services, trade unions and most other large organisations use PR to some extent to present themselves in the best way possible to the press, public, local communities, parliament, local councils, employees etc. using a variety of means e.g. press releases, reports, magazines, speeches etc. PR Officers either work for an agency or are employed by an individual organisation. The Institute of Public Relations can provide an information pack which outlines what public relations is all about and gives information on career development.

### INSTITUTE OF TRAVEL AND TOURISM (ITT)
113 Victoria Street
St Albans
Herts AL1 3TJ
Tel: 0727 54395

The ITT can provide a basic information pack, mainly aimed at school leavers and those thinking of changing their careers towards travel and tourism. It contains useful advice and information, lists of ITT approved colleges and the courses they offer, recommended reading and useful further contacts. Current price is £3. Contact above to check details of price and availability.

## INTERCULTURAL EDUCATIONAL PROGRAMMES (IEP)
Ground Floor Suite
Arden House
Main Street
Bingley
West Yorkshire BD16 2NB
Tel: 0274 560677  Fax: 0274 567675

IEP is the UK partner of AFS Intercultural programmes, a large worldwide network offering exchange opportunities. IEP offers young people the opportunity not just to live with a family abroad, but to become part of it for a year, attending school, learning the language and making a whole new network of friends. Participants develop a greater independence and self-confidence by dealing with new situations.  Support is given throughout the programme by the local AFS office, volunteers and the selected host family.

**AGE RANGE:**
15-18
**NUMBERS PASSING THROUGH:**
60 in the UK – 30,000 worldwide (IEP are aiming to expand future UK involvement)
**HOW TO CONTACT:**
Write or phone for information and an application form
**REGIONS SERVICED:**
UK

**SPECIAL NEEDS PROVISION:**
Each person is treated individually
**COSTS/WAITING LISTS:**
The full cost of participation on the year
programme is £3,450. Some scholarship
finance is available and applicants are
encouraged to seek sponsorship.
Applications for August departure need to be
in by December and Jan/Feb departures need
to apply by the end of October

## INTERNATIONAL ASSOCIATION FOR THE EXCHANGE OF STUDENTS FOR TECHNICAL EXPERIENCE (IAESTE)

Central Bureau for Educational Visits and
Exchanges
Seymour Mews
London W1H 9PE
Tel: 071 486 5101  Fax: 071 935 5741

IAESTE is an independent, non-political
worldwide organisation which arranges course-
related paid work placements for degree level
students in fields such as engineering, sciences,
agriculture and the applied arts. Most last for up
to 12 weeks during the summer, although longer
placements may be available.  Contact the
Central Bureau at the above address for more
information.

## INTERNATIONAL DIRECTORY OF
## VOLUNTARY WORK (publication)
Vacation Work Publications
9 Park End Street
Oxford OX1 1HJ
Tel: 0865 241978  Fax: 0865 790885

Directory which includes details of over 500
organisations wanting help from all types of
people for all types of work. Covers both short
and long term residential work in Britain and
around the world, and non-residential work in
the UK for those with the time to help a local
organisation or charity. Opportunities exist for
both skilled and unskilled people – dentists can
work for two years on a development project in
Malawi, or students can work on an
archaeological dig in France for a few weeks, or
can help an inner-city shelter for homeless
people.
ISBN 1 85458 085 X Available through libraries,
bookshops (price £8.95), or direct from the
above address (price £9.95 inc p&p).

## INTERNATIONAL HEALTH AND BEAUTY
## COUNCIL (IHBC)
109a Felpham Road
Felpham
West Sussex PO22 7PW

The International Health and Beauty Council
can provide a general careers information pack

covering the full range of jobs in the beauty industry, plus job-profiles and suggested career paths.

**AGE RANGE:**
Any
**HOW TO CONTACT:**
SAE to above address
**REGIONS SERVICED:**
UK

---

### INTERNATIONAL SOCIAL AND EDUCATION EXCHANGES (ISEE)
150 Bonnyton Drive
Eaglesham
Glasgow G76 0LU
Tel: 041 429 8722  Fax: 041 429 2117

ISEE can provide information, contacts, support, training, resources and general advice on any aspect of international youth mobility.

**REGIONAL ADDRESSES:**
Contact through above address
**AGE RANGE:**
In practice over 90% of those using ISEE are aged 12-27 but anyone can use the sevice
**HOW TO CONTACT:**
By letter or telephone to above address for further information
**REGIONS SERVICED:**
UK and abroad

**SPECIAL NEEDS PROVISION:**
ISEE has taken a special interest in the opening up of access to international opportunities to socially and physically disadvantaged groups

**COSTS/WAITING LISTS:**
No costs or waiting lists, but some replies at certain times of the year may take some time

---

## INTERNATIONAL STUDENT PLAYSCRIPT COMPETITION (ISPC)
World Student Drama Trust
20 Lansdowne Road
Muswell Hill
London N10 2AU
Tel: 081 883 4586  Fax: 081 883 7142

This annual competition is open to current or recent students. Applicants must have been full or part-time students on or after the 1st January of the year before the year of entry and scripts must be entered by 30th November. There are no restrictions on length, subject, setting etc. but scripts must be in English, or translated into English and be unperformed. All scripts will be considered for first performance by the National Student Theatre Company (see separate entry) or the young professional Springboard Theatre Company and each entry will receive a written criticism. The winner receives the World Student Drama Trust Award of £400 and, if practicable, a rehearsed reading at the following National

Student Drama Festival (see separate entry).

**AGE RANGE:**
Any
**HOW TO CONTACT:**
Details and entry forms available from above
address (but do not send scripts there)
**REGIONS SERVICED:**
UK and abroad
**COSTS/WAITING LISTS:**
Entry is free

## INTERNATIONAL THEATRE EXCHANGE (ITE)

Marjorie Havard
19 Abbey Park Road
Grimsby
Humberside DN32 0HJ
Tel: 0472 343424

International Theatre Exchange is the UK centre
of the International Amateur Theatre Association,
an organisation whose main aim is to promote
cultural exchange in the area of the performing
arts and arts education. It organises and conducts
international theatre workshops, festivals and
theatrical exchange visits, many of which are
based around youth and student theatre. All the
work of the ITE is carried out by experienced
people volunteering their services and funding
is provided by 'friends' – individuals and groups
involved in theatre in any of its forms, whether

student, amateur, professional, puppet, school,
fringe or community theatre. Write to the above
address for details of forthcoming events.

**AGE RANGE:**
Any
**HOW TO CONTACT:**
Contact the secretariat at the above address
for further information
**REGIONS SERVICED:**
UK
**SPECIAL NEEDS PROVISION:**
Not all venues are fully accessible
**COSTS/WAITING LISTS:**
Individual annual subscription is £6; group
subscription is £12. International work
involves costs such as air fares and groups
need to fund-raise to cover costs. It is often
worthwhile approaching businesses for
sponsorship and Local Authorities sometimes
assist with educational projects. Exchanges
and visits can take 12 months or more to fully
organise

## INTERNATIONAL VOLUNTARY SERVICE (IVS)

IVS aims to provide ways for individuals from
various countries to work together on socially
useful projects, in the hope of promoting peace
and understanding between people of different
nations. Each year they operate around 60

workcamps in Britain and hundreds abroad. Workcamps bring together a mix of volunteers, aged 18 and over, from different countries and backgrounds. The volunteers live and work co-operatively. Workcamps typically last between 2-4 weeks, with a wide range of projects being offered from camp to camp. They could involve work with children or disabled people, conservation, renovation, or solidarity with disadvantaged minorities. Wherever possible the workcamps offer a small 'study element' to allow volunteers to find out about the underlying issues that make the work important.

**REGIONAL ADDRESSES:**
North of England: IVS (North), 188 Roundhay Road, Leeds LS8 5PL
South of England: IVS (South), Old Hall East, Bergholt, Nr Colchester CO7 6TQ.
Scotland: IVS (Scotland) St John's Church, Princes Street, Edinburgh EH2 4BJ
Northern Ireland: see separate entry below
**AGE RANGE:**
18+
**HOW TO CONTACT:**
Letter plus SAE to appropriate regional office for information pack
**REGIONS SERVICED:**
England and Wales. See also entries for IVS SCOTLAND and IVS NORTHERN IRELAND
**SPECIAL NEEDS PROVISION:**
IVS promote open access and equal

opportunities in all their activities. Some projects, however, may not be suitable for people with disabilities – further information available on request

**COSTS/WAITING LISTS:**

Volunteers pay for their own travel to workcamps – assistance may be available, more details from IVS. Workcamp fees range from £45-£85

---

### INTERNATIONAL VOLUNTARY SERVICE (NORTHERN IRELAND)
122 Great Victoria Street
Belfast BT2 7BG
Tel: 0232 238147

IVS, through the Teenage Workcamp Scheme (TWS), provides opportunities for 16-19 year-old volunteers to work together with their European peers, through a programme of weekends and 2-week work camps. The emphasis of the TWS is on young people who would not normally have the opportunity to travel. After one year, opportunities exist to become more involved in organising your own activities, using the IVS international network. International Workcamps consist of an international group of volunteers. They last for 2-3 weeks and take place throughout Europe and America. Volunteers pay their own way to the camp and are offered food and accommodation in exchange for their labour.

**AGE RANGE:**
16-19 for Teenage Workcamp Scheme (TWS);
18+ for International Workcamps and
Regional voluntary work; 21+ for Asia/Africa
exchange

**NUMBERS PASSING THROUGH:**
c 150 per year

**HOW TO CONTACT:**
Telephone or in person for advice and
information. Also information available on
other organisations

**REGIONS SERVICED:**
Nothern Ireland

**SPECIAL NEEDS PROVISION:**
Some opportunities available. Varies
according to workcamp programme

**COSTS/WAITING LISTS:**
TWS is £2.50 per residential night in
Northern Ireland. TWS workcamps in Europe
cost £80 including all travel. International
Workcamps membership and registration
costs from £10 to £20 depending on income
(volunteer is responsible for own travel).
Camps in Eastern Europe cost an extra £30.
Apply for TWS from January to March

**INTERNSHIPS USA 1993 (publication)**
Vacation Work Publications
9 Park End Street
Oxford OX1 1HJ
Tel: 0865 241978  Fax: 0865 790885

Internship is the American word for short term work experience that enables students and graduates to get invaluable on-the-job training for a possible future career by acquiring the skills, ability and experience that can only be gained by a genuine period of work with an established organisation.  38,000 career-orientated positions in the USA are listed in fields ranging from business to theatre, communications to science.  Many are open to British students.  The book explains when, where and how to apply for both positions and work permits.

ISBN 1 56079 149 7. Available through libraries, bookshops (price £15.95), or direct from the above address (price £16.95 inc p&p).

## JOBCENTRES

Jobcentres have the largest computer-based vacancy system in the country, displaying local job vacancies and vacancies from other parts of the country and overseas.  If you find a suitable vacancy one of the staff will be happy to discuss it with you and then phone the employer to arrange an interview.  Jobcentres can also offer advice to help with your job search through things like jobclubs and Job Search Seminars, as well as information on opportunities to become self-employed.  Consult your local telephone directory for your nearest Jobcentre.

## JOHN HALL PRE-UNIVERSITY INTERIM COURSE

12 Gainsborough Road
Ipswich
Suffolk
IP4 2UR
Tel: 0473 251223  Fax: 0473 288009

The pre-university interim course has been running for 25 years. It lasts about seven weeks running from late January to mid March. It is about European Civilization. The course begins with an introduction in London, and thereafter in Venice. There are optional extensions to the course held in Florence and Rome. The course is for students who have just left school – the average age is 18. It is open to Arts and Science students alike. No previous knowledge of European art or music history is required. It offers a foretaste of a university style of learning and living. The course is a programme of lectures, classes, walk-abouts and special study visits, language teaching, photography, and life-drawing and painting classes, and free time and individual visits.

**AGE RANGE:**
c 18
**HOW TO CONTACT:**
Write to above
**REGIONS SERVICED:**
UK

**COSTS/WAITING LISTS:**
1993 – c £3,000. Scholarships offered by
The National Association of Decorative and
Fine Arts Societies (NADFAS), but only to
applicants who have been members of Young
NADFAS for at least 2 consecutive years and
who are under 19 at the time of application

## JUBILEE SAILING TRUST (JST)
Test Road, Eastern Docks
Southampton
Hants SO1 1GG
Tel: 0703 631395/631388  Fax: 0703 638625

Jubilee Sailing Trust offers young people aged
16 and over the opportunity to experience the
challenge and adventure of crewing a 490-ton
tall ship at sea for up to 10 days regardless of
their physical ability. Voyages comprise an
equal number of physically handicapped and
able-bodied people aged 16 to 70.

**AGE RANGE:**
16+
**HOW TO CONTACT:**
Telephone or letter (with SAE) to the Public
Relations Department
**REGIONS SERVICED:**
UK, Channel Islands, Republic of Ireland,
Overseas
**SPECIAL NEEDS PROVISION:**
Provision for physically disabled

**COSTS/WAITING LISTS:**
UK voyages range from £200 (3 days) to £695 (10 days), Canaries voyages from £295 (8 days) to £600 (19 days). Associate membership is £15pa. There are various bursaries and Trusts from which some funding is available – details from JST. Applications should be made two months in advance

### JUNIOR ASTRONOMICAL SOCIETY (JAS)
36 Fairway
Keyworth
Nottingham NG12 5DU

The JAS is open to beginners and more experienced amateur astronomers of all ages. There are four meetings each year in London and occassional meetings and weekend courses away from London. Publications include the *Popular Astronomy* magazine four times a year as well as news circulars usually about six times a year. The society also provides a GCSE advisory service and an instrument advisory service, and society officials are pleased to correspond with young people to provide help and guidance. Members may contribute to specialist observing sections.

**AGE RANGE:**
Any
**NUMBERS PASSING THROUGH:**
Nearly 3,000 members

**HOW TO CONTACT:**
Write with SAE to above address for
information leaflet and an application form
**REGIONS SERVICED:**
UK and overseas
**SPECIAL NEEDS PROVISION:**
Require notice of attendance as some
activities may not be accessible
**COSTS/WAITING LISTS:**
Annual UK subscription is £10 per year
which includes all publications. Weekend
courses are charged at cost for
accommodation, food etc.

---

### KIBBUTZ REPRESENTATIVES
1A Accommodation Road
London NW11 8ED
Tel: 081 458 9235  Fax: 081 455 7930

An opportunity to live and work on a Kibbutz in
Israel. A Kibbutz is a co-operative community
and in exchange for working you will be provided
with accommodation, meals and all the leisure
facilities and activities of the Kibbutz.
Occasional trips around the country will be
arranged and a small allowance provided to
cover essentials. You need to be in good
physical and mental health, have at least eight
weeks to spare and be interested in participating
in an alternative and communal lifestyle.

**AGE RANGE:**
18-32

**NUMBERS PASSING THROUGH:**
3,000
**HOW TO CONTACT:**
SAE to address above for information and
application forms
**REGIONS SERVICED:**
UK
**SPECIAL NEEDS PROVISION:**
No provision
**COSTS/WAITING LISTS:**
Registration fee approx £40; Return fare to
Israel (varies according to time of year);
insurance £32-£80.  Costs are the same
whether you go for 8 weeks or 6 months
(present maximum).  Applications normally
take 3-6 weeks to process but applications for
July and August should be sent by April

---

**KIBBUTZ VOLUNTEER (publication)**
Vacation Work Publications
9 Park End Street
Oxford OX1 1HJ
Tel: 0865 241978  Fax: 0865 790885

A guide to life on a Kibbutz.  The book gives
details of 200 Kibbutzim, and describes what to
expect when working in one.  Also gives details
of other vacation and short term work available
in Israel – the Moshav Movement, conservation,
archaeological digs, fruit picking, voluntary work
with Palestinian refugees, au pair work, and
hotel jobs in Eilat.  Sections devoted to Kibbutz

Ulpan, money, customs, food and drink, where to stay, and generally how to see the country as an insider rather than a tourist.
ISBN 1 85458 021 3. Available through libraries, bookshops (price £5.95), or direct from the above address (price £6.95 inc p&p).

### LABOUR PARTY
150 Walworth Road
London SE17 1JT
Tel: 071 701 1234

### LAND USE VOLUNTEERS (LUV)
c/o Horticultural Therapy
Goulds Ground
Vallis Way, Frome
Somerset BA11 3DW
Tel: 0373 464782  Fax: 0373 464782

If you have experience and/or basic qualifications in horticulture, have worked in some capacity with people with special needs, and are looking for a way to use your skills LUV will help. They help projects use horticulture as therapy for people with disabilities, by providing a volunteer with horticultural skills. You may help in preparing a new site for a horticultural therapy unit, or train clients and care staff in basic horticultural tasks. LUV will place you in a project that reflects your own particular skills and interests. Minimum period of service is six months, the maximum one year. Board, lodging and pocket money provided throughout your stay.

**AGE RANGE:**
18+
**HOW TO CONTACT:**
Letter, telephone to above address for application form and fuller details
**REGIONS SERVICED:**
England, Wales, Northern Ireland. See entry for HORTICULTURAL VOLUNTEERS IN SCOTLAND for Scottish equivalent
**SPECIAL NEEDS PROVISION:**
LUV act as a clearing house, matching volunteers with projects. Any volunteer with special needs would be carefully placed in a project which had committed their support

## LAURA ASHLEY FOUNDATION
33 King Street
London WC2
Tel: 071 497 2503

The Laura Ashley Foundation will consider applications for course fees in cases of hardship for any course held at a further education college, e.g. City and Guilds, foundation courses, nursery nursing, 'A' level, GCSE or BTEC.

**AGE RANGE:**
18+
**NUMBERS PASSING THROUGH:**
150

**HOW TO CONTACT:**
Telephone or letter for information and an
application form
**REGIONS SERVICED:**
UK
**SPECIAL NEEDS PROVISION:**
Anyone can apply
**COSTS/WAITING LISTS:**
Apply before the course begins

---

### LAW SOCIETY
Careers Office
227-228 The Strand
London WC2R 1BA
Tel: 071 242 1222.

The Law Society produce a range of careers
leaflets and brochures and can provide advice
and information about training and developing
a career as a solicitor.

**REGIONAL OFFICES:**
Scotland: Legal Education Department, 26
Drumsheugh Gardens, Edinburgh EH3 7YR
Tel: 031 226 7411
Northern Ireland: 98 Victoria Street, Belfast
BT1 3JZ  Tel: 0232 231614

---

### LIBERAL DEMOCRATS
4 Cowley Street
London SW1P 3NB
Tel: 071 222 7999

## LITTLE THEATRE GUILD OF GREAT BRITAIN (LTG)
Secretariat
Ann Mattey
Flat 6, 34 Broadwater Down
Tunbridge Wells
TN2 5NX

LTG members are independent, non-commercial companies producing several plays a year. There are 64 member theatres most of which have a youth or junior section and provide some form of training for young people, workshops and student productions. If you have an interest in any aspect of theatre, the LTG can direct you to your nearest suitable member company or alternatively look up the theatres in your area at your local library.

**REGIONAL ADDRESSES:**
Three regional offices – Northern (including Scotland), Midland and Southern – details from above

**AGE RANGE:**
Any

**HOW TO CONTACT:**
Send SAE to above address or call 0472 343424 for further information including details of the nearest suitable LTG member

**REGIONS SERVICED:**
UK

**SPECIAL NEEDS PROVISION:**
Each member theatre of the LTG varies in

facilities and provision
**COSTS/WAITING LISTS:**
Annual subscriptions/membership fees vary
as do course and workshop fees.  There is
often a limit to the number of training places
available and those wishing to participate
join a waiting list.  6 months is a usual
waiting time

---

### LIVEWIRE
Hawthorn House
Forth Banks
Newcastle-upon Tyne NE1 3SG
Tel: 091 261 5584  Fax: 091 261 1910

Livewire can provide information, advice and
support to young people who are thinking of
starting up in business, and to those already
established in business.  Sponsored by Shell
(UK) Limited, there are three key elements to the
Livewire service:

The Enquiry and Link Up Service: young people
anywhere in the UK can be linked to appropriate
local advice and support on starting up in
business.

The Business Start Up Awards: £175,000 worth
of cash awards and help in kind is available
through this awards competition in a series of
county, regional, national and UK events.  It is
based on submission of a business plan for a
new business and awards are made by
independent judging panels.

Business Growth Challenge: a management development programme for young owner managers of established businesses.

**REGIONAL ADDRESSES:**
Livewire England: The Fishergate Centre, 4 Fishergate, York YO1 4AB  Tel: 0904 613696 Fax: 0904 613696
Livewire Scotland: Romano House, 43 Station Road, Corstorphine, Edinburgh EH12 7AF Tel: 031 334 9876  Fax: 031 316 4521
Livewire Northern Ireland: Young Business Centre, 103-107 York Street,
Belfast BT15 1AB  Tel: 0232 328000  Fax: 0232 439666
Livewire Cymru: Greenfield Valley Enterprise Centre, Greenfield Road, Greenfield, Holywell, Clwyd CH8 7QB  Tel: 0352 710199

**AGE RANGE:**
16-25 for enquiry service and Start Up awards.  Up to 35 for Business Growth Challenge

**NUMBERS PASSING THROUGH:**
£175,000 worth of awards shared between approx. 300 young businesses nationally. 10,000 young people linked to information/ advice.  500 people helped through the Business Growth Challenge

**HOW TO CONTACT:**
Telephone UK or national Livewire offices above.  Information is usually available in Careers Offices, Jobcentres and Local

Enterprise Agencies. Or write to one of the
following Freepost adresses:-
Livewire UK, FREEPOST, Newcastle-upon-
Tyne NE1 1BR
Livewire Cymru, FREEPOST,
Holywell CH8 7YZ
Livewire Scotland, FREEPOST,
Edinburgh EH12 0PE
Livewire Northern Ireland, FREEPOST,
Belfast BT15 1BR
**REGIONS SERVICED:**
UK
**SPECIAL NEEDS PROVISION:**
Support is available to any young person
regardless of ability
**COSTS/WAITING LISTS:**
No costs. All enquiries are dealt with
promptly

---

## LIVEWIRE
## BUSINESS START UP AWARDS
for contact details see main LIVEWIRE entry

This awards scheme is open to entrants aged 16-
25 who submit a business plan to their local
Livewire co-ordinator which is then assessed by
independent judging panels. Over 80 awards
presentations take place each year at county,
regional and national levels leading to the
prestigious Livewire UK finals. Each year up to
£175,000 is given in awards. The scheme
provides an opportunity for young businesses,

advisers, organisers and sponsors to mix and learn from one another.

## LLOYDS BANK THEATRE CHALLENGE
Education Department
Royal National Theatre
South Bank
London SE1 9PX

The Lloyds Bank Theatre Challenge is a year-round scheme to promote and celebrate young people's theatre across the country, culminating in an annual three-day summer showcase at the Royal National Theatre. Any company of 2 to 50 members aged 11-19 can take part and when you've prepared your production, Royal National Theatre assessors will come and visit you. Every company visited receives a written report and verbal advice on its production. For full details of the challenge and information on a series of workshops run in connection with the scheme, contact the above address.

**AGE RANGE:**
11-19
**HOW TO CONTACT:**
Send a large SAE to the above address for further details and an application form
**REGIONS SERVICED:**
UK
**SPECIAL NEEDS PROVISION:**
Applications welcome

**COSTS/WAITING LISTS:**
No costs for entry.  The closing date for
applications is usually around the end of
October each year

## LOCAL ENTERPRISE COMPANIES
## (SCOTLAND)
Contact through Jobcentre or telephone
directory.

Youth Training, Employment Training and
Enterprise Allowance schemes in Scotland are
all managed by Local Enterprise Companies.
Their programmes are structured for the area in
which they operate, and they can provide advice,
information on all aspects of youth training in
Scotland.

## LOCAL ENTERPRISE DEVELOPMENT UNIT
## (LEDU)
LEDU House
Upper Galwally
Belfast BT8 4TB
Tel: 0232 491031  Fax: 0232 691432

As well as offering financial assistance, LEDU
can provide advice, guidance and information
to anyone in Northern Ireland on setting up in
business.

**REGIONAL ADDRESSES:**
Six regional offices throughout Northern

Ireland – full details from the above address

**AGE RANGE:**
17+

**NUMBERS PASSING THROUGH:**
400-500

**HOW TO CONTACT:**
Contact through any local LEDU regional
office or direct to above address

**REGIONS SERVICED:**
Northern Ireland

**SPECIAL NEEDS PROVISION:**
Disabled programmes available

**COSTS/WAITING LISTS:**
None

## THE LOCAL GOVERNMENT MANAGEMENT BOARD
Arndale House
Arndale Centre
Luton LU1 2TS
Tel: 0582 451166

There are three main types of employment in
local government; professionals such as
accountants and architects who train in their
own field first and take up employment in local
government; specialists who train in a specific
area of local government such as Environmental
Health Officers; and administrators and clerical
workers who carry out the day to day running of
local government affairs. The Local Government
Management Board can provide further

information about training and career structure for specialists, administrators and clerical workers.

## LONDON COLLEGE OF FASHION
20 John Prince's Street
London W1M 0BJ
Tel: 071 629 9401

The London College of Fashion, as well as offering a wide variety of training and courses in all aspects of fashion including clothing, tailoring, fashion hairstyling, embroidery etc., also produces a range of leaflets and can offer advice and information covering many aspects of the beauty industry including background information about starting up and developing a career in modelling.

## MARINE CONSERVATION SOCIETY
9 Gloucester Road
Ross-on-Wye
Herefordshire
HR9 5BU
Tel: 0989 66017  Fax: 0989 67815

Information on all aspects of marine conservation; factsheets for students/pupils; advice on careers in marine sciences; surveys and projects which encourage young people to take an active role e.g. Coastwatch UK, Dogwhelk survey, Marine curio survey; clothing with a conservation message.  MCS Sales Ltd stock many publications suitable for young people.

**REGIONAL ADDRESSES:**
List of local groups available from main office
**AGE RANGE:**
Any
**NUMBERS PASSING THROUGH:**
6,000 enquiries from young people
**HOW TO CONTACT:**
SAE to Enquiry Secretary for membership leaflet, factsheets and information
**REGIONS SERVICED:**
UK
**COSTS/WAITING LISTS:**
Annual membership fee – £12

---

### THE MERLIN TRUST
The Dower House
Boughton House
Kettering
Northamptonshire NN14 1BJ
Tel: 0536 82279

The Merlin Trust was set up in memory of keen naturalists Sir David Scott and his son Merlin, who was killed during the Second World War aged 20.  It offers practical assistance to young horticulturalists who are driven by their love of plants.  Assistance takes the form of grants of up to £500 for study projects either in Britain or abroad. Projects can involve photography, painting, written observations, seed collecting, or help with conservation projects, especially involving garden plants. Travelling and other expenses are paid. Please note that grants are not normally given for post-graduate study or to fund highly technical, laboratory-based research.

**AGE RANGE:**
18 – 30, though age matters less than a genuine keenness for plants, gardens or gardening. Applicants should be able to show that their proposed applications will help them in their careers

**NUMBERS PASSING THROUGH:**
An average of 25 a year

**HOW TO CONTACT:**
Write for application form, enclosing a large A4 SAE to the Hon. Secretary at the above address

**REGIONS SERVICED:**
UK

**COSTS/WAITING LISTS:**
No costs. Applications dealt with on a first come/first served basis

---

**MINORITIES ARTS ADVISORY SERVICE LTD
(MAAS)**
4th Floor
28 Shacklewell Lane
London E8 2EZ
Tel: 071 254 7295
(Advice and Information line)

MAAS is an arts development agency strongly involved in the advancing and promotion of the black arts sector by providing advice and information, research, initiating conferences and seminars and providing information on training opportunities for administrators, artists and cultural workers. The Advice and Information services are available to artists and arts organisations, students and researchers, educational and training agencies and members of the general public. They also publish an intercultural arts magazine, *Artrage*, containing interviews, articles, listings and reviews on fine arts, the performing arts, literature and the media arts.

**AGE RANGE:**
Any
**HOW TO CONTACT:**
Write or telephone for advice and information
**REGIONS SERVICED:**
UK

## MOBILITY INTERNATIONAL
228 Borough High Street
London SE1 1JX
Tel: 071 403 5688  Fax: 071 378 1292

Mobility International organises projects in the UK and abroad for disabled young people of different nationalities and with different abilities.

The aim is to give all young people – regardless of their needs – the chance to learn new skills and gain confidence through international travel. Some projects are only open to people with a particular disability, others can be enjoyed by everybody. If you are disabled MI may have a project for you – brush up on a foreign language, improve your employment prospects, meet new friends. Assistance available towards the cost of bringing a helper/companion with you. Full details of opportunities available are in the annual programme.

**AGE RANGE:**
16-30 (but this is flexible)
**HOW TO CONTACT:**
Telephone, letter, fax or in person for an annual programme of events and activities
**REGIONS SERVICED:**
UK
**SPECIAL NEEDS PROVISION:**
See above
**COSTS/WAITING LISTS:**
Costs of activities and events vary and some funding is available from various sources such as LEAs, Trusts etc.

**MUSIC IN SCOTLAND TRUST (MIST)**
PO Box 183
Glasgow G3 8DG
Tel: 041 204 1961

The Music in Scotland Trust is a unique charity which assists young people between 18 and 25 by securing funding and providing music-related information and advice to those wishing to set up in business in the Scottish music industry. The trust has close links with the Prince's Scottish Youth Business Trust and can assist with everything from helping with the development of a business plan to providing places at music industry seminars and helps in a wide variety of ways according to need.

**AGE RANGE:**
18-25
**NUMBERS PASSING THROUGH:**
500
**HOW TO CONTACT:**
Telephone or letter (with SAE) or by contacting the Prince's Scottish Youth Business Trust in your area
**REGIONS SERVICED:**
Scotland
**SPECIAL NEEDS PROVISION:**
Enquiries welcome
**COSTS/WAITING LISTS:**
No costs or waiting lists

---

**MUSICIANS UNION (MU)**
60-62 Clapham Road
London SW9 0JJ
Tel: 071 582 5566  Fax: 071 582 9805

The Musicians Union exists to support those who earn their living, or part of it from any kind of music. Any kind of musician is welcome, from early music specialists through to rappers. Benefits include access to legal advice about musical employment, contracts advice, career advice, insurance for equipment, and access to a wealth of information covering all aspects of the music industry.

**REGIONAL ADDRESSES:**
East/North East: 193 Dogsthorpe Road, Peterborough PE1 3AT  Tel: 0733 557555
Fax: 0733 898224
London: as Head Office above
Midlands: Unit A, Benson House, Lombard Street, Birmingham B12 0QR
Tel: 021 622 3870  Fax: 021 622 5361
North/North East: 327 Roundhay Road, Leeds LS8 4HT  Tel: 0532 481335
Fax: 0532 481292
North West: 40 Canal Street, Manchester M1 3WD  Tel: 061 236 1764  Fax: 061 236 0159
Scotland: 135 Wellington Street, Glasgow G2 2XD  Tel: 041 248 3723  Fax: 041 204 3510
South East: as Head Office above
South West: 131 St George's Road, Bristol BS1 5UW  Tel: 0272 265438
Fax: 0272 253729
**AGE RANGE:**
Any
**HOW TO CONTACT:**
Letter, telephone, fax for membership details

and application forms
**REGIONS SERVICED:**
UK
**SPECIAL NEEDS PROVISION:**
Enquiries welcome
**COSTS/WAITING LISTS:**
Membership costs vary depending on how
much you are earning from your music

---

### NATIONAL ASSOCIATION FOR THE CARE AND RESETTLEMENT OF OFFENDERS – YOUTH ACTIVITIES UNIT (NACRO)
169 Clapham Road
Stockwell
London SW9 0PU
Tel: 071 582 6500

NACRO can provide information concerning
criminal offences, the police, the courts and
criminal records. In nine areas of England
NACRO run Youth Activities Units where young
people participate in organising their own
activities when previously there were very few.
Projects recruit volunteers (including 15-21 year-
olds) to help develop new provision. NACRO
also has a number of Youth Training and
Employment Training Schemes.

**REGIONAL ADDRESSES:**
South: 2nd Floor, Cranmer House, 39 Brixton
Road, London SW9 6DZ Tel: 071 735 0744
Midlands: 2nd Floor, 16 Darlington Street,

Wolverhampton WV1 4HW  Tel: 0902
715557
**AGE RANGE:**
Any
**NUMBERS PASSING THROUGH:**
3,000
**HOW TO CONTACT:**
Letter to South or Midlands office for
information on current projects or suitable
alternatives
**REGIONS SERVICED:**
Criminal justice information service available
nationwide.  Location of youth projects vary
**SPECIAL NEEDS PROVISION:**
Young people with physical disabilities will
be accommodated wherever possible.  Those
with learning difficulties are especially
welcome if it is causing school, social or
integration problems
**COSTS/WAITING LISTS:**
Occasionally, contributions are required
towards the costs of activities

### NATIONAL ASSOCIATION OF BOYS
### CLUBS (NABC)
369 Kennington Lane
London SE11 5QY
Tel: 071 793 0787  Fax: 071 820 9815

Boys Clubs exist to encourage the development
of boys and young men – although 50% of clubs
welcome girls! – in a co-operative and enjoyable

environment. There is no typical type of Boys Club – most are just places where young people go for enjoyment. But there are also clubs of a specialist nature e.g. single activity groups for boxing, football etc. In more and more clubs the members are forging vital links with their local communities, perhaps by fund-raising for a local cause, or through helping the elderly and the disabled. Sport is important in Boys Clubs but there are also opportunities for other outdoor pursuits such as adventure schemes and exhibitions. Members are encouraged to participate in activities such as the Duke of Edinburgh's Award, Operation Raleigh, Community Sports Leader Award etc. There are also opportunities for creativity in the visual arts, drama and music using the latest techniques and technologies – airbrush, spray-painting, computers, film, video etc.

**AGE RANGE:**
c 11-19
**NUMBERS PASSING THROUGH:**
200,000
**HOW TO CONTACT:**
Letter, telephone for general information about NABC, and for details of clubs in your area
**REGIONS SERVICED:**
UK
**SPECIAL NEEDS PROVISION:**
Enquiries welcome

## NATIONAL ASSOCIATION OF
## EDUCATION DEVELOPMENT CENTRES
6 Endsleigh Street
London WC1H 0DX
Tel: 071 388 2670

Organisation which can give support and advice on exchange trips and other aspects of forging short and long-term links with peoples from around the world.

## NATIONAL ASSOCIATION OF VOLUNTEER
## BUREAUX (NAVB)
St Peter's College
College Road
Saltley
Birmingham B8 3TE
Tel: 021 327 0265  Fax: 021 327 3696

NAVB can give you details of your nearest Volunteeer Bureau.  Volunteer Bureaux offer advice and information on volunteering opportunities in your local area.  A Bureau will also be able to put you in touch with organisations in your local area who want to recruit volunteers.

**AGE RANGE:**
Any
**HOW TO CONTACT:**
Letter, telephone, fax to above address
**REGIONS SERVICED:**
England, Wales and Northern Ireland

**SPECIAL NEEDS PROVISION:**
Volunteer Bureaux cater for people with
special needs

---

### NATIONAL ASSOCIATION OF YOUTH
### ORCHESTRAS (NAYO)
Ainslie House
11 St Colme Street
Edinburgh EH3 6AG
Tel: 031 225 4606  Fax: 031 225 3568

The NAYO exists to represent youth orchestras
(including chamber, symphonic, wind and jazz
orchestras) throughout the country and to foster
their development.  The association organises
an Anglo-German youth music week each
summer for musicians of both countries aged
15-25, can arrange tuition/coaching for young
musicians and has a free ticket scheme for
Edinburgh and Glasgow Festivals of British Youth
Orchestras.  The NAYO publishes a news
bulletin, *Full Orchestra* containing news of youth
orchestras, courses, future events, foreign travel
etc., and can provide ideas for concert
programmes, advice on overseas travel,
exchange of platforms etc. and is happy to deal
with enquiries about youth music from anyone.

**AGE RANGE:**
No specific age range
**HOW TO CONTACT:**
By letter for advice and information

**REGIONS SERVICED:**
UK
**SPECIAL NEEDS PROVISION:**
Services open to all young people with an
interest in music

---

## NATIONAL ASSOCIATION OF YOUTH
## THEATRES (NAYT)
The Bond
180-182 Fazeley Street
Birmingham B5 5SE
Tel: 021 766 8920  Fax: 021 766 8505

The NAYT holds the most comprehensive list of
youth theatres in the UK (over 700 which involve
at least 40,000 young people). They can put
you in contact with your local group, provide
more information about youth theatre and give
informal advice regarding theatre as a hobby
and as a career. If you already have experience
and are interested in starting your own youth
theatre, NAYT has a range of services that can
help you.

**AGE RANGE:**
No specific age range.
**NUMBERS PASSING THROUGH:**
Indirectly, approximately 20,000
**HOW TO CONTACT:**
Easiest to contact by letter (with SAE) for
individual advice (if applicable), a copy of
NAYT magazine *React* and any other

information as appropriate

**REGIONS SERVICED:**

UK

**SPECIAL NEEDS PROVISION:**

Details available of youth theatres which cater for or work solely with young people with special needs, as well as specific advice relating to special needs

**COSTS/WAITING LISTS:**

Membership costs about £15 annually for groups and individuals. Course fees vary from £5 for a day course to £90 for a weekend. Substantial financial support is usually given to young people from various sources including the NAYT's own assistance fund, the Prince's Trust, local County Councils and Regional Arts Boards

---

### NATIONAL BOARD FOR NURSING, MIDWIFERY AND HEALTH VISITING

Contact the relevant national board for information on courses and careers in nursing including hospital nursing, midwifery, community nursing, occupational health nursing and working as a health visitor. You can also obtain information on training from the Regional Nursing Officer at your nearest NHS Regional Health Authority.

**NATIONAL BOARDS:**

England: Resource and Careers Services, Chantry

House, 798 Chesterfield Road
Sheffield S8 0SF   Tel: 0742 551064/5
Northern Ireland: RAC House, 79 Chichester
Street, Belfast BT1 4JR Tel: 0232 238152
Scotland: 22 Queen Street, Edinburgh EH2 1JX
Tel: 031 226 7371
Wales: 13th Floor, Pearl Assurance House,
Greyfriars Road, Cardiff CF1 3AG  Tel: 0222
395535

---

## NATIONAL COACHING FOUNDATION
### (NCF)
4 College Close
Beckett Park
Leeds LS6 3QH
Tel: 0532 744802

The NCF can give information about developing
a career as a sports coach – how to get in,
coaching courses, and lists of useful further
contacts.   The NCF provides courses and
publications on sports coaching.

**REGIONAL ADDRESSES:**
A list of national coaching courses across the
UK is available from the above address
**AGE RANGE:**
Any
**HOW TO CONTACT:**
Large SAE required for careers factsheets.
Letter, telephone for information and advice
**REGIONS SERVICED:**
UK

**SPECIAL NEEDS PROVISION:**
Enquiries welcome

---

### NATIONAL COUNCIL FOR DRAMA TRAINING (NCDT)
5 Tavistock Place
London WC1H 9SS
Tel: 071 387 3650

The NCDT can provide information on professional training courses in drama. Send SAE to the above address for an up-to-date list.

---

### NATIONAL COUNCIL FOR THE TRAINING OF JOURNALISTS (NCTJ)
Latton Bush Centre
Southern Way
Harlow
Essex CM18 7BL
Tel: 0279 430009

Trainee journalists study and train for professional qualifications approved by the NCTJ, who can provide information about courses in journalism – where they are held, entry requirements, duration etc. Please mark all written correspondence 'Pre-entry'.

## NATIONAL EXTENSION COLLEGE (NEC)
18 Brooklands Avenue
Cambridge
CB2 2HN
Tel: 0223 316644  Fax: 0223 313586

The National Extension College offers a wide range of courses which people of all ages can undertake in their own time, at their own pace, and in their own way. Independent Study courses leading to GCSEs, City and Guilds, BTEC, 'A' levels, RSA, Degrees etc. are available. 'Open Entry' to an independent study course means that you can start a course at any time. Students are given ongoing support by personal tutors – usually by letter or telephone – leading to examinations which can be taken when and if the student chooses. Full courses list available from NEC.

**AGE RANGE:**
Any
**HOW TO CONTACT:**
Telephone, letter or fax for information pack
**REGIONS SERVICED:**
UK
**SPECIAL NEEDS PROVISION:**
Enquiries welcome
**COSTS/WAITING LISTS:**
Price list of courses available from NEC

## NATIONAL FEDERATION OF CITY FARMS (NFCF)
AMF House
93 Whitby Road
Brislington
Bristol BS4 3QF
Tel: 0272 719109

NFCF brings the countryside to the city by setting up and running small farm holdings in built-up areas where many of us live. For more information about the work of NFCF, addresses of farms in your local area and advice on how to become involved in the city farm movement – either voluntarily or as a worker – contact the address above.

**AGE RANGE:**
Any
**HOW TO CONTACT:**
Letter to above address. SAE required for written information
**REGIONS SERVICED:**
UK

## NATIONAL FEDERATION OF GATEWAY CLUBS
117 Golden Lane
London EC1Y 0RT
Tel: 071 454 0454  Fax: 071 608 3254

Gateway clubs offer leisure opportunities to

people of all ages with a learning disability. The activities provided aim to advance the personal development of club members by promoting choice and independence. Members are encouraged to become involved in the wider community through the club. The Gateway Award incorporates these aims and activities into a progressive award scheme. Able-bodied volunteers always needed to help with the work of the clubs.

**REGIONAL ADDRESSES:**
South: as Head Office above
East: 4 Scotgate, Stamford, Lincs PE9 2YB
Tel: 0780 51199
West: 127b Pembroke Road, Clifton, Bristol
BS8 3ES  Tel: 0272 742547
North: 119 Drake Street, Rochdale OL1 1PZ
Tel: 0706 344800
Northern Ireland: Segal House, 4 Annadale
Avenue, Belfast BT7 3JH  Tel: 0232 691351
Wales: 169A City Road, Cardiff CF2 2JB  Tel:
0222 494933
**AGE RANGE:**
Any
**NUMBERS PASSING THROUGH:**
35,000 members
**HOW TO CONTACT:**
Letter or telephone to Head or Regional
Offices who will put you in touch with
nearest Gateway group
**REGIONS SERVICED:**
England, Northern Ireland, Wales

**SPECIAL NEEDS PROVISION:**
Exclusively for people with learning
disabilities, although any young people can
join clubs as volunteers
**COSTS/WAITING LISTS:**
Gateway clubs each set their own
membership fees which are usually very low
or even free

---

### NATIONAL FEDERATION OF MUSIC
### SOCIETIES (NFMS)
Francis House
Francis Street
London SW1P 1DE
Tel: 071 828 7320  Fax: 071 828 5504

NFMS is the national body covering all types of
music societies. They can put you in touch with
a local society or offer help and advice to
anyone who wants to set up a new music club
or society. Most of their member societies are
orchestras and choirs but they are keen to
encourage other types of music such as jazz,
steel bands, folk music, Indian music etc.

**REGIONAL ADDRESSES:**
12 regions – contact through Head Office
**AGE RANGE:**
Any
**HOW TO CONTACT:**
Telephone Head Office who will put you in
touch with a local regional contact

**REGIONS SERVICED:**
England, Wales and Scotland
**SPECIAL NEEDS PROVISION:**
Depends on individual societies
**COSTS/WAITING LISTS:**
Costs vary between societies

## NATIONAL FEDERATION OF YOUNG FARMERS CLUBS (NFYFC)
National Agricultural Centre
Stoneleigh Park
Kenilworth
Warwickshire CV8 2LG
Tel: 0203 696544  Fax: 0203 696559

The services provided by YFCs include; educational services e.g. courses, seminars, publications and training aids; many social functions; competitions held at regional and national level; the opportunity to travel via the international exchange programme; a wide range of sporting activities; encouragement for young people to take an interest in and express an opinion on farming and countryside issues.

**REGIONAL ADDRESSES:**
Wales: YFC Centre, Llanelwedd, Builth Wells, Powys LD2 3SY  Tel: 0982 553502
**AGE RANGE:**
10-26
**NUMBERS PASSING THROUGH:**
37,500 members

**HOW TO CONTACT:**
Telephone or letter to Head Office or any
County Office (listed in telephone book)
**REGIONS SERVICED:**
All of Wales and the majority of England
**SPECIAL NEEDS PROVISION:**
No special provision but every effort made to
accommodate special requirements when the
need arises
**COSTS/WAITING LISTS:**
Annual subscriptions vary between £5 and
£10

## NATIONAL MUSEUM OF PHOTOGRAPHY, FILM AND TELEVISION (NMPFT)

Pictureville
Bradford
West Yorkshire BD1 1NQ
Tel: 0274 727488 (Museum), 0274 725347
(Education Unit)  Fax: 0274 723155

The museum has six storeys of interactive
exhibitions and displays taking you into the
fascinating worlds of television, film and
photography. It also houses Britain's only IMAX
cinema – with daily showings of a changing
programme of films on the 52' x 64' screen –
and is the home to the first museum resident
theatre company, Action Replay, whose regular
performances around the Museum bring displays
and exhibitions to life.  The Education Unit
organises a programme of talks, workshops,

demonstrations etc. as well as special events and courses for young people including the Co-op Young People's Film and Video Festival, summer workshops and much more. The Museum, jointly with Bradford University, runs a B.Sc. course in Electronic Imaging.

**AGE RANGE:**
Any
**NUMBERS PASSING THROUGH:**
750,000 each year
**HOW TO CONTACT:**
By letter or phone call to the Education Unit or Museum switchboard. Group visits welcome and education packs available
**REGIONS SERVICED:**
UK
**SPECIAL NEEDS PROVISION:**
Museum is accessible to people with special needs with ramps and lifts to the entrance and all levels. IMAX cinema can accommodate two wheelchairs – advance booking for these spaces is strongly recommended
**COSTS/WAITING LISTS:**
Charges made for some events/workshops. School groups should make contact approx. one term in advance. Individuals should book for IMAX one week in advance

### NATIONAL RECORDER SCHOOL OF SCOTLAND (NYROS)
Scottish Amateur Music Association
7 Randolph Crescent
Edinburgh EH3 7TH
Tel: 0738 71574

Young musicians are invited to apply for the 1993 course which will be held at Craigie College, Ayr from 10-12 September. No audition required but players should be Grade 4 to benefit fully from the course. Auditions for the Advanced Group will be held during the first session.

**AGE RANGE:**
Any
**NUMBERS PASSING THROUGH:**
70
**HOW TO CONTACT:**
By telephone or letter for further information
**REGIONS SERVICED:**
UK but mainly Scotland
**SPECIAL NEEDS PROVISION:**
Special tuition at an advanced level available
**COSTS/WAITING LISTS:**
There is a course fee of £70 which includes tuition, accommodation and the services of a professional Director. Some local authority grants may be available. Waiting lists can be up to six months preceeding the next year's course

## NATIONAL RESOURCE CENTRE FOR
## DANCE (NRCD)
University of Surrey
Guildford
Surrey GU2 5XH
Tel: 0483 509316

NRCD was established to provide information on all aspects of dance and will direct enquiries to other sources where appropriate. Membership of NRCD offers access to a reference library/ archive (also open to visitors), courses and seminars, a range of directories/publications/ catalogues/periodicals, and to news of NRCD's latest activities/courses/plans etc.

**COSTS/WAITING LISTS:**
Full membership for individuals – £27.50 per year. Affiliated membership for individuals – £7.50 per year

## NATIONAL SOCIETY FOR EDUCATION IN
## ART AND DESIGN (NSEAD)
The Gatehouse
Corsham Court
Corsham
Wiltshire SN13 0BZ
Tel: 0249 714825

The NSEAD produce a *A Guide to Courses and Careers in Art, Craft and Design* (£12.15 inc p&p), a publication providing general information about all routes to gaining employment in the field of art, craft and design. A free booklist of publications related to art and design is also available on request.

---

## NATIONAL STUDENT DRAMA FESTIVAL (NSDF)
20 Lansdowne Road
Muswell Hill
London N10 2AU
Tel: 081 883 4586  Fax: 081 883 7142

The NSDF gives an annual national platform during the Easter vacation for the work of talented students, with productions often transferring to the Edinburgh Festival. You don't need to enter a production or be a student to attend and see the fourteen or so selected productions, join in the discussions, write for the daily Festival newspaper, join the Tech Team or help with the organisation, and participate in the professionally led workshops programme. Contact the NSDF at the above address for details of how to enter a production or participate in the Festival.

**AGE RANGE:**
Any, but usually about 17+
**HOW TO CONTACT:**
Contact above for further information
**REGIONS SERVICED:**
UK

## NATIONAL STUDENT THEATRE COMPANY (NSTC)

20 Lansdowne Road
Muswell Hill
London N10 2AU
Tel: 081 883 4586  Fax: 081 883 7142

The NSTC is open to all current British students or recent graduates and aims to channel the best student talents, especially those discovered through the annual National Student Drama Festival (NSDF – see separate entry), into an outsanding company, of which the hallmarks are excellence, professional discipline, total commitment and high entertainment value. The company mainly operates in the summer vacation and forms afresh after each NSDF (around Easter).  Technicians, admin and publicity personnel should ideally first apply to help at the Easter NSDF.  Actors and musicians should apply from the third week in April onwards with auditions held from May. Several productions are taken to the Edinburgh Fringe Festival each year, where the company has been particularly successful.

**AGE RANGE:**
17+
**HOW TO CONTACT:**
Contact above address
**REGIONS SERVICED:**
UK

**COSTS/WAITING LISTS:**

For the last two years the company has been unsponsored, which means that members have to be able to support themselves. Any profits are shared; but there is fierce competition for audiences at the Edinburgh Festival and no-one should rely on receiving anything back. So you will need to find accommodation costs (flat sharing can cost around £55 a week for four weeks in Edinburgh), travel and food costs, as well as any London rehearsal expenses. The NSTC can find you accommodation in Edinburgh, but not, usually, in London.

---

**NATIONAL TRUST (ACORN PROJECTS)**
PO Box 12
Westbury
Wiltshire BA13 4NA
Tel: 0373 826826  Fax: 0373 827162

If you have one or two weeks to spare, or even just a weekend, why not volunteer for an Acorn Working Holiday, helping on an outdoor conservation project on a site in the care of the National Trust. Projects cover a wide range of tasks and you could be helping to maintain woodland paths, dry stone walling, restoring farm buildings, or even surveying cliff vegetation. Food and accommodation are provided. There are over 420 projects taking place all year round. A comprehensive brochure is available free from the Volunteer Office at the above address.

**REGIONAL ADDRESSES:**
Available from Head Office
**AGE RANGE:**
16+
**NUMBERS PASSING THROUGH:**
3,500 per annum
**HOW TO CONTACT:**
Telephone or write to The National Trust Volunteer Office at the above address
**REGIONS SERVICED:**
England, Wales, Northern Ireland
**COSTS/WAITING LISTS:**
One week usually costs about £35; weekend projects about £10. Fees go towards the cost of food and accommodation. Volunteers pay their own travelling expenses

---

### NATIONAL TRUST FOR SCOTLAND CONSERVATION VOLUNTEERS (NTS)
The Conservation Volunteer Co-ordinator
5 Charlotte Square
Edinburgh EH2 4DU
Tel: 031 226 5922 Fax: 031 243 9302

Conservation volunteers carry out practical conservation work at countryside properties in the care of the Trust throughout Scotland. There are two ways to become involved – Thistle Camps and the local Conservation Volunteeers groups. Thistle Camps, lasting one or two weeks, take place between March and October each year and are located throughout Scotland on Trust properties. The five local groups – Glasgow, Lothian, Grampian, Tayside and Highland – work weekends, throughout the year, and undertake valuable conservation-related work that otherwise might never be possible. By taking part in projects you can learn such traditional skills as drystone walling, footpath construction, or woodland management and make a positive contribution to the care and protection of Scotland's countryside and wildlife. Opportunities are available to attend courses in countryside skills and to learn at first hand how the Ranger/ Naturalist service works.

**REGIONAL ADDRESSES:**
5 Regional Offices. Contact Head Office in the first instance
**AGE RANGE:**
16+
**HOW TO CONTACT:**
Write to the Conservation Volunteer Co-ordinator at the above address for full details
**REGIONS SERVICED:**
Scotland
**SPECIAL NEEDS PROVISION:**
No information
**COSTS/WAITING LISTS:**
The Thistle Camp programme is published in January and rapidly becomes fully booked;

applicants are advised to book early.  The five local group programmes are published twice yearly, in March and September

---

**NATIONAL UNION OF STUDENTS (NUS)**
Nelson Mandela House
461 Holloway Road
London N7 6LJ
Tel: 071 272 8900  Fax: 071 263 5713

NUS provides information and services to all young people continuing education after school, whether in further or higher education.  Advice and information can be provided on welfare matters such as student hardship, grants and housing, educational matters (although not on actual courses) and legal help plus much more.

**REGIONAL ADDRESSES:**
Available from Head Office
**AGE RANGE:**
Any
**HOW TO CONTACT:**
Telephone Head Office for advice and services.  Regional offices for union developments etc.
**REGIONS SERVICED:**
UK
**SPECIAL NEEDS PROVISION:**
Information service available
**COSTS/WAITING LISTS:**
No costs for information

### NATIONAL VOCATIONAL QUALIFICATIONS (NVQs)
National Council for Vocational
Qualifications
222 Euston Road
London NW1 2BZ
Tel: 071 387 9898

NVQs are work-related qualifications based on national standards set by industry and commerce, designed to reward individuals who can demonstrate competence in their performance at work. Each NVQ is made up of a number of units. Each unit is certificated separately which enables you to choose which units to study and at the pace that suits you best. It is up to you how and where you study, whether at work, at college or at home. More information on NVQs is available from schools careers services and Careers Offices (look in the phone book under 'C').

**AGE RANGE:**
Any
**HOW TO CONTACT:**
Letter, telephone to above address
**REGIONS SERVICED:**
England, Wales and Northern Ireland. See entry SCOTVEC for Scottish provision

## NATIONAL YOUTH AGENCY (NYA)
17-23 Albion Street
Leicester LE1 6GD
Tel: 0533 471200  Fax: 0533 471043

The National Youth Agency is the central agency providing information, advice and curriculum development materials for young people and all those who work with them. Its activities include answering enquiries using the agency's extensive library facilities, compiling regularly updated reading and resource lists and information packs, publishing a range of new materials on issues which affect young people, and generally providing an overview of what is going on for young people throughout the UK.

**HOW TO CONTACT:**
Letter, telephone, fax to above address
**REGIONS SERVICED:**
UK
**COSTS/WAITING LISTS:**
None for information

## NATIONAL YOUTH BRASS BAND OF SCOTLAND (NYBBS)
Scottish Amateur Music Association
7 Randolph Crescent
Edinburgh EH3 7TH
Tel: 0738 71574

Young brass musicians are invited to audition for a place in the NYBBS. The 1993 course will be held at St Andrew's College, Bearsden, Glasgow from 5-11 July. Candidates must have attained a standard equivalent to Grade 6 and be prepared to sight read, be proficient in scales and arpeggios and to perform two contrasting pieces.

**AGE RANGE:**
Up to 21
**NUMBERS PASSING THROUGH:**
73
**HOW TO CONTACT:**
By telephone or letter for further information
**REGIONS SERVICED:**
UK but mainly Scotland
**SPECIAL NEEDS PROVISION:**
Special tuition at an advanced level available
**COSTS/WAITING LISTS:**
There is a course fee of £185 which includes tuition, accommodation and the services of a professional conductor. Some local authority grants may be available. The Carnegie UK Trust has funded a special bursary scheme for those in need. Applications are treated on merit. Waiting lists can be up to six months preceeding the next year's course

---

**NATIONAL YOUTH JAZZ ORCHESTRA OF GREAT BRITAIN (NYJO)**
11 Victor Road
Harrow
Middx HA2 6PT
Tel: 081 863 2717  Fax: 081 863 8685

NYJO holds open rehearsals for anybody interested in a career in jazz. They can provide the opportunity for young people to rehearse with a professional Big Band and to go on to perform professionally. Applicants need a high level of musical aptitude, but this can be decided upon at rehearsals.

**AGE RANGE:**
Up to 25
**NUMBERS PASSING THROUGH:**
Approx 150
**HOW TO CONTACT:**
Letter, fax, telephone
**REGIONS SERVICED:**
UK
**SPECIAL NEEDS PROVISION:**
Enquiries welcome
**COSTS/WAITING LISTS:**
None

## NATIONAL YOUTH MUSIC THEATRE (NYMT)
Sadler's Wells
Roseberry Avenue
London EC1R 4TN
Tel: 071 278 6563  Fax: 071 837 2332

The NYMT's artistic policy is primarily to create and perform new music theatre works for performance by young people to the highest artistic standards. As well as cast and instrumental performers, an NYMT production will also involve young people in the tehnical, backstage and wardrobe departments, as well as front of house, box office, publicity and administration, offering them a valuable learning experience.   For those not selected through annual auditions, the NYMT hold residential weekend workshops in the spring and autumn which you do not need to audition for.

**AGE RANGE:**
Workshop courses 11-19: cast performers 11-19: instrumentalists mainly 11-19: technical staff, front of house, box office, press, PR, admin assistants 16-25

**NUMBERS PASSING THROUGH:**
400 in 1991 out of 3,000 who auditioned

**HOW TO CONTACT:**
By telephone or letter (with SAE) for information and application forms for workshops and/or national annual auditions

**REGIONS SERVICED:**
UK

**SPECIAL NEEDS PROVISION:**
No provision as yet

**COSTS/WAITING LISTS:**
A residential workshop weekend costs about £75.  Residential, rehearsal and performance weeks cost about £150 per week.  There are various possible sources of funding e.g. schools, Local Education Authorities, Prince's Trust, individual fund-raising activities, local sponsorship etc.  Contact in September for

auditions, anytime for workshops and in Jan –
April for working backstage, box office etc.

## NATIONAL YOUTH ORCHESTRA OF GREAT BRITAIN (NYO)
Causeway House
Lodge Causeway
Fishponds
Bristol BS16 3HD
Tel: 0272 650036  Fax: 0272 585311

Musicians under the age of 18 who play
orchestral instruments and have achieved Grade
8 with distinction in Associated Board
Examinations or are of an equivalent standard
can apply to join the NYO.  Auditions are held
each year for about 50 places and those selected
meet on three residential courses a year with
over 150 other young musicians to rehearse and
perform, with coaching from top professional
musicians and prestigious conductors.  Each
course lasts about ten days and ends with
concerts at venues such as the Proms in London,
Symphony Hall, Birmingham, Glasgow, Leeds,
Newcastle etc.

**AGE RANGE:**
18 and under
**NUMBERS PASSING THROUGH:**
155
**HOW TO CONTACT:**
Telephone or letter for further information

and an application form
**REGIONS SERVICED:**
UK
**SPECIAL NEEDS PROVISION:**
Applications welcome
**COSTS/WAITING LISTS:**
Course fees are £200 per course plus travel.
Funding is available from various sources e.g.
Local Education Authorities, Trusts, Local
Business, NYO Bursary Fund etc. The NYO
provides full board and travel to concerts.
About 400 people audition for approx 50
places each year. Applications must be
received by 30th June for auditions in
September/October and entry into the
Orchestra at Christmas

## NATIONAL YOUTH STRING ORCHESTRA OF SCOTLAND (NYSOS)

Scottish Amateur Music Association
7 Randolph Crescent
Edinburgh EH3 7TH
Tel: 0738 71574

Young musicians are invited to audition for a
place in the NYSOS. The 1993 course will be
held in Orkney from 10-17 July. Candidates
must have attained a standard equivalent to
Grade 7 and be prepared to sight read, be
proficient in scales and arpeggios and to perform
two contrasting pieces.

**AGE RANGE:**
Up to 21
**NUMBERS PASSING THROUGH:**
60
**HOW TO CONTACT:**
By telephone or letter for further information
**REGIONS SERVICED:**
UK but mainly Scotland
**SPECIAL NEEDS PROVISION:**
Special tuition at an advanced level available
**COSTS/WAITING LISTS:**
There is a course fee of £190 which includes
tuition, accommodation and the services of a
professional conductor. Some local authority
grants may be available. Waiting lists can be
up to six months preceeding the next year's
course

---

## NATIONAL YOUTH THEATRE OF GREAT BRITAIN (NYT)
443-445 Holloway Road
London N7 6LW
Tel: 071 281 3863  Fax: 071 281 8246

The NYT gives young people the chance to join
a team which mounts productions in professional
theatres. Productions may take place in London
or tour the country or occasionally visit a theatre
abroad. The NYT's members join in all
departments of theatre work – not just acting –
such as design, lighting and sound, costume
and stage management. Enthusiasm and an

interest in theatre are more important than talent.

**AGE RANGE:**
14-21
**NUMBERS PASSING THROUGH:**
c 500
**HOW TO CONTACT:**
By letter to above asking for an audition or interview depending on which area of theatre you are interested in.  Auditions are held throughout the UK
**REGIONS SERVICED:**
UK
**SPECIAL NEEDS PROVISION:**
To date no special provision has been necessary as all members have fitted in perfectly well regardless of ability
**COSTS/WAITING LISTS:**
Audition/Interview Fee – £6.  Acting courses for first year members: Junior Course – £115 (Two weeks), Senior Course – £165 (Three weeks).  After first year there is no fee, but members have to meet the cost of accommodation, travel and subsistence. Funding may be available from Local Education Authorities, Prince's Trust etc. and the NYT has its own bursary fund to help in difficult cases.  Apply in October of each year.  All applicants are seen and many re-apply the following year

## NATIONAL YOUTH WIND ENSEMBLE/
## NATIONAL YOUTH SYMPHONIC BAND
## OF SCOTLAND

Scottish Amateur Music Association
7 Randolph Crescent
Edinburgh EH3 7TH
Tel: 0738 71574

Young musicians are invited to audition for a place in the bands. A 1993 course for the bands will be held from 31 July-4 August in West Linton, followed by a tour to Paris from 5-11 August, ending with a concert in Edinburgh on 12 August. Candidates must have attained a standard equivalent to Grade 6 and be prepared to sight read, be proficient in scales and arpeggios and to perform two contrasting pieces.

**AGE RANGE:**
Up to 21
**NUMBERS PASSING THROUGH:**
90
**HOW TO CONTACT:**
By telephone or letter for further information
**REGIONS SERVICED:**
UK but mainly Scotland
**SPECIAL NEEDS PROVISION:**
Special tuition at an advanced level available
**COSTS/WAITING LISTS:**
There is a course fee of £360 which includes tuition, accommodation and the services of a professional conductor. Some local authority

grants may be available. Waiting lists can be up to six months preceeding the next year's course

---

## NORMAN HART MEMORIAL FUND
43 Northumberland Place
London W2 5AS

The Norman Hart Memorial Fund offers grants for young people undertaking study or work projects in European Countries. A limited number of grants to cover travel and related costs are offered each year to supplement finance from other sources, or as initial funding for applicants seeking further support elsewhere. Awards are made to young people who plan short periods of study or work on projects that further the aims of European unification. Particular stress is placed on the individual initiative shown by the applicants. The projects can be in the political, economic, social, cultural, professional, vocational, industrial or commercial fields and applicants, if awarded a grant, are asked to report to the trustees on the conclusion of their projects.

**AGE RANGE:**
18-25
**NUMBERS PASSING THROUGH:**
9 grants totalling £3,000 made in 1991
**HOW TO CONTACT:**
By letter only to the Secretary of the Trust for

a leaflet, explanatory notes and an
application form
**REGIONS SERVICED:**
UK
**COSTS/WAITING LISTS:**
Applications may be made at any time of the
year though submission in the early months is
recommended. Applications for grants for
projects to be undertaken during the summer
months should be submitted by 31 May at the
latest

---

**OCCUPATIONS (publication)**
Careers and Occupational Information Centre
(COIC)
Rockery Cottage
Sutton-cum-Lound
Retford
Nottinghamshire DN22 8PJ
Tel: 0777 705951

*Occupations* is one of the main reference books
used by careers advisers, listing over 600 different
types of jobs and careers from unskilled work to
professional occupations. Each entry describes
the type of work involved, the working
environment, pay and conditions, job
opportunities and prospects, personal
characteristics required, entry requirements and
training available as well as where to go to find
out more information. Price £19.50. Available
in bookshops, Careers Offices, public libraries

or direct from the above address (price £24.50 inc p&p).

---

### OCEAN YOUTH CLUB (OYC)
The Bus Station
South Street
Gosport
Hants PO12 1EP
Tel: 0705 528421; Bookings 0705 501211
Fax: 0705 522069

Ocean Youth Club aims to give young people from all backgrounds the fun, adventure and self-discipline of going to sea under sail. They take young people aged 12-24 to sea on ten large sailing vessels based around the UK and Northern Ireland to give them hands-on experience of sailing. It is a prime opportunity to meet new friends and learn new skills. They will be manning the helm, washing up for 17 other crew and polishing the brass to name but a few. Those who wish to continue sailing with the club as opposed to a once only experience, can partake in the OYC training scheme and to progress to skipper if they so wish, and young people are encouraged to get involved in the boats' winter refits and to attend reunions at the end of the sailing season.

**REGIONAL ADDRESSES:**
Northern Ireland: Barnett Dock, Belfast Harbour BT3 9AF  Tel: 0232 740008

Scotland: Kip Marina, Inverkip PA16 0AS
Tel: 0475 521294
North West: c/o Business Training Centre,
Windmill Lane, Denton, Tameside M34 3QS
Tel: 061 335 9032

**AGE RANGE:**
12-24

**NUMBERS PASSING THROUGH:**
4,900 sailed in 1990

**HOW TO CONTACT:**
By telephone to bookings number above or
by letter to central office, Gosport

**REGIONS SERVICED:**
UK and rest of Europe

**SPECIAL NEEDS PROVISION:**
OYC regularly run cruises for young people
with special needs. All yachts are fitted with
audio compasses to assist visually impaired
voyagers

**COSTS/WAITING LISTS:**
Cruises cost about £30-£40 a day depending
on the season. OYC does have a bursary
scheme but young people are encouraged to
raise funds themselves. Peak season always
books up early – telephone for berth
availability

---

**OCKENDEN VENTURE**
Constitution Hill
Woking
Surrey GU22 7UU
Tel: 0483 772012/3  Fax: 0483 750774

Volunteers are recruited to look after refugees at various homes and reception centres in the UK, giving them the opportunity, through working as part of a team and using initiative, to learn about others and themselves in all types of situations. Volunteers are normally recruited for one year, but shorter term vacancies do occasionally occur. The main recruitment period is in August/September. Volunteers receive board and lodging and between £22 and £25 a week pocket money.

**REGIONAL ADDRESSES:**
Contact through HQ
**AGE RANGE:**
18+
**NUMBERS PASSING THROUGH:**
8 volunteers at any one time
**HOW TO CONTACT:**
Letter with SAE for further information
**REGIONS SERVICED:**
UK
**SPECIAL NEEDS PROVISION:**
No provision
**COSTS/WAITING LISTS:**
Advisable to enquire a few months in advance

## ODYSSEY TRAVEL CLUB
Odyssey International
21 Cambridge Road
Waterbeach
Cambridge CB5 9NJ
Tel: 0223 861079  Fax: 0223 861079

The number of young people travelling or taking a year out from education is on the increase. Many others would like to travel but don't have anyone to go with or are put off by expensive single supplements. The Odyssey Travel Club can help by bringing together like-minded travellers with similar interests and plans. If you are seeking a companion or just travel advice contact the Odyssey Travel Club.

**AGE RANGE:**
17+
**NUMBERS PASSING THROUGH:**
2,000
**HOW TO CONTACT:**
Telephone or letter for further information
**REGIONS SERVICED:**
UK
**SPECIAL NEEDS PROVISION:**
No special provision
**COSTS/WAITING LISTS:**
Annual membership fee is £20 which includes contact service, advice line, quarterly newsletter, discounted activity breaks/holidays and discounted travel insurance

**THE OPEN COLLEGE (OC)**
Customer Services
St Paul's
781 Wilmslow Road
Didsbury
Manchester M20 8RW
Tel: 061 434 0007

The Open College offers a range of work skills courses through 'open learning'. This system allows you to study at your own pace using specially designed course books, audio and visual tapes. Open College training materials offer a valuable learning experience in their own right. However, to gain full benefit from studying our materials we recommend that you obtain tutor support from a local college or training centre. This is advisable for all learners, but it is usually essential if you wish to work towards a qualification.

**REGIONAL ADDRESSES:**
All enquiries through above address
**AGE RANGE:**
Any
**REGIONS SERVICED:**
UK
**SPECIAL NEEDS PROVISION:**
Anyone can use the Open College
**COSTS/WAITING LISTS:**
From £25 to over £120

### THE OPEN UNIVERSITY (OU)
Walton Hall
Milton Keynes MK7 6AA
Tel: 0908 274066

The Open University offers a different way of studying a degree level course. Learning is through radio and television broadcasts, course books and other learning packages as well as residential summer courses. The structure of the courses allows students to study at their own pace.

**AGE RANGE:**
Any
**HOW TO CONTACT:**
Write to the above address for further information
**REGIONS SERVICED:**
UK
**SPECIAL NEEDS PROVISION:**
The OU has a specialist adviser for students with disabilities
**COSTS/WAITING LISTS:**
Details of course fees are available from OU. Help may be available from the Local Education Authority

**OPERATION RALEIGH** see RALEIGH
INTERNATIONAL

**ORGANISATION FOR BLACK ARTS
ADVANCEMENT AND LEARNING
ACTIVITIES (OBAALA)**
Obaala House
225 Seven Sisters Road
London N4 2DA
Tel: 071 263 1918

OBAALA aims to create a greater awareness of
Black art, runs a bookshop and gallery, a summer
arts school, and an annual project for 11-16
year old African-Caribbean young people.

**OUTSET – Action on Disability**
18 Creekside
London SE8 3DZ
Tel: 081 692 7141  Fax: 081 469 2532

Outset is the national charity which develops
technology-related employment opportunities
for people with disabilities.  Through a network
of 12 centres they   provide information
technology and business skills training.  This is
backed by job-match and post-recruitment
support.  Outset's Consultancy Service works
with Local Authorities, Health Authorities, Trusts,
TECs and the private sector to improve local
opportunities and service provision.  Outset

also offers Disability Awareness Training and has an Initiatives Database providing information on all aspects of employment and disability. Outset's Business Services Division runs a mailing house and office services bureaux directly employing people with disabilities. The division offers a wide range of services to a variety of clients.

---

### OUTWARD BOUND TRUST
Chestnut Field
Regent Place
Rugby
Warwickshire CV1 2PJ
Tel: 0788 560423  Fax: 0788 541069

The Outward Bound Trust runs a wide range of adventure courses and expeditions, available to all.  The courses can be 'centre based' at one of Outward Bound's residential settings, or you can find yourself trekking through the wilderness with little more than a tent between you and the elements. The courses and programmes usually run for between a week and a month and they provide a range of opportunities for you to enjoy the experience and challenge of adventure. Activities include rock-climbing, abseiling, the Outward Bound ropes course, orienteering, sailing, Canadian canoeing and kayaking, caving, and expeditions. The expedition courses are probably the most challenging and demanding of the courses on offer.  They take place in wilderness areas, with every night spent under canvas, often far from civilisation. Outward Bound recommend that people attend courses as individuals although they will accept group enquiries. Whatever, you are encouraged to participate as part of a team and to stretch yourself to the limits on these courses. The Trust also run other types of schemes, including City Challenge courses where participants are given the opportunity for personal development through a series of challenging placements working with disadvantaged people in the community, or Urban Schemes which were developed to enable young people from the inner-cities to benefit from Outward Bound courses. A network of centres is developing throughout Europe, so there are opportunities abroad too. Contact Head Office for a brochure covering the full range of opportunities on offer.

**REGIONAL ADDRESSES:**
There are a number of regional centres.
Details of your nearest centre from Head Office
**AGE RANGE:**
Any. Minimum 14
**NUMBERS PASSING THROUGH:**
c 500
**HOW TO CONTACT:**
By letter or telephone to Head Office for advice, information and brochure
**REGIONS SERVICED:**
UK

**SPECIAL NEEDS PROVISION:**
Enquiries welcome

**COSTS/WAITING LISTS:**
The fees for all courses are fully inclusive of
all accommodation, specialist equipment,
tuition etc. They range from approx £250 –
£650. Young people between 15 and 24 may
qualify for financial help up to 50% of the
cost of a course. Details from the Trust.
Courses during the summer months do tend
to get filled quickly, so apply early

---

## OVERSEAS PLACING UNIT (EMPLOYMENT SERVICE) (OPU)

c/o Rockingham House
13 West Street
Sheffield S1 4ER

The OPU can give advice and guidance to
anyone who wants to take up employment
overseas – through Jobcentres.

**AGE RANGE:**
18+ for vacancy applications – 16+ for
information packs

**NUMBERS PASSING THROUGH:**
500-800 enquiries monthly

**HOW TO CONTACT:**
By visiting any Jobcentre for information on
specific countries

**REGIONS SERVICED:**
UK

**SPECIAL NEEDS PROVISION:**
Each enquiry dealt with individually
**COSTS/WAITING LISTS:**
The service is free. Contact your local
Jobcentre at least one month before you
intend travelling

## OVERSEAS VOLUNTEER SCHEME OF THE
## BRITISH AND FOREIGN SCHOOL SOCIETY
The Richard Mayo Hall
Eden Street
Kingston-upon-Thames KT1 1HZ
Tel: 081 546 2379

This Society offers financial help to school-
leavers who have established firm links with
peoples or projects in developing countries –
perhaps through a school exchange – and who
are interested in spending up to a year progressing
those links – mainly in teaching positions.

## PARTNERS IN EUROPE
The Prince's Trust
8 Bedford Row
London WC1R 4BA
Tel: 071 405 5799  Fax: 071 831 7280

Partners in Europe aims to support young people
in developing lasting links with European
counterparts. Small development grants
(maximum £500) called Go and See and more
substantial follow-up grants called Go Ahead

are available for young people with ideas for working with a European counterpart. Partners in Europe is part of The Prince's Trust and is sponsored by Severn Trent plc.

**AGE RANGE:**
Under 26 and out of full-time education.
Under 31 for people with disabilities
**NUMBERS PASSING THROUGH:**
Approximately 200 grants awarded each year
**HOW TO CONTACT:**
By phone or letter
**REGIONS SERVICED:**
UK

---

## PEAK PARK CONSERVATION VOLUNTEERS (PPCV)
The Volunteers Organiser
Peak Park Joint Planning Board
Aldern House
Baslow Road
Bakewell
Derbyshire DE45 1AE
Tel: 0629 814321 (ext 339)
Fax: 0629 812659

The National Park Ranger Service enables volunteers of all ages and backgrounds to become actively involved in many types of practical conservation projects throughout the Peak District National Park. The projects include footpath construction and erosion control, fencing, walling, tree planting, scrub clearance, simple nature reserve management and much more. The project tasks are led by a ranger/ supervisor and tools, materials and a lunchtime brew are provided. Tasks are arranged all year round for each weekend although limited opportunities exist during the midweek period.

**AGE RANGE:**
14-66
**NUMBERS PASSING THROUGH:**
Over 3,000 per year
**HOW TO CONTACT:**
Telephone, letter, fax or in person for information and leaflets
**REGIONS SERVICED:**
Peak National Park
**SPECIAL NEEDS PROVISION:**
Enquiries welcome
**COSTS/WAITING LISTS:**
Membership is 50p per year for individuals

---

### PENFRIENDS WORLDWIDE
PO Box 87
Douglas
Isle of Man
Tel: 0624 612035

International correspondence service accepting members of all ages from any country in the world. Special sections for stamp collectors, language students etc.

**AGE RANGE:**
Any
**HOW TO CONTACT:**
By letter for brochure containing full
information plus application form
**REGIONS SERVICED:**
UK
**COSTS/WAITING LISTS:**
16 and under – £5 fee; 17+ – £10 fee

---

### PETRA (EUROPEAN COMMUNITY PETRA
### PROGRAMME)
c/o The Central Bureau for Educational Visits
and Exchanges
Seymour Mews House
Seymour Mews
London SW1H 9PE
Tel: 071 486 5101

PETRA is a European Community programme
for the vocational training of young people and
their preparation for adult and working life. It
has recently been extended, and the revised
programme now incorporates the EC Young
Worker Exchange Programme. One of the ways
PETRA can be of direct benefit to young people
is by providing financial support for individuals
aged 16-27 to benefit from a vocational training/
work experience placement in another EC
Member State.

Short term placements are aimed at young
people in initial vocational training and are

normally of three weeks duration. Long term placements are aimed at those who are either in employment, available on the labour market or taking part in an advanced training programme after starting work. The average duration of these placements is three months.

Financial assistance is available as a contribution towards accommodation, food, insurance, pocket money, language tuition, local travel, travel costs to and from host country (normally 75% of economy fare). In the case of short term projects, grants will only be made payable to project organisers and not to individuals.

**AGE RANGE:**
16-27
**HOW TO CONTACT:**
Contact the Central Bureau at the above address for details of how to apply to take part in the programme
**REGIONS SERVICED:**
UK
**SPECIAL NEEDS PROVISION:**
Enquiries welcome
**COSTS/WAITING LISTS:**
No costs to individuals – placements are funded by the EEC and training organisations

---

**PHAB**
12-14 London Road
Croydon
Tel: 081 667 9443  Fax: 081 681 1399

PHAB is an organisation working towards the integration of physically handicapped people into the community via youth clubs, holidays and training facilities. Join a PHAB club and participate with young people with and without a physical disability in a wide range of activities, e.g. sailing, rock climbing, snooker, table tennis etc., as well as enjoying holidays together and weekends away. Enquiries from volunteers welcome.

**REGIONAL ADDRESSES:**
Details available from Head Office
**AGE RANGE:**
Any
**NUMBERS PASSING THROUGH:**
18,000
**HOW TO CONTACT:**
Letter, telephone or fax, ideally through regional divisions (see telephone directory), but can be contacted through Head Office for information on clubs, holidays, activities etc.
**REGIONS SERVICED:**
UK
**SPECIAL NEEDS PROVISION:**
All members can participate in any activity
**COSTS/WAITING LISTS:**
Small club subscription. Some activities/ holidays are subsidised by various trusts and funds

**PLAID CYMRU**
51 Cathedral Road
Cardiff CF1 9HD
Tel: 0222 231944

**THE POETRY SOCIETY**
22 Betterton Street
London WC2H 9BU
Tel: 071 240 4810 Fax: 071 240 4818

The society is a membership organisation which aims to promote all aspects of poetry and encourage interest in poetry including young people. They can provide advice and information on poetry competitions, workshops, contact names and addresses of relevant organisations as well as details on how to go about getting poetry published. The Society's Education Department administrates the WH Smith Poets in Schools Scheme and publishes the termly *School's Poetry Review*.

**AGE RANGE:**
Any
**NUMBERS PASSING THROUGH:**
400-500
**HOW TO CONTACT:**
By telephone or letter (with SAE) for advice and further information
**REGIONS SERVICED:**
UK

**SPECIAL NEEDS PROVISION:**
Anyone with an interest in poetry can use the
services of the society
**COSTS/WAITING LISTS:**
None

---

## POLICE RECRUITMENT DEPARTMENT
F5-Division
Room 516
Home Office
50 Queen Anne's Gate
London SW1H 9AT
Tel: 071 273 3797

The 40+ police forces in England and Wales
recruit independently so if you are interested in
joining a particular force write to the chief
officer of that force for further information. You
can contact the Police Recruitment Dept. above
(Police Division for Scotland, RUC Recruiting
Branch for Northern Ireland) for leaflets and
information about careers in the police force in
general covering the nature of the work, range
of opportunities and entry requirements.

**REGIONAL OFFICES:**
Scotland: Police Division, Scottish Office,
Home and Health Dept, St Andrews House,
Edinburgh EH1 3DE  Tel: 031 556 8400
Northern Ireland: RUC Recruiting Branch,
RUC Headquarters, Brooklyn, Knock Road,
Belfast BT5 6LE  Tel: 0232 451881

## THE PRINCE'S SCOTTISH YOUTH
## BUSINESS TRUST (PSYBT)
6th Floor
Mercantile Chambers
53 Bothwell Street
Glasgow G2 6TS
Tel: 041 248 4999 Fax: 041 248 4836

The aim of the Prince's Scottish Business Trust is to provide seedcorn finance and professional support to young people in Scotland, aged 18-25, whoever they are and wherever they come from, so that they can set up and continue to run their own businesses. The Trust has particular concern for the disadvantaged. Applicants must have a viable business idea, be unable to raise all or part of the finance necessary to set up their own business and be able to work at their business full-time. The Trust offers free professional advice; access to pre-start training; loans of up to £5,000 over a period of up to 5 years at 4% interest; grants of up to £1,000; assistance from professional advisers for a minimum period of two years.

**REGIONAL ADDRESSES:**
14 regional and 3 sub-regional managers – details available from Head Office
**AGE RANGE:**
18-25
**NUMBERS PASSING THROUGH:**
460 businesses were set up in the 90/91 financial year, 437 in 91/92

**HOW TO CONTACT:**
Contact nearest regional manager of which
there are 17 based in Enterprise Trusts
throughout Scotland
**REGIONS SERVICED:**
Scotland
**SPECIAL NEEDS PROVISION:**
Applications welcome
**COSTS/WAITING LISTS:**
There are no waiting lists but it normally
takes twelve weeks or more to prepare an
application/business plan and complete the
necessary training before the application is
ready to be processed

## THE PRINCE'S TRUST AND THE ROYAL
## JUBILEE TRUSTS
8 Bedford Row
London WC1R 4BA
Tel: 071 430 0524  Fax: 071 831 7280

Aim is to assist young people who are in
some way disadvantaged.  Grants up to £800
for an individual or £2,500 for a group are
provided to enable development of individual
potential or to be of service to others in the
community.  The Trusts' primary focus for
projects is on those that address needs that
are otherwise ignored and that are original in
provision.  Shortfall in statutory funding will
not be considered nor will general fund-
raising.

**REGIONAL ADDRESSES:**
59 local committees covering the UK, each
have their own contact number available
from the phone book or from the national
number above

**AGE RANGE:**
14 to 25 inclusive

**NUMBERS PASSING THROUGH:**
20,000 grants made 91/92

**HOW TO CONTACT:**
By telephone or letter which will be followed
up by a member of the local committee

**REGIONS COVERED:**
UK

**COSTS/WAITING LISTS:**
There are no costs to applicants and grants
are not repayable. Committees should be
able to act quickly, the majority providing
funding within one month of application

---

**THE PRINCE'S TRUST VOLUNTEERS**
8 Jockey's Fields
London WC1R 4BW
Tel: 071 430 0378  Fax: 071 404 5339

A national Programme which provides young
people with the opportunity for personal
development training and experience while
working with and in their local community.
Each 15-strong team of volunteers includes a
full mix of young people from different
backgrounds, all walks of life and those who are

employed, unemployed or in education. Each team participates in a 60-day programme which includes team building, a residential experience and 40 days of either individual placement or team project work in the community. These community opportunities will include environmental and caring experiences. Volunteers who successfully complete the Programme receive a City and Guilds Profile of Achievement, a Prince's Trust Volunteers Certificate and the opportunity during the Programme to attain personal skills qualifications such as the Community Sports Leader Award and a First Aid Certificate.

**AGE RANGE:**
16-24
**NUMBERS PASSING THROUGH:**
2,000 per year
**HOW TO CONTACT:**
Letter or telephone to the above address
**REGIONS SERVICED:**
UK

## THE PRINCE'S YOUTH BUSINESS TRUST (PYBT)
5 Cleveland Place
London SW1Y 6JJ
Tel: 071 321 6500  Fax: 071 839 6494

The Trust is a registered charity which aims to help young people, who would not otherwise have the opportunity, to develop their self-confidence, achieve economic independence and contribute to the community through the medium of self-employment. Loans up to £5,000 on easy repayment terms and grants up to £1,500 are awarded to young people with a good business idea but without adequate means to finance it. In addition to finance the Trust provides each supported business with a volunteer Business Adviser and directs the young people to suitable enterprise training. Applicants must have tried but failed to raise all their necessary finance elsewhere.

**REGIONAL ADDRESSES:**
38 regional addresses throughout England, Wales and Northern Ireland. Consult local telephone directory or call the Head Office at the above address
(for Scotland see PRINCE'S SCOTTISH YOUTH BUSINESS TRUST)

**AGE RANGE:**
18-26 (up to 30 for disabled people)

**NUMBERS PASSING THROUGH:**
Approx 25,000 enquiries each year leading to about 3,000 people receiving grants or loans

**HOW TO CONTACT:**
By letter or telephone

**REGIONS SERVICED:**
All parts of England, Wales and Northern Ireland

**SPECIAL NEEDS PROVISION:**
Applications from disabled people and people from ethnic minorities welcome

**COSTS/WAITING LISTS:**
There are no costs to the applicant in
applying and no waiting list. All proposals
are evaluated on their individual merits

---

### PROJECT 67
10 Hatton Garden
London EC1N 8AH
Tel: 071 831 7626 Fax: 071 404 5588

Project 67 arrange for over 2,000 people a year
to go to Israel on three types of working holiday
on a 'package holiday' basis; there are kibbutz
and moshav holidays which last for a minimum
of two months, and archaeological digs.
Departures take place throughout the year, with
placement guaranteed. Project 67 is the official
UK representative of the kibbutz movement and
arranges kibbutz holidays (age limits 18-32) on
which volunteers receive free accommodation,
meals, laundry, pocket money, recreational
facilities and occasional trips in exchange for
working a 6-day week.

On a moshav holiday (age limits 21-35) work is
mainly agricultural. Free accommodation is
provided (usually self-contained). In exchange
for their work volunteers receive a monthly
salary which may be increased if overtime is
worked.

Project's archaeological digs are organised in
conjunction with the Ministry of Antiquities and
Universities; a variety of programmes are offered

on several sites throughout Israel, in which anyone over the age of 18 can participate. Accommodation varies from site to site.

Project 67 has its own office in Tel Aviv which can take care of the needs of volunteers while they are in Israel.

**AGE RANGE:**
18-35
**NUMBERS PASSING THROUGH:**
c 4,000
**HOW TO CONTACT:**
For more details those interested can visit Project's London office to watch a video, otherwise telephone or send SAE for a brochure
**REGIONS SERVICED:**
UK
**SPECIAL NEEDS PROVISION:**
No special provision but enquiries welcome
**COSTS/WAITING LISTS:**
Cost is approx £270. This is for the minimum period for any holiday of 5 weeks. A one year placement might only be £20 more. Usually no waiting lists except in busy periods

**PROJECT TRUST**
The Hebridean Centre
Ballyhough
Isle of Coll
Scotland PA78 6TB
Tel: 08793 444  Fax: 08793 357

Project Trust is an educational Trust that places volunteers overseas each year in posts where they have the opportunity to do useful work for a year between school and higher education. Since 1968 it has sent over 2,000 volunteers to 39 different countries. Project aims to give young people a better understanding of the world outside Europe through living and working overseas. The three main categories of project are; teacher-aides, social services and outdoor activities. Projects are chosen which do not take work from a local person, and which offer work that is both satisfying to the volunteer and useful to the host nation.

**AGE RANGE:**
17-19
**NUMBERS PASSING THROUGH:**
180-200 each year
**HOW TO CONTACT:**
By letter to the Director at above address for an information leaflet and application form
**REGIONS SERVICED:**
UK
**SPECIAL NEEDS PROVISION:**
No provision
**COSTS/WAITING LISTS:**
The average cost is about £3,250, Project Trust provides about £500 – volunteers need to raise £2,750. The Trust has a finance officer who can advise how to go about fund-raising, through sponsored events, charities, industry, local business etc. Projects start in

August/September and you can apply 18
months before. Applications close usually in
the previous October

---

### QUAKER INTERNATIONAL SOCIAL
### PROJECTS (QISP)
Friends' House
Euston Road
London NW1 2BJ
Tel: 071 387 3601  Fax: 071 388 1977

QISP projects bring together people of different
nationalities, backgrounds and cultures who
would like to be involved in a 1-3 week voluntary
project. The projects are innovative and are
initiated by a local community who need
volunteers to help them carry out some task that
aims to make life more positive for others. There
are many different types of projects e.g.
playschemes, in psychiatric hospitals, manual
projects, women only projects, study projects
etc. QISP projects offer you the chance to meet,
live and work with people you might not
otherwise meet, learn from each other, develop
new skills and find out for yourself just what a
group of 12 or so complete strangers from all
over the world can do when they work together.

**AGE RANGE:**
18+ (16-18 for International Youth Projects)
**NUMBERS PASSING THROUGH:**
200 young people in UK, 100 sent abroad

**HOW TO CONTACT:**
In person, by telephone, SAE or fax for
information about current projects
**REGIONS SERVICED:**
UK
**SPECIAL NEEDS PROVISION:**
QISP is open to volunteers of all abilities and
any special needs are considered when
planning projects
**COSTS/WAITING LISTS:**
There is a small registration fee from £3 to
£25 depending on income. Food and
accommodation are free and some travel
subsidies are available. Apply in January for
Easter projects and in April/May for summer
projects

---

### RAC MOTOR SPORTS ASSOCIATION (RAC MSA)
Motor Sports House
Riverside House
Tel: 0753 681736

The RAC MSA produce a comprehensive booklet
about starting up in the various types of motor
sports, and about the different types of jobs that
are available. It can give information about
schools, circuits and a range of other specialized
contact information covering motor sports
throughout the UK.

## RALEIGH INTERNATIONAL
(formerly Operation Raleigh)
Raleigh House
27 Parsons Green Lane
London SW6 4HS
Tel: 071 371 8585  Fax: 071 371 5116

Raleigh International is a charity which aims to develop young people through a valuable programme of community, conservation and scientific projects in remote parts of the world. Raleigh is recruiting over 1,000 young people between the ages of 17-25 and over 350 members of staff aged 25+ for expeditions in 1993/94 to Chile, Guyana, Namibia, Zimbabwe, Mauritius, Russia and Malaysia.  No skills are necessary except the ability to swim and speak basic English.

**REGIONAL ADDRESSES:**
Contact through Head Office
**AGE RANGE:**
17+
**NUMBERS PASSING THROUGH:**
1,000+
**HOW TO CONTACT:**
Send an A4 SAE to Head Office
**REGIONS SERVICED:**
Worldwide
**SPECIAL NEEDS PROVISION:**
Participants must be physically capable of looking after themselves.  Raleigh cannot accommodate young people with severe

learning difficulties but physical disabilities do not present a problem

**COSTS/WAITING LISTS:**
Participants are asked to raise £2,950 through sponsorship and fund-raising events. Many companies send employees as part of a training programme

---

### REMPLOY LTD
415 Edgware Road
Cricklewood
London NW2 6LR
Tel: 081 452 8020  Fax: 081 452 6898

Remploy Ltd, a state-funded manufacturing and services company with 9,500 severely disabled employees, provides special needs training, sheltered employment and progression to jobs in open industry and commerce.

**REGIONAL ADDRESSES:**
Check with local Jobcentres for Remploy factories in your area

**AGE RANGE:**
16+

**NUMBERS PASSING THROUGH:**
Approximately 150 disabled young people take part in Remploy YT and ET courses each year. While there is no guarantee of a permanent job, approximately 100 are employed at the end of their training

**HOW TO CONTACT:**
Applicants, registered as severely disabled

(Category 2, Green Card) must be referred to
Remploy by the Disability Employment
Adviser at a Jobcentre

**REGIONS SERVICED:**
There are 96 Remploy factories throughout
the country

**SPECIAL NEEDS PROVISION:**
A wide range of courses available including
those aimed at providing vocational
qualifications to national standards

**COSTS/WAITING LISTS:**
There are more young people applying than
places available

---

## ROAD TRANSPORT INDUSTRY TRAINING BOARD (RTITB)

The RTITB can offer advice and supply
information brochures covering courses and
careers throughout the road transport industry.
They are a good first point of contact whether
you want to be a mechanic, auto electrician, car
fitter, driver, car salesperson, transport manager
etc.

**REGIONAL ADDRESSES:**
England and Wales: Capitol House, Empire
Way, Wembley, Middx HA9 0NG  Tel: 081
902 8880
Northern Ireland: Nutts Corner Training
Centre, 15 Dundrod Road, Crumlin, Co
Antrim BT29 4SS  Tel: 0232 825653

Scotland: Training Services, Hardie Road,
Livingstone, West Lothian EH54 8AR  Tel:
0506 416355

---

## ROTARY YOUTH EXCHANGE
## PROGRAMME
Rotary International
Kinwarton Road
Alcester
Warwickshire B49 6BP
Tel: 0789 765411  Fax: 0789 765570

The object of the Rotary Youth Exchange
Programme is to promote international
understanding and goodwill by bringing young
people into contact with each other so that they
can understand other ways of life, learn the
thinking and culture of other countries and
open lasting friendships. Youth exchanges give
an opportunity for travel, education and self-
dependence. Young people have to be selected
by an interviewing panel of the local Rotary
Club and they have to be sponsored by the
Rotary Club.

**REGIONAL ADDRESSES:**
Over 1,700 clubs around Britain and Ireland
**AGE RANGE:**
16-22
**NUMBERS PASSING THROUGH:**
10,000 worldwide

**HOW TO CONTACT:**
Send SAE to Head Office who will put you in
contact with a local club
**REGIONS SERVICED:**
UK
**SPECIAL NEEDS PROVISION:**
Enquiries welcome
**COSTS/WAITING LISTS:**
Individuals are responsible for transport,
insurance/registration and spending money

## ROUGH GUIDE TO CAREERS
BSS
PO Box 29 (SEDO)
Manchester M12 6AD
Tel: 061 272 7722

BSS publishes guides to various careers to
accompany the 'Rough Guides to Careers' series
shown on BBC2. There are a number of titles
available covering a wide range of career
opportunities. Each guide gives details of the
different jobs and careers available in a particular
field (e.g. sport and leisure, finance, tourism,
working in Europe), what each job actually
involves told by people who do it and the
training opportunities available. For details of
the guides available, contact BSS at the above
address.

**COSTS/WAITING LISTS:**
Guides cost between £1.50 and £2.25

## ROYAL ACADEMY OF DANCING (RAD)
36 Battersea Square
London SW11 3RA
Tel: 071 223 0091  Fax: 071 924 3129

RAD caters for dancing for anyone whether as a pastime or professional career.  Students can attend lessons at HQ or at any of the registered teachers schools located worldwide – lists available from above.  The Academy caters for dancers at every stage of their professional career from dancing examinations, to awards that help entry into companies, to training as teachers.  There are summer schools for all ages and a Junior Friends club and magazine.

**REGIONAL ADDRESSES:**
Details available from Head Office
**AGE RANGE:**
Any
**HOW TO CONTACT:**
Telephone, letter or in person
**REGIONS SERVICED:**
UK
**SPECIAL NEEDS PROVISION:**
There is provision for teaching students with special needs
**COSTS/WAITING LISTS:**
Membership of the academy is £35.  Ballet classes and course fees vary.  Funding is sometimes available from local councils and the Council for Dance Education and Training

## ROYAL ACADEMY OF DRAMATIC ART
## (RADA)
62/64 Gower Street
London WC1E 6ED
Tel: 071 636 7076  Fax: 071 323 3865

RADA offer courses in acting, stage management, and specialist diploma courses. They also offer a 4-week summer vacation Drama Workshop in Shakespearean acting, and a 2-week course in Set Design. Competition for places is tough, although the entry criteria for each course is different. Fuller details in the college prospectus.

**AGE RANGE:**
18+
**HOW TO CONTACT:**
Letter plus large SAE for further information and prospectus
**REGIONS SERVICED:**
UK
**COSTS/WAITING LISTS:**
Application forms should be submitted by the November prior to the year for which entry is sought

## ROYAL AIR FORCE CAREERS

Contact your nearest RAF Careers Information Office (see telephone directory) for details of careers and training in the RAF or alternatively if you are still at school contact the RAF Schools

Liaison Officer through your careers department.

## ROYAL INSTITUTE OF BRITISH
## ARCHITECTS (RIBA)
Education Department
66 Portland Place
London W1N 4AD
Tel: 071 580 5533

Architecture involves a mixture of artistic skill and technology. As well as designing a building to look attractive an architect also needs the necessary technical knowledge to ensure that it is practical to build the structure he or she has designed so training is quite a lengthy process. The majority of architects work in private practice but many also work for local authorities and government departments. Contact RIBA for information on training and career development. Opportunities also exist for architectural technicians working as part of a team assisting architects on a particular project. Contact the British Institute of Architectural Technicians for its training requirements at 397 City Road, London EC1V 1NE Tel: 071 278 2206/8

## ROYAL LIFE SAVING SOCIETY UK
## (RLSS UK)
Mountbatten House
Studley
Warwicks B80 7NN
Tel: 0527 85 3943  Fax: 0527 85 4453

If you want to learn to look after yourself – or take care of others – in the water, RLSS have courses for you, ranging from very basic to professional level qualifications for lifeguards, which can lead to a job in the leisure industry or active membership of a volunteer lifeguard club. Whatever your swimming ability a lifesaving course will make you safer in the water. People with special needs welcome.

**REGIONAL ADDRESSES:**
Details from Head Office
**AGE RANGE:**
Any
**NUMBERS PASSING THROUGH:**
200,000
**HOW TO CONTACT:**
Phone, letter, fax, or in person to Head Office for advice, information, leaflets etc. about the work of RLSS UK, and for local contact information
**REGIONS SERVICED:**
UK
**SPECIAL NEEDS PROVISION:**
No special provision but participation welcome
**COSTS/WAITING LISTS:**
Club membership – up to £5. Programmes cost from nothing to £5. Exam fees range from 75p – £4. No waiting lists, but some programmes only run at particular times of the year

## ROYAL NATIONAL COLLEGE FOR THE BLIND (RNCB)
College Road
Hereford HR1 1EB
Tel: 0432 265725  Fax: 0432 353478

The RNCB is the major further education establishment in the UK offering preparation for open employment and higher education for visually handicapped students. The college offers specialist training, development of independence and mobility skills, experience with the latest technology, employment counselling and much more. Entry is via an assessment and the emphasis is on potential rather than qualifications.

**AGE RANGE:**
16+
**NUMBERS PASSING THROUGH:**
220
**HOW TO CONTACT:**
Contact direct by telephone, fax or letter or through the Specialist Careers Officer in the Careers Centre or the Disablement Resettlement Officer in the Jobcentre
**REGIONS SERVICED:**
UK
**SPECIAL NEEDS PROVISION:**
Exclusively for visually handicapped students
**COSTS/WAITING LISTS:**
Course fees may be paid by Local Education Authorities

**ROYAL NATIONAL THEATRE EDUCATION**
Upper Ground
South Bank
London SE1 9PX
Tel: 071 261 9808  Fax: 071 620 1197

The Education Department of the Royal National Theatre is responsible for a range of activities and resources including: main stage productions for young people; mobile touring productions which visit schools, colleges and theatres throughout the UK; printed study packs and resource materials; weekend courses for students and teachers; and cut-price ticket schemes (see also, LLOYDS BANK THEATRE CHALLENGE and WH SMITH INTERACT).  Joining Royal National Theatre education means you will receive regular information about forthcoming events.

**AGE RANGE:**
Any
**HOW TO CONTACT:**
By letter or fax to the Education Department at the above address
**REGIONS SERVICED:**
UK
**SPECIAL NEEDS PROVISION:**
Variety of workshops planned according to special needs
**COSTS/WAITING LISTS:**
Small voluntary contribution for regular

newsletter.  Workshops are usually charged for

---

## ROYAL NAVY AND ROYAL MARINES CAREERS

For information on careers in the Royal Navy and Royal Marines contact your local Royal Navy Careers Information Office – address of your nearest one is available from the telephone directory.  If still at school you can contact the Navy Schools Liaison Officer through the Careers Department.  Alternatively you could write to – Officer Enquiry Section, DNR, Ministry of Defence, Old Admiralty Building, London SW1A 2BE

---

## ROYAL SOCIETY FOR THE PREVENTION OF CRUELTY TO ANIMALS (RSPCA)
Causeway
Horsham
West Sussex RH12 1HG
Tel: 0403 64181  Fax: 0403 41048

The RSPCA is a charity concerned with animal welfare.  It receives no money from the government and has no direct link with any political party.  It works to prevent cruelty and to encourage kindness to animals.  You can become involved by joining the Society as a member, helping to raise funds, helping out at events, raising awareness etc.  RSPCA is a very good source of information about all aspects of animal welfare.

**REGIONAL ADDRESSES:**
Contact Head Office for regional addresses
**AGE RANGE:**
Any
**HOW TO CONTACT:**
Letter, telephone, fax for general information and membership forms
**REGIONS SERVICED:**
UK
**SPECIAL NEEDS PROVISION:**
Enquiries welcome
**COSTS/ WAITING LISTS:**
Junior membership (up to 17 years) £2.50 per year

### RSA EXAMINATIONS BOARD (RSA)
Progress House
Westwood Way
Coventry CV4 8HS
Tel: 0203 470033  Fax: 0203 468080

With over one million candidates every year, RSA Examinations Board is one of the UK's leading providers of vocational and non-vocational qualifications. Courses are available in more than 8,000 centres, including schools, further education colleges, higher education colleges and the workplace. There are more than 200 schemes and courses in subjects ranging from business or office skills through language courses to warehousing and wholesaling. RSA is the awarding body for many NVQs and the new GNVQs. Its standards are recognised by employers and education institutions at home and abroad.

**REGIONAL ADDRESSES:**
Midlands/Anglia: Bradford Court, Bradford Street, Birmingham B12 0NX
North: 1 Albion Place, Leeds LS1 6JL
South East: 8 John Adam Street, London WC2N 6EZ
South West: contact Coventry Head Office
**AGE RANGE:**
14+
**NUMBERS PASSING THROUGH:**
More than 1,000,000 candidates in 1992
**HOW TO CONTACT:**
Write to or call RSA or contact colleges and training organisations direct
**REGIONS SERVICED:**
UK and Ireland
**SPECIAL NEEDS PROVISION:**
RSA publishes a booklet outlining its pro-active approach to special needs. Call RSA for a copy
**COSTS/WAITING LISTS:**
Costs vary according to the course concerned. Call RSA or the centre concerned for details

## THE RSNC WILDLIFE TRUSTS
## PARTNERSHIP
The Green
Witham Park
Waterside South
Lincoln LN5 7JR
Tel: 0522 544400  Fax: 0522 511616

The RSNC is a voluntary organisation concerned with all aspects of wildlife protection. There are many opportunities for getting involved in local conservation projects and initiatives which aim to create a better future for wildlife. Contact RSNC for information about activities in your area and how you can get involved. RSNC also produce information about careers in the environment.

**REGIONAL ADDRESSES:**
Branches throughout the UK
**AGE RANGE:**
Any
**HOW TO CONTACT:**
Letter, telephone, fax to above address for general information and details of your nearest branch
**REGIONS SERVICED:**
UK

## RURAL DEVELOPMENT COMMISSION
### (New Entrants Training Scheme)
141 Castle Street
Salisbury
Wiltshire SP1 3TP
Tel: 0722 336255  Fax: 0722 332769

The commission promotes and assists jobs and communities in rural areas of England. They provide training opportunities for young employees of small rural businesses in a wide variety of occupations e.g. upholstery, forgework, plastics, woodworking machinery, saddlery, thatching, furniture making etc.

**REGIONAL ADDRESSES:**
Details available from Head Office
**AGE RANGE:**
Any
**NUMBERS PASSING THROUGH:**
300 (on training scheme)
**HOW TO CONTACT:**
Telephone or letter to Head Office
**REGIONS SERVICED:**
Rural areas of England only (i.e. where the population does not exceed 10,000 people)
**SPECIAL NEEDS PROVISION:**
Provision is dependent on the nature of the course
**COSTS/WAITING LISTS:**
There is no cost to the trainee under the New Entrants Training Scheme

## RYA SEAMANSHIP FOUNDATION
RYA House
Romsey Road
Eastleigh
Hampshire SO5 4YA
Tel: 0703 629962  Fax: 0703 629924

The Young Skippers scheme, run by the Seamanship Foundation, is designed to give young people (14-23) the opportunity to skipper a yacht and experience the responsibility of command. It provides small cruising yachts and invites young people to sail them at a price which just covers running costs. The Challenger scheme, also run by the Seamanship Foundation, gives young people and adults with a physical disability the opportunity to sail trimarans at a number of centres around the country. The blind sailing course, run each year for visually impaired people aged 17+, lasts for a week and is structured for beginners through to experienced sailors.

**AGE RANGE:**
14+
**HOW TO CONTACT:**
Letter or telephone for general information
**REGIONS SERVICED:**
UK
**SPECIAL NEEDS PROVISION:**
See above
**COSTS/WAITING LISTS:**
Young Skipper Scheme cruise fees are £100-

£140 for 7-10 day cruise.  Blind Sailing Week fees are about £120.  Challenger fees vary with each boat

---

## SAIL TRAINING ASSOCIATION
### (STA Schooners)
2a The Hard
Portsmouth PO1 3PT
Tel: 0705 832055/6  Fax: 0705 815769

The aim of the STA is to help young people learn about themselves, their capabilities and awareness of others in an exciting and demanding voyage on the UK's largest sail-training schooners – the 150ft 'Sir Winston Churchill' and 'Malcolm Miller'. The voyage is designed as an outlet for your spirit of adventure; you do not need any previous experience of the sea or sailing, just an awareness that you are undertaking a challenge, both physically and psychologically, that will stand you in good stead for the rest of your life.  During the two weeks on board you and 38 other trainees of varying backgrounds will take a large sailing ship across nearly 1,000 miles of unpredictable sea.  You will be part of the ship's company and as such will take an active part in the care and maintenance of the ship as well as Watch duties, including look-out, steering, sail-trimming, galley work and ship cleaning.  All voyages count towards the Duke of Edinburgh Award scheme – Gold Award Residential qualification or the scheme's interest section.

**REGIONAL ADDRESSES:**
Comprehensive list of regional committees
available from Head Office
**AGE RANGE:**
16-24
**NUMBERS PASSING THROUGH:**
c 1,000
**HOW TO CONTACT:**
Telephone, letter or fax to Head Office for
advice and information
**REGIONS SERVICED:**
UK
**SPECIAL NEEDS PROVISION:**
Each case is dealt with individually
**COSTS/WAITING LISTS:**
Low season – 2 weeks £500, high season –
£770, inclusive of all food and equipment,
raised from own activities.  STA volunteer
committees around the country hold fund-
raising events and Head Office can advise on
funds and Trusts.  It is advisable to book as
early as possible

---

**SAMA SUMMER SCHOOL**
Scottish Amateur Music Association
7 Randolph Crescent
Edinburgh EH3 7TH
Tel: 0738 71574

Young musicians are invited to apply for the
1993 course which will be held at Craigie

College, Ayr from 11-17 July. No audition is required. Coaching in Chamber Music (ensembles and orchestra), Choir Training, Vocal Training, Opera Workshop, Conducting and Piano Accompanying.

**AGE RANGE:**
18+, senior school pupils may be considered
**NUMBERS PASSING THROUGH:**
50
**HOW TO CONTACT:**
By telephone or letter for further information
**REGIONS SERVICED:**
UK but mainly Scotland
**SPECIAL NEEDS PROVISION:**
Special tuition at an advanced level available
**COSTS/WAITING LISTS:**
There is a course fee of £250 (students £200) which includes tuition, accommodation and the services of professional musicians. Some local authority grants may be available. Waiting lists can be up to six months preceeding the next year's course

## SAVE THE CHILDREN FUND (SCF)
17 Grove Lane
Camberwell
London SE5 8RD
Tel: 071 703 5400

SCF is the UK's largest international voluntary agency concerned with child health and welfare.

It operates major projects in more than 30 countries overseas, as well as many programmes in the UK. For survival it depends on financial support from the general public, and on volunteers in over 800 fund-raising branches throughout the UK.

**AGE RANGE:**
Any
**HOW TO CONTACT:**
Letter, telephone to above address
**REGIONS SERVICED:**
UK

---

### SCOTS FIDDLE SCHOOL
Scottish Amateur Music Association
7 Randolph Crescent
Edinburgh EH3 7TH
Tel: 0738 71574

Young musicians are invited to attend the 1993 course which will be held at Craigie College, Ayr from 11-15 July. No audition is required.

**AGE RANGE:**
Any
**NUMBERS PASSING THROUGH:**
20
**HOW TO CONTACT:**
By telephone or letter for further information
**REGIONS SERVICED:**
UK but mainly Scotland

**SPECIAL NEEDS PROVISION:**
Special tuition at all levels available
**COSTS/WAITING LISTS:**
There is a course fee of £130 which includes
tuition, accommodation and the services of
professional musicians.  Some local authority
grants may be available.  Waiting lists can be
up to six months preceeding the next year's
course

---

**SCOTTISH ARTS COUNCIL**
12 Manor Place
Edinburgh EH3 7DD
Tel: 031 226 6051

See entry for ARTS COUNCIL

---

**SCOTTISH ASSOCIATION OF YOUNG
FARMERS (SAYF)**
Young Farmers Centre
Ingliston
Edinburgh EH28 8NE
Tel: 031 333 2445

Young Farmers care about the countryside, and
delve into all kinds of rural issues for 'grass
roots' information.  There are some 120 clubs
throughout Scotland which organise activities
such as discos and parties, drama and
international travel, sporting competitions
(anything from curling to tug-of-war, football
and ten pin bowling), speechmaking contests

and craft-making. They organise special courses which help young people to develop leadership skills and confidence in public speaking. They are part of an international network of young people whose interests lie in meeting people and caring for the countryside. Members make friends worldwide – exchange visits are arranged between clubs in the UK and as far away as Australia, Finland, Sweden, Switzerland, Canada and America.

**AGE RANGE:**
14-26
**HOW TO CONTACT:**
Letter, telephone to Head Office for information about your nearest Young Farmers Club
**REGIONS SERVICED:**
Scotland

---

## SCOTTISH BUSINESS IN THE COMMUNITY (SBC)
Romano House
43 Station Road
Corstorphine
Edinburgh EH12 7AF
Tel: 031 334 9876  Fax: 031 316 4521

SBC can give general information on all aspects of setting up and maintaining your own business, plus details of agencies in your local area from where you can obtain more specific information and advice.

**AGE RANGE:**
Any
**HOW TO CONTACT:**
Letter, telephone, fax for general information
**REGIONS SERVICED:**
Scotland
**SPECIAL NEEDS PROVISION:**
Enquiries welcome

---

## SCOTTISH CONSERVATION PROJECTS TRUST (SCP)
Balallan House
24 Allan Park
Stirling FK8 2QG
Tel: 0786 479697  Fax: 0786 465359

Action Breaks are 7-14 day practical, residential, conservation projects for people aged 16+ held throughout Scotland. Midweek Groups are one day projects for mainly unemployed volunteers aged over 16.  Operation Brightwater projects are water-based projects carried out by groups in various parts of Scotland, mainly for over 16s but there are some opportunities for younger people. There are also weekend training courses in environment skills and 6- and 8-month Vocational Training Courses leading to a recognised City and Guilds Certificate.  There are also long-term volunteering and leadership opportunities.

**REGIONAL ADDRESSES:**
Contact through Head Office

**AGE RANGE:**
16+
**NUMBERS PASSING THROUGH:**
5,000 total volunteers (about 3,000 young people)
**HOW TO CONTACT:**
Telephone or letter to Head Office
**REGIONS SERVICED:**
Scotland (volunteers taken from anywhere)
**SPECIAL NEEDS PROVISION:**
Some provision on certain schemes
**COSTS/WAITING LISTS:**
Student membership is £6. Action Breaks cost £3 per day. There are no costs for Midweek Projects or Operation Brightwater. Training courses cost £16 per weekend

---

### SCOTTISH CO-OPERATIVES DEVELOPMENT COMMITTEE (SCDC)
Building 1, 1st Floor
Templeton Business Centre
Templeton Street
Bridgeton
Glasgow G40 1DA
Tel: 041 554 3797

The SCDC is an organisation which can give free advice to anyone proposing to start a business and who might be interested in a co-operative structure. Free advice from SCDC will explain what a co-operative is and how it could work for your business. They can assist in preparing a business plan, and ultimately can help you to register your company. After start-up SCDC will stay on hand with advice and assistance through the early months.

**AGE RANGE:**
Any
**HOW TO CONTACT:**
Telephone, letter to Head Office for details of regional offices
**REGIONS SERVICED:**
Scotland

---

## SCOTTISH COUNCIL FOR EDUCATIONAL TECHNOLOGY (SCET)
Dowanhill
74 Victoria Crescent Road
Glasgow G12 9JN
Tel: 041 334 9314  Fax: 041 334 6519

SCET provide information and advice on all aspects of open and flexible learning. They run training workshops and have an extensive range of education and training films and videos. They also have a large library of learning packages and opportunities open to the public.

**AGE RANGE:**
Any
**HOW TO CONTACT:**
Telephone, letter, fax or in person to the Information Resource Centre for information

or referral to another agency if appropriate
**REGIONS SERVICED:**
UK
**SPECIAL NEEDS PROVISION:**
Information database available on the use of
microelectronics for learners with special
educational needs.  Visual Impairment
Service – an information service designed for
the use of the visually impaired community
and those working in the field – also available
**COSTS/WAITING LISTS:**
There is no charge for information.  Costs for
services vary

---

### SCOTTISH NATIONAL ASSOCIATION OF YOUTH THEATRE (SNAYT)
Old Athenaeum Theatre
179 Buchanan Street
Glasgow G1 2JZ
Tel: 041 332 5127  Fax: 041 333 1021

---

The SNAYT is a resource and development
service for youth theatre in Scotland and can
provide information and advice to anyone with
an interest in young people's theatre, either
directly or by referring to other organisations.

**AGE RANGE:**
12-25
**HOW TO CONTACT:**
Letter, phone or fax for further information
**REGIONS SERVICED:**
Scotland, but can provide information outside

Scotland e.g. on theatre exchanges
**SPECIAL NEEDS PROVISION:**
Can put people in touch with relevant
organisations
**COSTS/WAITING LISTS:**
None for information

---

## SCOTTISH NATIONAL PARTY (SNP)
6 North Charlotte Street
Edinburgh
Lothian EH2 4FH
Tel: 031 226 3661

---

## SCOTTISH SILVER JUBILEE & CHILDREN'S BURSARY FUND
1 Woodside Road
Tullibody
Alloa
Clackmannanshire FK10 2QQ
Tel: 0259 723935

If you are under 25 and have an idea that would benefit the community in some way this bursary fund may be able to give you a grant to help with your project. You can apply on your own or with others (you don't have to be a member of a club or organisation). If you want to apply, write down your plans, find out how much it will cost and get in touch with the Fund.

**AGE RANGE:**
Under 25

**NUMBERS PASSING THROUGH:**
20 grants awarded
**HOW TO CONTACT:**
Telephone or letter for information and an
applicaton form
**REGIONS SERVICED:**
Scotland
**SPECIAL NEEDS PROVISION:**
Anyone under 25 can apply for grants
**COSTS/WAITING LISTS:**
Applications are usually dealt with as
received

## SCOTTISH SPORTS COUNCIL
Caledonia House
South Gyle
Edinburgh EH12 9DQ
Tel: 031 317 7200  Fax: 031 317 7202

The Scottish Sports Council provides information
on sport in Scotland and initiates opportunities
for people to participate in sport at any level of
ability.

**AGE RANGE:**
Any
**HOW TO CONTACT:**
Telephone or letter for information,
publications and contact addresses of sports
organisations
**REGIONS SERVICED:**
Scotland

**SPECIAL NEEDS PROVISION:**
Information on disabled sports
**COSTS/WAITING LISTS:**
There is a charge for some publications
although many are free

---

## SCOTTISH VOCATIONAL EDUCATION COUNCIL (SCOTVEC)
Hanover House
24 Douglas Street
Glasgow G2 7NQ
Tel: 041 248 7900

SCOTVEC is the broad equivalent in Scotland of BTEC. They approve a wide range of work-related courses and exams suitable for part-time or full-time study depending on the type of course. They can provide information on the large range of vocational courses available throughout Scotland – what you need to get on, how long it will take, what you will gain, and where the courses are held. Information about the range of courses in your area is also available at your local Careers Office. Look in the phone book under 'Careers'.

**AGE RANGE:**
Any
**HOW TO CONTACT:**
Write to the above address
**REGIONS SERVICED:**
Scotland. For England, Wales and Northern

Ireland see entry for BUSINESS AND
TECHNICAL EDUCATION COUNCIL (BTEC)

## SCOTTISH YOUNG PERSONS VIDEO COMPETITION
Learning Systems Division
Scottish Council for Educational Technology
74 Victoria Crescent Road
Glasgow G12 9JN

This video competition is an annual event with
prizes for an overall winner and for the best
programmes in the primary, secondary and
further education sectors. It is open to those
aged 21 and under who are at an established
school or college in Scotland and who are not
involved professionally in broadcast media.
Each year there is a theme for entries and also a
category for scripts/storyboards so you can enter
even if you don't have access to production
equipment. Write to the above address for
further information.

## SCOTTISH YOUTH DANCE FESTIVAL (SYDF)
The Assembly Rooms
54 George Street
Edinburgh EH2 2LR
Tel: 031 220 6320

The SYDF runs the annual youth dance festival
in Scotland which includes all types of dance

plus the chance to perform alongside professional companies. They also administrate the Mitchell Trust Dance Bursary as well as promoting young people's participation in dance through information networking.

**AGE RANGE:**
14-25
**NUMBERS PASSING THROUGH:**
300 directly involved
**HOW TO CONTACT:**
Telephone or letter with SAE for information on the dance festival and other activities as well as opportunities for dance in Scotland
**REGIONS SERVICED:**
Mainly Scotland, but also UK and Europe
**SPECIAL NEEDS PROVISION:**
Enquiries welcome
**COSTS/WAITING LISTS:**
Cost of attendance at the 1993 Festival in Dundee is £155 + VAT residential and £95 + VAT non-residential. Information and advice is free

---

### SCOTTISH YOUTH THEATRE (SYT)
Old Athenaeum Theatre
179 Buchanan Street
Glasgow G1 2JZ
Tel: 041 332 5727  Fax: 041 333 1021

SYT wants to hear from anyone, anywhere in Scotland, aged 12-21, who is interested in the performing arts. They offer the chance to experience all aspects of performance art while working with theatre professionals. A very wide range of activities is available including touring workshops, youth theatre festivals, a playwright festival, professional training and much more.

**AGE RANGE:**
12-21
**NUMBERS PASSING THROUGH:**
10,000+
**HOW TO CONTACT:**
Letter, telephone, fax or in person for details of activities
**REGIONS SERVICED:**
UK but mainly Scotland
**SPECIAL NEEDS PROVISION:**
Extensive provision e.g. a variety of mixed ability projects and workshops
**COSTS/WAITING LISTS:**
Costs for festivals, courses, tuition etc. vary and SYT can offer advice on fund-raising

## THE SCOUT ASSOCIATION
The Scout Association
Baden-Powell House
Queen's Gate
London SW7 5JS
Tel: 071 584 7030  Fax: 071 581 9953

Scouts are young men and women who take part in a very wide range of outdoor activities including climbing, abseiling, canoeing, sailing, hiking, mountaineering etc., as well as community work, international projects throughout the world, training in a variety of different areas and a personal development programme.

**REGIONAL ADDRESSES:**
Available from HQ
**AGE RANGE:**
Venture Scouts 15-20 years, other sections 6-15 years
**NUMBERS PASSING THROUGH:**
556,000 members
**HOW TO CONTACT:**
Contact local group (Local Authority has list of Scout groups in area) or Headquarters above
**REGIONS SERVICED:**
UK with international projects throughout the world
**SPECIAL NEEDS PROVISION:**
Scout Link Clubs deal specifically with special needs scouting
**COSTS/WAITING LISTS:**
Subscriptions vary from group to group

**SEA CADET CORPS (SCC)**
202 Lambeth Road
London SE1 7JF
Tel: 071 928 8978

The Sea Cadet Corps is a voluntary youth organisation comprised of 400 units scattered throughout the country, providing facilities for the Cadets to take part in activities in which self-discipline, leadership and a sense of responsibility to the community are encouraged. The accent is on the sea; sailing and boatwork have a high priority and most units have access to water and boats. Other activities include, band training, communications, engineering, model making, swimming, visits to ships, expeditions and much more. All cadets can take part in adventure training, map reading and the Duke of Edinburgh Award Scheme.

**REGIONAL ADDRESSES:**
Six regional addresses – details available from Head Office
**AGE RANGE:**
12-18
**NUMBERS PASSING THROUGH:**
17,000 members
**HOW TO CONTACT:**
Telephone, letter or fax to Head/Regional Office or contact local Sea Cadet Unit
**REGIONS SERVICED:**
UK
**SPECIAL NEEDS PROVISION:**
Some restriction on physical disability
**COSTS/WAITING LISTS:**
Voluntary monthly contribution. Part assistance with travel costs for selected field trips

**SEA RANGER ASSOCIATION (SRA)**
HQTS 'Lord Amory'
Dollar Bay
301 Marsh Wall
London E14 9TF
Tel: 071 987 1757

The SRA gives girls and young women the chance to canoe, row, sail-board and dinghy off-shore; camp, learn first-aid etc; help the community, e.g. at hospitals, childrens homes; fund-raise for other charities; make new friends, meet regularly and have fun.

**REGIONAL ADDRESSES:**
Available through General Secretary
**AGE RANGE:**
10-21
**NUMBERS PASSING THROUGH:**
750
**HOW TO CONTACT:**
Telephone or SAE to General Secretary, Vera Simpson, 91 Sherwood Ave, Streatham Vale, London SW16 5EL  Tel: 081 764 3694 for advice and information plus details of local contact
**REGIONS SERVICED:**
England
**SPECIAL NEEDS PROVISION:**
Enquiries welcome
**COSTS/WAITING LISTS:**
Annual subscription – £3; membership fees –

25p-50p per week; payments for specific
events, e.g. £5 for regatta and activity
weekend camp

### SHELL BETTER BRITAIN CAMPAIGN
Red House
Hill Lane
Great Barr
Birmingham B43 6LZ
Tel: 021 358 0744  Fax: 021 358 5250

The Shell Better Britain Campaign provides
advice and support for any voluntary group that
is carrying out a practical project to improve
their local environment.   There is a free
information pack which includes a 68-page
booklet, *Getting Help For Community
Environmental Projects* and details of their grant
scheme. The grant scheme is only applicable to
voluntary groups.

**AGE RANGE:**
Any
**NUMBERS PASSING THROUGH:**
85 young people's groups received grants.
1,500 schools and youth groups asked for the
information pack
**HOW TO CONTACT:**
Letter to Head Office for an information pack
and details of grant scheme
**REGIONS SERVICED:**
UK

**SPECIAL NEEDS PROVISION:**
No special provision
**COSTS/WAITING LISTS:**
None

---

### SHELL TECHNOLOGY ENTERPRISE PROGRAMME (STEP)
Shell (UK) Ltd
Shell Mex House
Strand
London WC2R 0DX
Tel: 071 257 3185

STEP offers selected university and polytechnic students placements with a host company for eight weeks during the summer vacation to complete a project which is specified by and benefits the firm. The scheme gives students an insight into how business works and the opportunity to learn about teamwork, problem solving, communication and decision making. Students make presentations about their projects at local awards ceremonies and the winners compete at the STEP National Awards ceremony.

**AGE RANGE:**
No specific age-range – open to students in their penultimate year of a degree or Higher Diploma Course
**NUMBERS PASSING THROUGH:**
400 in 1991, 800 in 1992
**HOW TO CONTACT:**
The best way to contact is through one of the

various agencies around the country that deal with the STEP programme – Careers Offices, TECs, universities, colleges etc. A full list is available from the above address or ask at your Careers Office for an application form

**REGIONS SERVICED:**
UK

**SPECIAL NEEDS PROVISION:**
No special provision

**COSTS/WAITING LISTS:**
No costs. Students receive a weekly training allowance of £100 for the eight weeks

---

### SHEPLEY-SHEPLEY TRUST
12 Manor Place
Edinburgh EH3 7DD
Tel: 031 226 6051  Fax: 031 225 9833

The Trust can offer grants from their Youth Arts Fund ranging from £50 to £2,000 for arts projects which show enterprise, innovation and potential for development. Applicants must be resident in Scotland and applying in connection with projects to be undertaken in Scotland. Projects can involve anything from film, video and rock music, to dance, drama, literature and the visual arts and crafts.

**AGE RANGE:**
16-25

**NUMBERS PASSING THROUGH:**
Approx 100 applications from 500 enquiries

**HOW TO CONTACT:**
Letter for further information and an
application form
**REGIONS SERVICED:**
Scotland
**SPECIAL NEEDS PROVISION:**
All applications are dealt with on an equal
opportunities basis
**COSTS/WAITING LISTS:**
Closing dates are three times per year (exact
dates available on request) and applicants
hear results within one month of closing date

---

## SKILL: NATIONAL BUREAU FOR STUDENTS WITH DISABILITIES
336 Brixton Road
London SW9 7AA
Tel: 071 274 0565  Fax: 071 274 7840

Skill provides an information/advice service for
people with disabilities or learning difficulties,
and the professionals who work with them, on
all aspects of post-16 education, training and
employment.  A range of other help including
staff development as well as free information
sheets and priced publications is available.
Membership fee includes subscription to two
newsletters and one journal.

**REGIONAL ADDRESSES:**
Contact through central office

**AGE RANGE:**
Any
**HOW TO CONTACT:**
Telephone or letter for information
**REGIONS SERVICED:**
UK
**SPECIAL NEEDS PROVISION:**
See above
**COSTS/WAITING LISTS:**
Annual membership starts at £7 and
publications cost £3-£10

---

**SOCIAL DEMOCRATIC AND LABOUR
PARTY (SDLP)**
38 University Street
Belfast BT7 1FZ
Tel: 0232 323428

---

**SOCIAL INVENTIONS COMPETITION**
The Institute for Social Inventions
20 Heber Road
London NW2 6AA
Tel: 081 208 2853  Fax: 081 452 6434

The Institute of Social Inventions runs an annual
competition, with prizes for both adults and
young people, for novel ideas and projects that
will improve the quality of life within our society.
A social invention is defined as a new and
imaginative solution to a social problem – not a
product, nor a technological invention, nor a
patentable device – but a means by which

society can be improved upon. Good examples of past social inventions include the Open University, and *Which?* magazine – new combinations of existing ideas, new ways for people to relate to each other, new organisational structures or whatever. ISI offer £1,000 a year for the best social invention, and they are editors of *The Book of Visions – An Encyclopaedia of Social Innovations* (price £17.99 inc p&p).

**AGE RANGE:**
Any
**HOW TO CONTACT:**
Letter, telephone, fax to above address
**REGIONS SERVICED:**
UK
**SPECIAL NEEDS PROVISION:**
Enquiries welcome

---

### SOCIETY OF VOLUNTARY ASSOCIATES (SOVA)
1-4 Brixton Hill Place
London SW2 1HJ
Tel: 081 671 7833

SOVA is a national charity which has schemes throughout the country that recruit and train volunteers to befriend people who have offended. The aims of this are to give support and advice, to encourage independence, and to break the cycle of re-offending. SOVA specialises in training local volunteers to work with the probation service. The volunteers in return give their time, committment and enthusiasm to assist in supporting offenders and their families in the community, thereby helping to reduce crime. The tasks that volunteers undertake are likely to be influenced by their location, and individual interests and skills. Some examples are: befriending of people on probation; supporting the partners and families of people in prison; teaching literacy or numeracy skills; providing support to individuals or families in court etc.

**SPONSORSHIPS '93 (publication)**
Careers and Occupational Information Centre
(COIC)
Rockery Cottage
Sutton-cum-Lound
Retford
Nottinghamshire DN22 8PJ
Tel: 0777 705951

Many companies help young people financially with their studies. *Sponsorships '93* contains a list of employers offering sponsorship to young people while they take professional or technical degrees. It lists rare opportunities for young people to gain extra financial support and work experience at a time when finances are stretched and experience at a premium. The book is divided into various categories, including accountancy, textile technology, transport and distribution.  Available from COIC (price £3.56 inc p&p).

---

**SPORTS COUNCIL**
16 Upper Woburn Place
London WC1H 0QP
Tel: 071 388 1277  Fax: 071 383 5740

The Sports Council Information Service provides contact addresses and information on all aspects of sport.  Details of career opportunities and courses are available.

**REGIONAL ADDRESSES:**
12 regional offices – addresses available from Head Office
**AGE RANGE:**
Any
**HOW TO CONTACT:**
Letter with SAE to Information Centre
**REGIONS SERVICED:**
UK (see separate entries for Scotland, Wales and Northern Ireland)
**SPECIAL NEEDS PROVISION:**
Information on disabled sports
**COSTS/WAITING LISTS:**
None

## SPORTS COUNCIL FOR NORTHERN IRELAND
House of Sport
Upper Malone Road
Belfast BT9 5LA
Tel: 0232 381222  Fax: 0232 682757

The aims of the Sports Council are to further sport and physical recreation in Northern Ireland. If you need any general advice or information about a particular sport and how to get involved, the Sports Council will either be able help or point you in the right direction.

**AGE RANGE:**
Any
**HOW TO CONTACT:**
By letter to the Information Officer
**REGIONS SERVICED:**
Northern Ireland
**SPECIAL NEEDS PROVISION:**
Information on disabled sports
**COSTS/WAITING LISTS:**
No costs for information

## SPORTS COUNCIL FOR WALES
Information Centre
Sophia Gardens
Cardiff CF1 9SW
Tel: 0222 397571

The Sports Council for Wales can provide

information on all sports provision throughout Wales – special needs provision, minority interest sports, major sporting events etc. They can give information about provision in your local area, and can give advice about developing a career in sport and related occupations.

**AGE RANGE:**
Any
**HOW TO CONTACT:**
By telephone or letter for further information on any aspect of sport
**REGIONS SERVICED:**
Wales

---

### SPRINGBOARD
1 Denmark Street
London WC2H 8LP
Tel: 071 497 8654

Springboard is the careers advice centre for Hotels, Catering, Leisure and Tourism. It can provide advice and up to date information on the wide variety of opportunities within this industry, training and qualifications that may be required, where to find the training, what your typical career path could be – all tailored to your own individual needs and aspirations. At the Springboard offices there are computer storyboards which you can go through in your own time, looking at job descriptions of more than 200 different types of career. These can be printed out for you to take away. This is backed up with our careers advisers' firsthand knowledge of the industry and literature from a variety of progressive companies within Hotels, Catering, Leisure and Tourism.

**AGE RANGE:**
All ages
**NUMBERS PASSING THROUGH:**
Approximately 10,000 per year
**HOW TO CONTACT:**
Either call in or contact the above address by letter or telephone
**REGIONS COVERED:**
Greater London area, but written and telephone enquiries are handled on a national basis

### STAGIAIRES
The UK Offices of the European Commision
Information Office
Jean Monnet House
8 Storey's Gate
London SW1P 3AT

The European Commission, the European Parliament and the Economic and Social Committee all run schemes of in-service training for about 300 trainees each year, known as 'stagiaires'. The largest one is run by the European Commission. The training period begins with a general introduction to Community matters, followed by attachments to departments with advisers to supervise your work. That gives you the opportunity to see how the Commission works from the inside. At the end of each 'stage', the work of each stagiaire is assessed and given a certificate. Trainees need to be under 30 and with either university degrees or equivalent. It is an advantage to have shown an interest in European affairs in your work or studies. For full information contact the above address.

---

### ST JOHN'S AMBULANCE
National Headquarters
1 Grosvenor Crescent
London SW1X 7EF
Tel: 071 235 5231 Fax: 071 235 0796

As a member of St John Ambulance you can learn everything from first aid to abseiling, from camping to working in the community and much more. St John Cadets aims for a balance of fun and responsibility. You can participate in the Duke of Edinburgh's Award Scheme and 'The Challenge' – an award scheme covering various activities, open to all 15-25 year-olds, not just St John members. There is also a St John connected society called 'Links', which operates in universities, polytechnics and higher and further education colleges.

**REGIONAL ADDRESSES:**
Organised on a county basis; all counties

have an HQ listed in the telephone directory.
Wales and Northern Ireland have their own
national HQs and in Scotland St John
Ambulance operates through a sister
organisation:-
Scotland: St Andrew's, Milton Street, Glasgow
Tel: 041 332 4031
Wales: Priory for Wales, Lisvane Road,
Llanishen, Cardiff CF4 5XT  Tel:
0222 750222
Northern Ireland: Erne Purdysburn Hospital,
Saintfield Road, Belfast BT8 8RA  Tel:
0232 799393

**AGE RANGE:**
Badgers 6-10; Cadets 10-18; Adult members
18+

**NUMBERS PASSING THROUGH:**
22,000 members

**HOW TO CONTACT:**
By letter or telephone to Cadet and Training
Department at National HQ or contact
County HQ via telephone directory

**REGIONS SERVICED:**
UK

**SPECIAL NEEDS PROVISION:**
Membership is open to all young people who
can learn first aid

**COSTS/WAITING LISTS:**
Small weekly divisional subscription plus
some uniform costs

**THE STOCK EXCHANGE**
Careers and Employment Office
The Stock Exchange
Old Broad Street
London EC2N 1HP
Tel: 071 588 2355

The main opportunities on the stock exchange or in the financial markets are as a market maker, stockbroker, investment analyst or in administration. Market makers deal in stocks and shares on the stock exchange in order to make a profit. Stockbrokers work on behalf of clients wishing to make investments by either advising on the value of stocks and shares or directly by buying from or selling to market makers. Investment analysts investigate and advise on the investment prospects of companies or particular industries usually either for stockbroking firms or for large investors such as pension funds. Administrative and clerical staff carry out back-up duties such as processing transactions etc. Market makers, stockbrokers and investment analysts study for the professional examinations of the Stock Exchange Council. For further information on careers and training in the stock exchange or financial markets contact either the Stock Exchchange at the above address or individual companies (see telephone directory under 'Investment Consultants' or 'Stockbrokers and Market Makers').

**STRATHCLYDE INTERNATIONAL RESOURCES CENTRE**
St Patrick's Primary School
10 Perth Street
Glasgow G3 8UQ
Tel: 041 227 3889  Fax: 041 227 2085

The International Resources Centre can provide information, advice, publications, training, contacts and any other type of help requested on any aspect of international work, e.g. exchanges, working abroad, job placements, European legislation, European Community schemes and much more.

**AGE RANGE:**
Any
**NUMBERS PASSING THROUGH:**
Over 3,000 per year
**HOW TO CONTACT:**
Telephone, letter, fax or in person for leaflets, information, local visits, details of courses etc.
**REGIONS SERVICED:**
Specifically Strathclyde, but will deal with enquiries from anywhere in the UK
**SPECIAL NEEDS PROVISION:**
The Centre has particular interest and expertise in special needs areas
**COSTS/WAITING LISTS:**
Service is free.  Enquiries are dealt with as they are received

## STUDENT CHRISTIAN MOVEMENT (SCM)
186 St Paul's Road
Balsall Heath
Birmingham B12 8LZ
Tel: 021 440 3000  Fax: 021 446 4060

SCM supports the initiatives and programmes of over 70 groups which meet regularly in universities and colleges. Each local group has its own programme of events, run by students and for students, usually involving invited speakers, discussions and visits.  There are regional and national conferences and training events. SCM is an ecumenical movement which encourages open enquiry into the nature of Christian faith and action. It is a member of the World Student Christian Federation and arranges regular exchanges and visits between students of different national movements.

**REGIONAL ADDRESSES:**
Midlands: 186 St Paul's Road, Balsall Heath, Birmingham B12 8LZ  Tel: 021 440 7138
North: St Peter's House, Precinct Centre, Oxford Road, Manchester M13 9GH
Tel: 061 273 5752
South: 52 Ladbroke Road, London W11 2PB
Tel: 071 792 1218
Scotland: University Chaplaincy Centre, 1 Bristo Square, Edinburgh EH8 9AL
Tel: 031 667 4321
Wales: Crwys Chapel, 77 Richmond Road, Cardiff CF2 3BR  Tel: 0222 463880

**AGE RANGE:**
Any
**REGIONS SERVICED:**
England, Scotland and Wales

## STUDENT INDUSTRIAL SOCIETY (SIS)
Quadrant Court
Calthorpe Road
Edgbaston
Birmingham B15 1TH
Tel: 021 454 6769  Fax: 021 456 2715

The SIS is part of the Industrial Society, an independent, non-political charity which works towards raising awareness of Industry and Commerce, and improving links with people in full-time education.  The SIS is run on campus by students for students, and they organise a variety of activities for their members including, visits to companies, presentations by companies, business games and skills training, all designed to promote industrial and commercial involvement in higher education and prepare students for the transition from higher education to employment.

**REGIONAL ADDRESSES:**
There are about 60 societies based at various universities and colleges around the country
**AGE RANGE:**
Any
**HOW TO CONTACT:**
Contact SIS at your institution if there is one

or alternatively contact address above
**REGIONS SERVICED:**
UK
**SPECIAL NEEDS PROVISION:**
No special provision, but this is an area the
society is developing
**COSTS/WAITING LISTS:**
None for information

---

### STUDENT LOAN COMPANY LTD
100 Bothwell Street
Glasgow G2 7GD
Tel: 041 306 2000  Fax: 041 306 2005

The Student Loans Scheme is a Government
funded loans scheme which is administered by
Student Loan Company Ltd. It provides for
loans to be made towards students' living costs.
There are different amounts of loan available,
depending on whether you are living at home or
away from home, and on whether you are
studying in London or outside London. For full
details of the scheme contact Student Loan
Company.

---

### STUDENTS ABROAD LTD
11 Milton View
Hitchin
Herts SG4 0QD
Tel: 0462 438909  Fax: 0462 438919

The agency places au pairs, mothers' helps and

nannies in Austria, Belgium, France, Germany, Greece, Holland, Italy, South Africa, Spain, USA and UK (minimum age 18, minimum period 2-3 months in summer except USA where stay must be 12 months). Also places mothers' helps in Israel where the minimum age is 19 and the minimum stay is one year, and qualified or experienced nannies over 18 in Canada for at least one year.

**AGE RANGE:**
18-27
**NUMBERS PASSING THROUGH:**
More than 600
**HOW TO CONTACT:**
Send a large SAE for information leaflets, an application form and a selection of positions currently available. Telephone enquiries welcome
**REGIONS SERVICED:**
UK
**SPECIAL NEEDS PROVISION:**
Rarely able to find placements for people with special needs due to the nature of the work
**COSTS/WAITING LISTS:**
There is an optional information pack (costs approx £40) available from the agency giving further information about working abroad, travel and insurance information

**STUDY HOLIDAYS (publication)**
Central Bureau for Educational Visits and
Exchanges
Seymour Mews
London W1H 9PE
Tel: 071 486 5101  Fax: 071 935 5741
Tel: 071 725 9402 (credit card orders)

If you need to brush up language skills in
preparation for exams, want to learn another
language for enjoyment or to further knowledge
of the country and culture, then *Study Holidays*
has details of a European language course that
can provide just what you are looking for.
Actually being in another country, learning
formally or informally, is an ideal way to become
confident and fluent in a second language.
*Study Holidays* has just about all the information
you need on holiday courses in 26 European
languages, where you can receive expert tuition
and stay in an area where you can put your
language skills into practice.  There is also
practical information on accommodation, travel,
sources for bursaries, grants and scholarships
and language teaching resources.
ISBN 0 90087 90 0.  Price £7.95.  Available
through bookshops or direct from the above
address (price £9.45 inc p&p).

## STUDYING FILM AND TELEVISION
### (publication)
British Film Institute
21 Stephen Street
London W1P 1PL
Tel: 071 255 1444

A guide to academic courses in higher education. Gives details of both undergraduate and postgraduate courses in universities and polytechnics in which film/television is a major, substantial or minor component. Updated annually. ISBN 0 85170 285 6 Available through public libraries, bookshops (price £3.75) or direct from the above address (price £4.25 inc p&p).

## SUE RYDER FOUNDATION
Cavendish
Suffolk CO10 8AY
Tel: 0787 280252

The Sue Ryder Foundation is an international charity formed in 1953. They run 80 homes in 24 different countries for the sick and disabled and offer opportunities for voluntary service which allow young people to work alongside staff and to meet other volunteers, some of different nationality. Volunteers do whatever work is necessary which may include helping with patients, domestic, office or other duties and in return receive free simple accommodation and meals plus pocket money.

**AGE RANGE:**
16+
**NUMBERS PASSING THROUGH:**
c 50 volunteers per year
**HOW TO CONTACT:**
By letter or telephone to Mr Wilkinson at the
above address for information on the
foundation and an application form
**REGIONS SERVICED:**
UK and abroad
**SPECIAL NEEDS PROVISION:**
No provision
**COSTS/WAITING LISTS:**
Volunteers have to meet their own travel
costs

---

**SUMMER JOBS USA 1993 (publication)**
Vacation Work Publications
9 Park End Street
Oxford OX1 1HJ
Tel: 0865 241978  Fax: 0865 790885

Thousands of jobs listed at employers request
for students in the United States and Canada.
Ranches, summer camps, national parks,
theatres, resorts, restaurants etc. Information is
given on board and lodging. Wages up to £750
per month.  Includes special section giving
advice on legal requirements and visa procedure
for non-US citizens, plus comments from
employers on the specific advantages of

particular jobs. Many US summer employers
welcome applicants from Britain and Europe.
ISBN 1 56079 148 9 Available through libraries,
bookshops (price £9.95) or direct from the
above address (price £10.95 inc p&p).

### SUMMER MUSIC
22 Gresley Road
London N19 3JZ
Tel: 071 272 5664

Summer Music arrange courses and classes for
musicians and singers throughout the year at
various locations. There is a programme of
weekend courses for singers (solo and choral),
guitarists, cellists, violinists, flautists, pianists,
trumpeters plus Tai Chi and story writing. There
is an 8-day summer school at Wellington College
in Berkshire offering classes in, amongst others,
string quartets, symphony orchestra, choirs, story
writing, composing, wind ensembles, sight
singing, opera, music theatre, conducting and
contemporary music.

**REGIONAL ADDRESSES:**
All enquiries to London Office
**AGE RANGE:**
14+
**NUMBERS PASSING THROUGH:**
Over 400
**HOW TO CONTACT:**
By telephone or letter for details of courses

available
**REGIONS SERVICED:**
UK
**SPECIAL NEEDS PROVISION:**
Most venues are fully accessible
**COSTS/WAITING LISTS:**
The 8-day summer school currently costs
£190 plus VAT for residents and £150 plus
VAT for non-residents. Weekend courses
cost from £75

---

## SURVIVAL INTERNATIONAL
310 Edgware Road
London W2 1DY
Tel: 071 723 5535  Fax: 071 723 4059

Survival International is a worldwide movement
to support tribal peoples. It stands for their right
to decide their own future and helps them
protect their lands, environment and way of life.
Their work is wholly funded by subscriptions
from members, and donations from supporters.
You can help by becoming a member and
taking an active part in one of their letter-writing
campaigns.

---

## TANGENTS
Central Hall
West Tollcross
Edinburgh EH3 9BP
Tel: 031 229 1950  Fax: 031 229 0339

The broad aim of Tangents is to bring together the young people of Scotland in a variety of ways to ensure their active participation, and a voice, in all issues relating to young people – homelessness, the environment, the law etc. The emphasis is on young people working for themselves to become actively involved and make their opinions and views known on a local, regional and national level. Tangents work with many youth projects in Scotland and can offer young people access to a variety of resources including training, support (from national staff or local workers), representation and access to a national network of young people. Membership is open to any young person in Scotland aged 16-25.

**AGE RANGE:**
16-25
**HOW TO CONTACT:**
Telephone, letter or in person
**REGIONS SERVICED:**
Scotland
**SPECIAL NEEDS PROVISION:**
Any young person can participate in
Tangents' activities
**COSTS/WAITING LISTS:**
None

## TEACHING ENGLISH ABROAD
### (publication)
Vacation Work Publications
9 Park End Street
Oxford OX1 1HJ
Tel: 0865 241978  Fax: 0865 790885

Guide to short and long-term opportunities for both trained and untrained teachers in the booming field of teaching English as a Foreign Language. The book contains chapters on over 20 countries where EFL is a major industry including Spain, Greece, Eastern Europe, Turkey, Japan, Taiwan etc., plus surveys of the range of possibilities in Africa and Latin America. Each country chapter discusses the ways in which native speakers of English can find work, the red tape involved, contracts and salaries, plus a list of language schools which hire English teachers. The introduction covers general topics such as how to become qualified in EFL, the role of recruitment agencies, and the possible risks and how to avoid them.

ISBN 1 85458 048 5. Available through libraries, bookshops (price £8.95), or direct from the above address (price £9.95 inc p&p).

## TEENAGERS' VACATION GUIDE TO WORK, STUDY AND ADVENTURE
**(publication)**
Vacation Work Publications
9 Park End Street
Oxford OX1 1HJ
Tel: 0865 241978  Fax: 0865 790885

Information on the wide range of jobs, study courses and adventure holidays that are available for teenagers in Britain and abroad during the school holidays. Lists hundreds of employers – language schools and other educational establishments, adventure holiday and multi-activity companies, and non-profit making youth organisations which arrange courses, expeditions, homestays, exchanges and termstays in Britain, Europe and worldwide. Provides information on youth travel, health, money and red tape etc, plus practical advice on choosing a project.
ISBN 1 85458 044 2. Available through libraries, bookshops (price £6.95), or direct from the above address (price £7.95 inc p&p).

## THEATRE WORKSHOP EDINBURGH (TW)
34 Hamilton Place
Edinburgh EH3 5AX
Tel: 031 225 7942 (Administration),
031 226 5425 (Box Office & Minicom)
Fax: 031 220 0112

TW run two youth theatre groups which meet on a weekly basis throughout the year. They operate a 'Theatre in Education' programme which they take out to schools and youth groups. They put on youth productions which go out on tour and they can offer vocational training opportunities for a small number of young people each year.

**AGE RANGE:**
Any
**HOW TO CONTACT:**
Telephone or letter for further information
**REGIONS SERVICED:**
Scotland
**SPECIAL NEEDS PROVISION:**
All projects are designed to be accessible to people with special needs. Two members of staff work specifically in this area. The workshop regularly employs performers with special needs
**COSTS/WAITING LISTS:**
£2 per session to participate in youth theatre activities. May be waiting lists

---

**THISTLE CAMPS**
see NATIONAL TRUST FOR SCOTLAND CONSERVATION VOLUNTEERS

**TOC H**
1 Forest Close
Wendover
Aylesbury
Bucks HP22 6BT
Tel: 0296 623911  Fax: 0296 696137

Toc H runs short-term residential projects throughout the year in the UK and Germany, usually from a weekend up to 3 weeks in duration. Project work undertaken can include: work with people with different disabilities; work with children in need; playschemes and camps; conservation and manual work; study and/or discussion sessions.  These projects provide those who take part with opportunities to learn more about themselves and the world we live in.

**REGIONAL ADDRESSES:**
Eight regional offices, details from Head Office
**AGE RANGE:**
Any
**NUMBERS PASSING THROUGH:**
500+
**HOW TO CONTACT:**
Contact regional co-ordinators or Head Office
**REGIONS SERVICED:**
UK
**SPECIAL NEEDS PROVISION:**
Dependent on the physical limitations

imposed by each individual project
**COSTS/WAITING LISTS:**
£5 registration fee to cover administration
costs. Toc H raises money to enable
volunteers to pay as little as possible. Places
are offered on a first-come first-served basis.
Contact can be maintained at any time. A
continuous update of vacancies is
maintained

---

### TRADE UNION CONGRESS (TUC)
Congress House
Great Russell Street
London WC1B 3LS
Tel: 071 636 4030  Fax: 071 636 0632

The TUC provides an information service for
young people at school or college wishing to
know more about trade unions, either as part of
their studies or when considering employment.
The TUC can also help individual schools to
twin with local union branches as part of the
TUC 'adopt a school' scheme. This can lead to
work experience, work shadowing and trade
unions taking part in projects. In addition,
many trade unions provide special services for
young people who join them. This can range
from special advice on training and education
to special conferences on youth issues. The
TUC itself has an advisory committee and
conference bringing together young trade
unionists.

**REGIONAL ADDRESSES:**
Details available from Head Office
**AGE RANGE:**
14+
**HOW TO CONTACT:**
By letter for information about trade unions
e.g. for school projects or for those leaving
school considering joining a union,
information about government training
schemes and their rights
**REGIONS SERVICED:**
UK
**SPECIAL NEEDS PROVISION:**
Most information is generally suitable for all
young people
**COSTS/WAITING LISTS:**
There is no charge for using the information
service

---

## TRAINING AND ENTERPRISE COUNCILS
## (TECs)
Contact through nearest Jobcentre or Careers
Office

Training and Enterprise Councils are responsible
for schemes and opportunities such as youth
training, employment training and training for
business enterprise. TECs operate on a local
basis which enables them to structure training
to suit their own area. For the address of your
local TEC look in the phone book under
'Training'.

## TRANS-EUROPEAN EXCHANGE AND TRANSFER CONSORTIUM (TEXT)
University of Derby
Kedleston Road
Derby DE3 1GB
Tel: 0332 47181  Fax: 0332 203221

TEXT arranges academic places in Europe for students in higher education.  The scheme is open to students attending one of 60 TEXT member institutions throughout Europe.

**AGE RANGE:**
No specific age range
**NUMBERS PASSING THROUGH:**
c 50
**HOW TO CONTACT:**
Direct contact with TEXT office or through the TEXT co-ordinator in your institution
**REGIONS SERVICED:**
Europe
**SPECIAL NEEDS PROVISION:**
Dealt with on an individual basis
**COSTS/WAITING LISTS:**
TEXT member institutions are approached on behalf of the student in order to assist in finding an appropriate placement.  Costs are negotiated directly between the student and the institution where they will study.  Apply at least six months in advance

## TRANS-EUROPEAN MOBILITY PROGRAMME FOR UNIVERSITY STUDIES (TEMPUS)
British Council
Medlock Street
Manchester M15 4PR

TEMPUS offers financial support for joint European projects which link enterprises and/or universities in Central or Eastern European countries with partners in at least two EC countries. It gives mobility grants for HE staff and students and support for youth exchanges. Applications may involve Albania, the Baltic States, Bulgaria, Croatia, the Czech and Slavak states, Hungary, Poland, Romania and Slovenia. Contact the above address for more details.

## TRAVELLERS' SURVIVAL KIT series (publications)
Vacation Work Publications
9 Park End Street
Oxford OX1 1HJ
Tel: 0865 241978  Fax: 0865 790885

A range of books covering various countries for both the independent traveller and package tourists and containing the latest information on all aspects of travel from finding the best value accommodation, public transport and food and drink to health precautions, personal safety and border crossings in some of the less accessible areas covered as well as background information on the people, culture, history and language.

Current titles available in the series are:-
*South America* (672pp) – £12.95 ISBN 1 85458 069 8
*Europe* (288pp) – £6.95 ISBN 1 85458 033 7
*Soviet Union and Eastern Europe* (544pp) – £8.95 ISBN 1 85458 010 8
*The East* (for travellers between Turkey and Indonesia) (448pp) – £6.95 ISBN 1 85458 031 0
*Australia and New Zealand* (512pp) – £8.95 ISBN 1 85458 065 5
*USA & Canada* (416pp) – £9.95 ISBN1 85458 089 2
*Central America* (480pp) – £8.95 ISBN 1 85458 052 3
*Cuba* (216pp) – £9.95 ISBN 1 85458 091 4

All available in libraries, bookshops or direct from the above address (add £1 for p&p).

---

**UK COUNCIL FOR MUSIC EDUCATION AND TRAINING (UKCMET)**
13 Back Lane
South Luffenham
Oakham
Leicestershire LE15 8NQ
Tel: 0780 721115   Fax: 0780 721401

Although the UK Council for Music Education and Training cannot offer specific careers advice, they can deal with general enquiries, usually by pointing enquirers in the direction of relevant reference books through which they can pursue their own particular interests.

**AGE RANGE:**
Any
**HOW TO CONTACT:**
Letter
**REGIONS SERVICED:**
UK
**SPECIAL NEEDS PROVISION:**
Enquiries welcome
**COSTS/WAITING LISTS:**
None for general information

---

### UK LINGUA UNIT
Central Bureau for Educational Visits and
Exchanges
Seymour Mews House
Seymour Mews
London W1H 9PE
Tel: 071 224 1477

LINGUA is the 'European Community Programme for the Promotion of the Teaching and Learning of Foreign Languages within the Community'. Its aims are to improve the quality and amount of language teaching in the EC by helping trainee language teachers, students and young people to take part in exchanges or to train or study abroad as well as encouraging language learning in industry.

**AGE RANGE:**
No specific age range
**HOW TO CONTACT:**
Write to above address for further information
**REGIONS SERVICED:**
UK

---

### UK ONE WORLD LINKING ASSOCIATION (UKOWLA)
c/o Oxford Development Education Unit
Westminster College
Oxford OX2 9AT
Tel: 0865 791610

UKOWLA organises conferences, publishes newsletters and handbooks, and supports and advises generally on all aspects linking young people from the UK with their counterparts in countries throughout the world.

---

### ULSTER UNIONIST PARTY
3 Glengall Street
Belfast BT12 5AE
Tel: 0232 324601

## UNDER 26
c/o National Youth Agency
17-23 Albion Street
Leicester LE1 6GD
Tel: 0533 471200  Fax: 0533 471043

Under 26 is a new scheme covering England and Wales which is open to all young people under the age of 26. For an annual subscription of £6 you will receive the Under 26 card. This card can save you money on travel, holidays, eating out, clothes, records and sports goods. When you apply for a card you will receive the Under 26 Discount Directory which lists all the places that offer discounts on production of the card. The card is also valid in over 150,000 places throughout Europe, where it is very popular. At present some 3.5 million young Europeans are carrying the card. As well as discounts, cardholders will receive a regular magazine with features on current issues, plus news of the latest discounts, offers and competitions open to members, and information about the large number of exchange trips, projects and events organised for cardholders. Membership of Under 26 also gives you access to a 24-hour legal advice line whereby you can speak to a trained legal adviser at anytime.

**REGIONAL ADDRESSES:**
Under 26 Cymru, 5 Washington Chambers, Stanwell Road, Penarth, South Glamorgan CF6 2AF  Tel: 0222 705611

**REGIONS SERVICED:**
England and Wales
**COSTS/WAITING LISTS:**
£6 per year

---

### UNDERSTANDING INDUSTRY (UI)
Enterprise House
59-65 Upper Ground
London SE1 9PQ
Tel: 071 620 0735  Fax: 071 928 0578

UI is a national education/industry partnership organisation which specialises in bringing business people into the classroom to work with young people as part of the school timetable. It aims to give students a greater understanding of how interesting and exciting business and industry can be. UI courses are different, active, and fun, and quite often involve visits to companies to gain firsthand experience. They usually take about 11 hours, broken into nine different sessions covering marketing, design, people at work and management. They take place at school or college during normal hours, so your approach should be through your school/ college.

**AGE RANGE:**
16-19
**NUMBERS PASSING THROUGH:**
c 25,000
**HOW TO CONTACT:**
Through teacher

**REGIONS SERVICED:**
UK
**SPECIAL NEEDS PROVISION:**
Enquiries welcome

---

### UNITED WORLD COLLEGES (UWC)
London House
Mecklenburgh Square
London WC1N 2AB
Tel: 071 833 2626  Fax: 071 837 3102

United World Colleges offer students of all races and creeds the opportunity of developing international understanding through combining high quality, internationally orientated academic study with activities which encourage a sense of adventure and social responsibility. Colleges in Swaziland, USA, Canada, Singapore, Italy, Venezuela and Hong Kong offer broad-based curricula for students drawn from the widest possible variety of national and social backgrounds. Study programmes include full secondary education, the International Baccalaureate Diploma, and vocational training. Selection for places, usually following a strong recommendation from a head teacher or similar, is based on ability, academic achievement prior to entry, and a strong personal desire to further the aims of UWC.

**AGE RANGE:**
16-18

**COSTS/WAITING LISTS:**
Most students will be holders of scholarships
for which high academic and personal
qualifications are required.  Further details
from UWC

## UNIVERSITIES CENTRAL COUNCIL ON
## ADMISSIONS (UCCA)

PO Box 28
Cheltenham
Gloucester GL50 3SA
Tel: 0242 222444  Fax: 0242 221622

UCCA process applications to all UK universities
and affiliated colleges. It is open to people of all
ages, but the majority of applicants are school
leavers of 17/18 years old.

**AGE RANGE:**
Any
**NUMBERS PASSING THROUGH:**
220,000 applicants
**HOW TO CONTACT:**
Telephone or letter to the Enquiries and
Information Division
**REGIONS SERVICED:**
UK
**COSTS/WAITING LISTS:**
The best time to apply is September of the
year before you wish to go to university.  The
deadline date for receipt of application forms
is 15 December of the preceding year of
entry

**VACATION TRAINEESHIPS FOR STUDENTS
1993 (publication)**
Vacation Work Publications
9 Park End Street
Oxford OX1 1HJ
Tel: 0865 241978  Fax: 0865 790885

Details of over 7,000 summer jobs in business, industry and the professions.  It tells young people at all stages of school and college education how they can try out a future career during their vacation, and provides information on recruitment methods, application procedure, tax regulations etc.  Vacation traineeships offer students the chance to earn money while discovering whether a particular career suits them, and also to acquire valuable work experience. Jobs in business and management, publishing, accountancy, marketing, banking and financial services, computers and electronics, construction and engineering, insurance, tourism, medicine, law, the Civil Service, the Police, the Armed Forces etc. are included.  ISBN 1 85458 063 9.  Available through libraries, bookshops (price £6.95), or direct from the above address (price £7.95 inc p&p).

**VACATION WORK PUBLICATIONS**
9 Park End Street
Oxford OX1 1HJ
Tel: 0865 241978  Fax: 0865 790885

Vacation Work publications produce a wide range of books covering jobs at home and abroad, travel and adventure. Their comprehensive list covers topics such as summer jobs in Britain and abroad, working your way around the world, teaching English as a second language, international voluntary work and studying abroad. They also publish the *Travellers Survival Kit* range of books, offering up-to-date information on travel in Central America, Cuba, USA and Canada, Australia and New Zealand, Europe, Eastern Europe and Asia. Contact Vacation Work for a current list of publications.

## VENTURE SCOTLAND
10 Randolph Crescent
Edinburgh EH3 7TU
Tel: 031 220 4026

A challenging programme of outdoor activities, problem solving and practical conservation which incorporates weekend and week-long residential courses in remote parts of Scotland. There are opportunities for young people to participate in activities or lead them as volunteers.

**AGE RANGE:**
15-25
**NUMBERS PASSING THROUGH:**
150 participants; 60 volunteers
**HOW TO CONTACT:**
Telephone or letter for information on current

activities and how to get involved

**REGIONS SERVICED:**
Strathclyde Region, predominantly around
Glasgow; Lothian Region, within Edinburgh;
Grampian Region, within Aberdeen

**SPECIAL NEEDS PROVISION:**
Limited provision

**COSTS/WAITING LISTS:**
Weekend residential course fee is £6; week-
long residential course fee is £20.  Ideally,
apply two months in advance

---

**VISA SHOP LTD**
1 Charing Cross Underground
London WC2
Tel: 071 379 0419  Fax: 071 497 2590

Visa Shop offers a comprehensive service of
visas and passports including information on
requirements for world travel as well as work
permits for students and details of working
holidays.

**AGE RANGE:**
Any

**NUMBERS PASSING THROUGH:**
200 per week

**HOW TO CONTACT:**
Telephone, letter, fax or in person for
information and advice plus visa or passport
forms if appropriate

**REGIONS SERVICED:**
UK

**COSTS/WAITING LISTS:**
Information is free. There is a general charge
of £14 for most visas or passports

---

### VOLUNTARY SERVICE BELFAST (VSB)
70-72 Lisburn Road
Belfast BT9 6AF
Tel: 0232 329499 Fax: 0232 321797

VSB provide opportunities for voluntary work
placements with children, the elderly and
disabled and those most in need, as well as
opportunities to take part in challenging
conservation and practical tasks. VSB also
provide vocational skills training for 18-25 year-
olds in areas such as horticulture, working with
children, computing, job search etc.

**AGE RANGE:**
16+
**NUMBERS PASSING THROUGH:**
280
**HOW TO CONTACT:**
Telephone, letter or in person for further
information and an application form
**REGIONS SERVICED:**
Mainly serves the Belfast area but anyone
willing to travel there at their own expense
can apply
**SPECIAL NEEDS PROVISION:**
Staff are available to provide support
**COSTS/WAITING LISTS:**
Apply about four weeks in advance

## THE VOLUNTEER CENTRE UK
29 Lower King's Road
Berkhamsted
Hertfordshire HP4 2AB
Tel: 0442 873311  Fax: 0442 870852

The Volunteer Centre is a resource centre for anyone involved or wanting to become involved in volunteer work at any level of participation. They can provide information on opportunities for volunteering as well as information about matters relating to voluntary work e.g. welfare benefits, expenses, insurance etc. A selection of volunteering opportunities is shown weekly on BBC2 Ceefax.  The centre produces a wide range of publications and information sheets – write to the above address for further information.

**AGE RANGE:**
Any
**HOW TO CONTACT:**
By letter (with SAE) to the Advisory Team for further information on volunteering
**REGIONS SERVICED:**
UK
**SPECIAL NEEDS PROVISION:**
Provision varies – depends on the individual volunteering opportunity
**COSTS/WAITING LISTS:**
Cost of publications vary

## VOLUNTEER DEVELOPMENT SCOTLAND (VDS)
80 Murray Place
Stirling
FK8 2BX
Tel: 0786 79593

VDS is the national resource and development agency on volunteering in Scotland. It mainly provides support services to agencies and individuals who work with volunteers. It also holds information about volunteer bureaux in Scotland so although it is unable to advise on individual placements it can point potential volunteers in the right direction.

**AGE RANGE:**
Any
**HOW TO CONTACT:**
Telephone or letter for general information
**REGIONS SERVICED:**
Scotland
**SPECIAL NEEDS PROVISION:**
Enquiries welcome within the limit of the available service
**COSTS/WAITING LISTS:**
There are no costs for information

**VOLUNTEER WORK (publication)**
Central Bureau for Educational Visits and
Exchanges
Seymour Mews House
Seymour Mews
London W1H 9PE
Tel: 071 486 5101  Fax: 071 935 5741
Tel: 071 725 9402 (credit card orders)

A period of voluntary work can be enriching, involving you in improving the quality of community life and environment. Opportunities exist in developed and developing countries, and *Volunteer Work* gives information on those recruiting and placing volunteers for medium and long-term service in Britain and abroad. Agency profiles, countries of operation and projects are given together with the qualifications and skills required of volunteers, terms of service, briefing and relevant literature; development workers and returned volunteers offer valuable insights through their experiences. The guide encourages volunteers to consider their motivation and commitment, and offers practical advice on preparation and training, understanding development, travel, health and insurance.
ISBN 0 900087 92 7.  Price £7.99.  Available through bookshops, or direct from the above address (price £9.49 inc p&p).

## WAR ON WANT
37-39 Great Guildford Street
London SE1 0ES
Tel: 071 620 1111 Fax: 071 261 9291

War on Want, the campaign against world poverty, tackles poverty at its roots, funding practical long-term development projects. Aiming to change attitudes in the richer nations and conditions in the poorer ones, War on Want supports people seeking change in their own localities. Young people who wish to help can volunteer at the Head Office in London, or collect used stamps and send them to War on Want.

## WATCH TRUST FOR ENVIRONMENTAL EDUCATION LTD (WATCH)
The Green
Witham Park
Waterside South
Lincoln LN5 7JR
Tel: 0522 544400 Fax: 0522 511616

WATCH is the wildlife and environment club that gets you involved. Once you are a member you receive the club magazine, *Watchword,* three times per year plus your local newsletter which gives you details of activities and groups in your area. You also have the opportunity to take part in national projects.

**AGE RANGE:**
7+
**NUMBERS PASSING THROUGH:**
33,000 members – 150,000 taking part in activities
**HOW TO CONTACT:**
SAE to above address for information
**REGIONS SERVICED:**
UK
**SPECIAL NEEDS PROVISION:**
No special provision
**COSTS/WAITING LISTS:**
Annual membership is £5 per year.  Local group costs vary – typically 50p per session

---

## WATERWAY RECOVERY GROUP (WRG)
114 Regent's Park Road
London NW1 8UQ
Tel: 071 723 7217  Fax: 071 723 7213

WRG is the national organisation which arranges restoration and conservation work throughout Britain's canals and waterways.  Young people are welcome to join in on week-long, weekends or single day workparties and events held along the waterway system.  WRG provide working holidays throughout the year for minimal charges.

**REGIONAL ADDRESSES:**
Leighton Buzzard, Beds, LU7 7XN  Tel: 0525 382311

London: Lesley McFadyen, 35 Silverster Road, East Dulwich, London SE22 9PB  Tel: 081 693 3266.

North West: Roger Evans, 45 Hattons Lane, Liverpool L16 7QR  Tel: 051 722 6216

North East: Martin Johnson, 38 Wesley Garth, Beeston, Leeds LS11 8RF  Tel: 0532 711215

Midlands: Jonathan Smith, 4a Walford Street, Tividale, Warley, West Midlands B69 2LB  Tel: 021 557 2353

South: Tim Lewis, 5 Heronsgate Road, London E12 5EJ  Tel: 081 530 7926

**AGE RANGE:**

16+

**NUMBERS PASSING THROUGH:**

1,000-2,000

**HOW TO CONTACT:**

For general enquiries contact main address above for an information pack covering all activities of the group

**REGIONS SERVICED:**

UK

**SPECIAL NEEDS PROVISION:**

No special provision

**COSTS/WAITING LISTS:**

Annual subscription is a minimum of £1.50. A working holiday costs about £28 per week which covers food and accommodation

**WATERWAYS FOR YOUTH (WFY)**
Inland Waterways Association
114 Regent's Park Road
London NW1 8UQ
Tel: 071 586 2510/2566 Fax: 071 722 7213

Waterways for Youth campaign to encourage greater participation by young people in a variety of water orientated sports and leisure pursuits. They provide free activity experience at all major events throughout the country. These include canoeing, sailing, rowing, sailboarding, ecology, water safety, knot tying, painting, nature trails, digger and dredger driving, angling, restoration and conservation (see also WATERWAY RECOVERY GROUP).

**REGIONAL ADDRESSES:**
Chairman: Ivor Caplan, 152 Castle Road, Cookley, Kidderminster DY10 3TB  Tel: 0562 851256.
London: Marion Waters, 5 Harpenden Road, Wanstead E12 5HJ  Tel: 081 530 4767
West Midlands: Matthew Cooper, Gorsey Lane Farm, Little Wyrley, Pelsall, Walsall WS3 5AQ  Tel: 0543 371769
Manchester: Ben Williams, 9 Warren Drive, Swinton, Manchester M27 3EA
Milton Keynes: Richard Hyde, 68 Glebe Road, Deanshanger MK19 6LU
South West: Kay Jennings, 1 Frazer Court, Moorfield Street, Hereford HR4 9JL
Tel: 0432 270907

Eastern: Phil Dowrick, 22 Gazelle Court,
Highwoods, Colchester CO4 4RW
Tel: 0206 751751

**AGE RANGE:**
Up to 17

**NUMBERS PASSING THROUGH:**
5,000

**HOW TO CONTACT:**
By telephone or letter to Ivor Caplan (address
above), the London office or any regional
representative for details of current and future
events

**REGIONS SERVICED:**
UK

**SPECIAL NEEDS PROVISION:**
Some WFY activities are easily available and
in some instances specially adapted
equipment can be provided

**COSTS/WAITING LISTS:**
No costs

---

## WEEKEND ARTS COLLEGE (WAC)
Dalby Street
Kentish Town
London NW5 3NG
Tel: 071 267 9421

The main aim of WAC is to provide professional
training for young people who are seriously
thinking about a career in the performing arts.
WAC runs classes for young people to teach
them basic skills and techniques necessary to

gain further full-time training. Classes are held in dance, drama and music. Young people have the opportunity to participate in creative sessions, perform, receive advice and help with auditions and interviews and gain experience in different styles of work.

**AGE RANGE:**
6-26
**NUMBERS PASSING THROUGH:**
c 500
**HOW TO CONTACT:**
Telephone or letter for advice, information and a prospectus
**REGIONS SERVICED:**
UK
**SPECIAL NEEDS PROVISION:**
Young people with special needs can partake of all the activities at the college
**COSTS/WAITING LISTS:**
There is a waiting list for courses and it is advisable to apply as early as possible

---

**WELSH ARTS COUNCIL**
Holst House
Museum Place
Cardiff CF1 3NX
Tel: 0222 394711

See separate ARTS COUNCIL entry.

## WELSH COLLEGE OF MUSIC AND DRAMA (WCMD)
Castle Grounds
Cathays Park
Cardiff CF1 3ER
Tel: 0222 342854  Fax: 0222 237639

College for training in the performing arts. Courses offered range from acting, music (all instruments and voice) – all styles, stage-management and stage-design.  Also offers training for those wishing to work as music or drama teachers, or in 'theatre-in-education'.

**AGE RANGE:**
Any
**NUMBERS PASSING THROUGH:**
c 700 students at present
**HOW TO CONTACT:**
Telephone, letter, fax to above address for information about courses
**REGIONS SERVICED:**
UK and overseas
**SPECIAL NEEDS PROVISION:**
If college is informed in advance of special needs requirements they can usually accommodate
**COSTS/WAITING LISTS:**
Full list of course fees available from the college.  The college has a small number of scholarships and prizes on offer to cover course fees.  Also, some LEAs give grants for certain courses.  Further details available in

college prospectus. Auditions held between
October and April for entry on to full-time
courses the following September.
Applications for part-time courses usually
dealt with as they arrive

## THE WESTON SPIRIT
85a Bold Street
Liverpool L1 4HF
Tel: 051 709 6620  Fax: 051 709 6620

The Weston Spirit is an organisation that offers
its members the opportunity to learn how to live
and work together, to respect other peoples'
views but to gain the confidence to challenge
those views and to express their own point of
view.  Members take part in voluntary work in
their own areas and away in residential centres
with disabled people.  The Weston Spirit offers
'drop-in' facilities and a programme of social,
educational and fund-raising opportunities. It is
about gaining self-confidence and control of
their own lives.

**REGIONAL ADDRESSES:**
Wales: Shand House, 20 Newport Road,
Cardiff CF2 1BD  Tel: 0222 462992
Newcastle: Tyne Theatre and Opera House,
Westgate Road, Newcastle upon Tyne  Tel:
091 232 1322
**AGE RANGE:**
16 or 17 at recruitment

**NUMBERS PASSING THROUGH:**
340
**HOW TO CONTACT:**
Telephone or letter to your local office
**REGIONS SERVICED:**
Merseyside, Cardiff and Newcastle/Gateshead
**SPECIAL NEEDS PROVISION:**
Enquiries welcome but unable to work with
physically disabled people because of
problems with access and the nature of the
residential course
**COSTS/WAITING LISTS:**
There are no costs or waiting lists

---

### WH SMITH INTERACT
Education Department
Royal National Theatre
South Bank
London SE1 9PX
Tel: 071 928 5214

WH Smith Interact is a scheme where
professionals from the National Theatre visit
schools and colleges to give workshops based
on a subject of your choice covering any aspect
of theatre. Groups of any age, level or experience
can benefit from an Interact session.

**AGE RANGE:**
Any
**HOW TO CONTACT:**
Write or telephone for further information

**REGIONS SERVICED:**
UK
**SPECIAL NEEDS PROVISION:**
Special needs groups welcome
**COSTS/WAITING LISTS:**
Preferably, contact at least 10 weeks before
you want to have your workshop

---

### WHITBREAD YOUNG VOLUNTEER AWARDS
FREEPOST (BS6647)
Bristol BS1 4YU
Tel: 0272 252000

The Whitbread Volunteer Action Award Scheme
is designed to recognise and reward young
people who give up their own time for the
benefit of others, especially those disadvantaged
by disability, sickness, situation or age. There
are two categories in the award, one for
individual volunteers and one for volunteering
groups with a prize of £1,000 for each category.

**AGE RANGE:**
Under 25
**NUMBERS PASSING THROUGH:**
Over 200 entries in 1992
**HOW TO CONTACT:**
Write to, or telehone above for a nomination
form
**REGIONS SERVICED:**
UK (excluding Northern Ireland)

**SPECIAL NEEDS PROVISION:**
No special provision but applications
welcome

**COSTS/WAITING LISTS:**
No costs or waiting lists. The award scheme
is usually launched in April each year and the
winners are announced in November

---

### WILDFOWL & WETLANDS TRUST (W&WT)
Slimbridge
Gloucester GL2 7BT
Tel: 0453 890333  Fax: 0453 890827

The Wildfowl & Wetlands Trust is an
environmental organisation which can offer
opportunities for young people to gain
experience in various aspects of conservation.
On the practical side you could help with
weeding, hedge trimming, clearing silt etc -
messy but absolutely vital! On the administrative
side, you might help with cataloguing of press-
cuttings, photocopying, stuffing appeals
envelopes and so on. Or on the 'people' side of
conservation you may help to staff the
Information Desk, help with preparation of
graphic displays/teaching aids, or just generally
help the public with their enquiries.

**REGIONAL ADDRESSES:**
Regional Centres in Lancashire, West Sussex,
Cambridgeshire, Dyfed, Tyne and Wear,
Dumfriesshire, and County Down. Contact

the National Centre at Slimbridge for full
details
**AGE RANGE:**
Varies according to the work
**HOW TO CONTACT:**
Letter plus SAE to National Centre for further
information and leaflets
**REGIONS SERVICED:**
Enquiries welcome from throughout the UK
but most of the work of the Trust takes place
in the areas surrounding its Centres
**SPECIAL NEEDS PROVISION:**
Enquiries welcome
**COSTS/WAITING LISTS:**
If applicable, costs will be explained. There
are no waiting lists

## WINANT CLAYTON VOLUNTEER ASSOCIATION (WCVA)
38 Newark Street
London E1 2AA
Tel: 071 375 0547  Fax: 071 377 2437

WCVA provides an opportunity for people of all
ages and backgrounds to experience another
culture and people, by working within it for a
period of 3 months from June to September each
summer. Placements vary and examples include:
working with deprived inner city kids; working
with AIDS patients; helping in a children's
home; working in an adult psychiatric
rehabilitation centre. All placements are on the

east coast of America. Some voluntary
experience in the UK would be useful but
maturity and keenness are more important.

**AGE RANGE:**
18+
**NUMBERS PASSING THROUGH:**
c 20 aged 19-45
**HOW TO CONTACT:**
Letter or telephone for information
**REGIONS SERVICED:**
UK
**SPECIAL NEEDS PROVISION:**
No special provision but has an equal
opportunities policy
**COSTS/WAITING LISTS:**
Volunteers usually need £500 to pay for air
fare and insurance and a further £500 to
finance their 3-week holiday at the end of
their placement. Individuals often fund-raise
locally or apply to charities such as the
Rotary Club, Round Table, Prince's Trust etc.
Volunteers should apply from September to
January before the summer they wish to travel

---

**WINDSOR FELLOWSHIP**
47 Hackney Road
London E2 7NX
Tel: 071 613 0373  Fax: 071 613 0377

The Windsor Fellowship is a three-year personal
development and basic management skills

training programme for minority ethnic undergraduates. It is recognised that certain barriers exist in the area of employment particularly for young black and Asian people. Established in 1986, the Fellowship aims to overcome these by encouraging, supporting and preparing undergraduates for management careers in Industry, Commerce and Public Administration.

**AGE RANGE:**
16-27
**NUMBERS PASSING THROUGH:**
190
**HOW TO CONTACT:**
By telephone, letter, fax or in person for further information
**REGIONS SERVICED:**
UK
**COSTS/WAITING LISTS:**
No costs. Application forms must be returned to the Fellowship by the end of March in the year of application to university or college

**WINGED FELLOWSHIP TRUST**
Angel House
20-32 Pentonville Road
London N1 9XD
Tel: 071 833 2594  Fax: 071 278 0370

Volunteers are required for a week or two at five holiday centres for severely physically disabled people.  Duties may include lifting, washing, dressing, feeding and pushing wheelchairs. Some domestic work is required of each helper as well as helping on daily outings and helping to entertain guests during their stay. Volunteers need to be fairly fit, cheerful and enthusiastic. Hard work and some late hours are involved in the job. Overseas and touring holidays are also arranged.

**AGE RANGE:**
17-75

**NUMBERS PASSING THROUGH:**
6,000 volunteers looking after 5,000 disabled people

**HOW TO CONTACT:**
Telephone, letter or fax for a booklet on what to expect, an application form and brochure

**REGIONS SERVICED:**
UK

**SPECIAL NEEDS PROVISION:**
Usually take on one or two people with disabilities to help as volunteers in the centres by special arrangement with the centre manager

**COSTS/WAITING LISTS:**
Volunteers should apply at least one month in advance

---

**WINSTON CHURCHILL MEMORIAL TRUST**
15 Queen's Gate Terrace
London SW7 5PR
Tel: 071 584 9315

Travelling fellowships given to UK citizens to travel overseas with air fares and all expenses paid for projects which will benefit you and your country on your return (awards do not cover courses or academic studies).

**AGE RANGE:**
Any
**NUMBERS PASSING THROUGH:**
100 fellowships are given each year
**HOW TO CONTACT:**
Telephone or letter (with SAE) for information on how to apply
**REGIONS SERVICED:**
UK
**SPECIAL NEEDS PROVISION:**
Enquiries welcome
**COSTS/WAITING LISTS:**
Apply from July to October to travel the following year

---

**WOMEN AND MANUAL TRADES (WAMT)**
52-54 Featherstone Street
London EC1Y 8RT
Tel: 071 251 9192/2519193

Women and Manual Trades was set up in 1970 by women carpenters, plumbers, electricians – women in all the skilled trades – to provide information on training available in these trades for young women, and provide support to help young women handle working in male-dominated occupations. If you're interested in learning more about the exciting work to be done in the manual trades – what it's like, both good and bad – WAMT will send you information, written by women who've done it. WAMT work mainly through schools, producing exercises, videos, cartoon stories, posters etc., but they also answer individual enquiries.

**AGE RANGE:**
Any
**NUMBERS PASSING THROUGH:**
c 250 individual enquiries; c 500 through school talks and careers conventions
**HOW TO CONTACT:**
Letter or telephone
**REGIONS SERVICED:**
UK
**SPECIAL NEEDS PROVISION:**
No specific provision. Enquiries are dealt with on an individual basis
**COSTS/WAITING LISTS:**
No costs involved

---

## WOMEN'S ENVIRONMENTAL NETWORK (WEN)
Aberdeen Studios
22 Highbury Grove
London N5 2EA
Tel: 071 354 8823

WEN is a non-profit organisation which educates, informs and empowers women who care about the environment. It runs seminars, workshops and public meetings, and researches and produces a range of action packs and leaflets on all aspects of environmental issues. They rely on memberships and donations for their survival. Membership entitles you to receive newsletters, briefings and notice of public events, plus information on playing an active role. WEN encourages both men and women to join, but looks at environment issues from womens' perspective.

**AGE RANGE:**
Any
**HOW TO CONTACT:**
Letter, telephone to above address
**REGIONS SERVICED:**
UK
**SPECIAL NEEDS PROVISION:**
Enquiries welcome
**COSTS/WAITING LISTS:**
Membership rates vary between £7 and £20

---

**WOODCRAFT FOLK**
13 Ritherdon Road
London SW17 8QE
Tel: 081 672 6031  Fax: 081 767 2457

The Woodcraft Folk is an educational movement for children and young people designed to develop self-confidence and activity in society with the aim of building a world based on equality, friendship, peace and co-operation. Weekly meetings take place and other activities include international exchanges, non-competitive games, outdoor activities and environmental work.

**REGIONAL ADDRESSES:**
Midlands: Birmingham and Midland Institute, Margaret Street, Birmingham B3 3BS
Tel: 021 236 4361
North: 252 York Road, Leeds LS9 9DN
Tel: 0532 498359
Scotland: Co-op Union, 95 Morrison Street, Glasgow  Tel: 041 429 0952
Wales: Manora, Cwmystwyth, Dyfed SY23 4AF  Tel: 097 422437

**AGE RANGE:**
No specific age range

**NUMBERS PASSING THROUGH:**
25,000+ members

**HOW TO CONTACT:**
Telephone or letter for information on activities

**REGIONS SERVICED:**
UK

**SPECIAL NEEDS PROVISION:**
All groups encourage full participation by all members of the community

**COSTS/WAITING LISTS:**
Weekly subscription up to 16 is 40-50p.  16+ annual subscription is £10 waged, £4 unwaged

**WOODLARKS CAMP SITE TRUST**
Tilford Road
Farnham
Surrey GU10 3RN
Tel: 0252 716279

Woodlarks Camp is a campsite for physically handicapped people with facilities specially designed for their needs. Enquiries are welcome from people interested in helping for a week. Individuals are invited to write in giving details of their age and interests. They will then be put in touch with the leader of a week's camp where extra help is needed.

**AGE RANGE:**
Any
**NUMBERS PASSING THROUGH:**
About 500 volunteers
**HOW TO CONTACT:**
SAE to above address for more information and a list of camps where extra help may be needed
**REGIONS SERVICED:**
UK
**SPECIAL NEEDS PROVISION:**
See above
**COSTS/WAITING LISTS:**
Costs vary from camp to camp – usually between £25-£50. Camps run from May to September. Contact in the new year for details of camps

**WOOLWICH YOUNG RADIO
PLAYWRIGHTS' FESTIVAL**
see INDEPENDENT RADIO DRAMA
PRODUCTIONS

**WORK YOUR WAY AROUND THE WORLD
(publication)**
Vacation Work Publications
9 Park End Street
Oxford OX1 1HJ
Tel: 0865 241978  Fax: 0865 790885

A guide for the working traveller which includes hundreds of recent firsthand accounts and offers authorative advice on how to find work around the world, either in advance or on the spot. Includes sections on teaching English in Eastern Europe, work in Greek tourism and agriculture, a summer job programme in Jamaica, au pairing throughout Europe and Canada, grape picking in France and Australia and more.  Gives up-to-date information on how to travel free by working a passage, dates and details of harvests, and how to survive when the money runs low. Realistic advice on how to become a barman/woman, kiwifruit picker, ski guide, jackaroo, teacher, fish packer etc.
ISBN 1 85458 074 4. Available through libraries, bookshops (price £9.95), or direct from the above address (price £10.95 inc p&p).

**WORKING HOLIDAYS 1993 (publication)**
Central Bureau for Educational Visits and
Exchanges
Seymour Mews House
Seymour Mews
London W1H 9PE
Tel: 071 486 5101  Fax: 071 935 5741
Tel: 071 725 9402 (credit card orders)

Holiday jobs are excellent ways of experiencing
life in other countries and, if you are prepared
for a complete change, seasonal work can take
you almost anywhere in the world.  You could
for example pick pears in Australia, teach on a
summer camp in North America, cut trails
through a rain cloud forest in Costa Rica, be a
holiday courier in Spain, pick grapes in France,
work on a steam railway in Britain or crew a
yacht in the Mediterranean.  Well researched
and revised annually, *Working Holidays* has over
300 pages of information on over 99,000 paid
and voluntary seasonal work opportunities in
70 countries including Britain. Full information
for each job is given together with details on
work/residence permits, travel, insurance,
accommodation and further sources of
information.
ISBN 0 900087 91 9.  Price £7.95.  Available
from bookshops, or direct from the above address
(price £9.45 inc p&p).

## WORKING IN SKI RESORTS – EUROPE
### (publication)
Vacation Work Publications
9 Park End Street
Oxford OX1 1HJ
Tel: 0865 241978  Fax: 0865 790885

Guide which contains the information on how to find work as a ski instructor, chalet girl, teacher, au pair, shop assistant, courier, disc jockey, snow cleaner, ski technician, office worker or resort representative in a ski resort. The first part of the book – 'A Job Before You Go' – describes how to pre-arrange work with over 90 British ski tour operators, school ski party organisers, and other organisations. The second part – 'Finding A Job On The Spot', gives reports on over 40 resorts, explaining where the jobs are and how to get them, plus information on accommodation and nightlife.
ISBN 0 907638 87 2. Available through libraries, bookshops (price £5.95), or direct from the above address (price £6.95 inc p&p).

## WORKNET
Twin Spires
155 Northumberland Street
Belfast BT13 2JF
Tel: 0232 246211  Fax: 0232 320898

Worknet is a community-based employment and training organisation established to develop the potential of the human resource in the Belfast area by means of a series of inter-related programmes. Aimed mainly at the long-term unemployed Worknet provides free training, advice and counselling. Worknet employs 45 staff and is a registered charity.

**AGE RANGE:**
18-65
**NUMBERS PASSING THROUGH:**
600+
**COSTS/WAITING LISTS:**
There are no costs. All interested individuals are immediately interviewed

---

### WORLD CHALLENGE EXPEDITIONS
Walham House
Walham Grove
London SW6 1QP
Tel: 071 386 9828  Fax: 071 386 5022

WCE plans and runs expeditions, lasting approximately one month to far-flung destinations including India, Borneo, Ecuador and Venezuela for school groups mainly and individual applicants. An average team comprises 16-20 members, with fully-trained, qualified leaders at a ratio of 1 leader to 8 team members. As well as the leadership training we adopt educational aims including cultural exchange and physical challenge, all at an acceptable, fully-inclusive price.

**AGE RANGE:**
16-20
**NUMBERS PASSING THROUGH:**
c 250
**HOW TO CONTACT:**
By telephone or letter for a brochure and
application form, either individually or
through school
**REGIONS SERVICED:**
UK
**SPECIAL NEEDS PROVISION:**
No provision
**COSTS/WAITING LISTS:**
Expeditions cost approx £2,000 for
individuals. Similar price bracket for school
groups but varies according to numbers and
destination

---

### WWOOF (Working Weekends on Organic Farms)
19 Bradford Road
Lewes
Sussex BN7 1RB
Tel: 0273 476286

The aims of WWOOF are to give you first hand
experience of organic farming and growing, to
help the organic movement, which is often
labour intensive, and to make contact with
other people in the organic movement.
WWOOF is an exchange; in return for working
on organic farms, gardens and smallholdings

(full time and quite hard) you will receive meals, somewhere for your sleeping bag and, if necessary, transport to and from the local station. Members receive a newsletter every two months which lists details of places needing help each weekend. The newsletter also gives details of events, developments, training and job opportunities in the organic movement and contributions from members.

**REGIONAL ADDRESSES:**
Contact main office for details
**AGE RANGE:**
16+
**NUMBERS PASSING THROUGH:**
2,500 members of which about half are 18-25
**HOW TO CONTACT:**
SAE to main office for brochure and application form
**REGIONS SERVICED:**
UK
**SPECIAL NEEDS PROVISION:**
No provision
**COSTS/WAITING LISTS:**
Annual membership is £8

## A YEAR BETWEEN (publication)

Central Bureau for Educational Visits and
Exchanges
Seymour Mews House
Seymour Mews
London W1H 9PE
Tel: 071 486 5101  Fax: 071 935 5741
Tel: 071 725 9402 (credit card orders)

A complete guide for those taking a year out between school and higher education or work, or higher education and a career. A year out is a rare chance to stand back, assess where life has brought you so far, and seize the freedom offered to learn new skills and develop existing ones. *A Year Between* provides full details of over 100 organisations offering placements in industry, research, business, teaching, community/social service and youth work in Britain and overseas as well as opportunities for discovery, leadership, conservation projects and further study. Authoritative advice and information is included together with practical hints, discussion of the pros and cons, and details on planning and preparation. *A Year Between* will help you make the most of a year out.

ISBN 0 900087 88 9. Price £7.99. Available through bookshops, or direct from the above address (price £9.49 inc p&p).

**YEAR IN INDUSTRY**
Simon Building
University of Manchester
Oxford Road
Manchester M13 9PL
Tel: 061 275 4396  Fax: 061 275 3844

A scheme offering students a pre-degree taste of industry – paid, challenging work in a company, backed by comprehensive 'off the job' training. The scheme, designed to stimulate students' interest in industry and to help companies spot future graduate talent, is open to students of any discipline but is particularly suited to those interested in any branch of engineering, science, computing, mathematics etc – acknowledged shortage skills. If you are expecting, or already have an offer of a place on a degree course, Year in Industry can put you in contact with participating companies – the companies choose who they will interview/employ – and you will spend up to a year gaining experience and learning skills in your chosen discipline. At the end you may be offered sponsorship to do your degree course, or you may be offered future employment or summer vacation work with the company. If your placement involves living or working away from home Year in Industry can provide advice and support. 85% of graduates from the pilot scheme returned to industry on completing their degree course – 26% with Firsts, 40% Upper Seconds. Deferred entry on to the scheme is possible.

**REGIONAL ADDRESSES:**
Year in Industry has12 regional offices,
contact Head Office at above address for
your local details
**AGE RANGE:**
Usually 17-20
**NUMBERS PASSING THROUGH:**
300 +
**HOW TO CONTACT:**
Phone, letter, fax
**REGIONS SERVICED:**
UK
**COSTS/WAITING LISTS:**
No costs.  Contact during lower 6th year – 6-
12 months before pre-degree starts

---

**YOUNG ARCHAEOLOGISTS CLUB (YAC)**
Homerton College
Cambridge CB2 2HE
Tel: 0223 411141

YAC is for young people who are interested in
finding out about archaeology as well as getting
practically involved.  Members can go on field
study holidays, join one of the club's local
branches, take part in archaeological digs, visits
and talks and enter national competitions such
as 'Young Archaeologist of the Year'.  Members
receive a quarterly magazine with news from
around Britain and abroad.

**REGIONAL ADDRESSES:**
Contact through address above
**AGE RANGE:**
9-18
**NUMBERS PASSING THROUGH:**
2,410 members
**HOW TO CONTACT:**
Write to above address
**REGIONS SERVICED:**
UK
**SPECIAL NEEDS PROVISION:**
No provision
**COSTS/WAITING LISTS:**
Membership is £5 per year

---

### YOUNG BRITISH ESPERANTISTS
### (JUNULARO ESPERANTISTA BRITA) (JEB)
Esperanto Centre
140 Holland Park Avenue
London W11 4UF
Tel: 071 727 7821 Fax: 071 229 5784 (office
hours only)

Esperanto is the international language created
in 1887 and which now has an estimated 8
million speakers around the world. It avoids
most of the difficulties which make other
languages hard to learn and thus eases
international communication. The JEB is the
youth section of the Esperanto Association of
Britain and the British section of the Worldwide
Youth Esperanto Organisation, which holds its

annual congress in places as far afield as Korea, Cuba and Canada. JEB organises regular weekend events around Britain, has its own magazine *Saluton!*, runs a worldwide pen-pal service for its members and can teach you the language by post through a free correspondence course. It also provides a list of 1,000 Esperanto speakers around the world who offer free accommodation in their homes to others who speak the language. JEB also enjoys links with an independent charitable Trust that offers grants for trips abroad to international Esperanto events.

**AGE RANGE:**
Up to 30
**HOW TO CONTACT:**
Write to the above address or telephone for further information.
**REGIONS SERVICED:**
UK
**COSTS/WAITING LISTS:**
Annual membership costs are: 18-30 – £5: Unemployed/student – £3: Under 18s – free

---

**YOUNG CONCERT ARTISTS TRUST (YCAT)**
14 Ogle Street
London W1P 7LG
Tel: 071 637 8743  Fax: 071 323 6985

YCAT is a unique charity set up to discover and launch the careers of outstanding young musicians. YCAT selects these musicians through a series of auditions held each year in London. YCAT selects only those musicians considered to possess the vital qualities needed for a major career. YCAT acts as agent to these musicians for an initial period of three years. YCAT depends entirely on sponsorship and contributions from Trusts, Foundations and individuals concerned with the artistic life of this country.

**AGE RANGE:**
Up to 28 for instrumentalists. Up to 32 for singers
**NUMBERS PASSING THROUGH:**
No specific numbers
**HOW TO CONTACT:**
Telephone, letter or fax
**REGIONS SERVICED:**
Worldwide but principally UK
**SPECIAL NEEDS PROVISION:**
No special provision
**COSTS/WAITING LISTS:**
£25 entry fee for auditions. YCAT artists are subject to commission on engagements

---

**YOUNG DISABLEMENT INCOME GROUP
(DIG)**
Millmead Business Centre
Millmead Road
London N17 9QU
Tel: 081 801 8013

Young DIG is the young people's section of the
Disablement Income Group and promotes the
financial welfare and independence of young
disabled people. It does this through advisory
services, fieldwork, information, publications
and training.

**AGE RANGE:**
16-24
**NUMBERS PASSING THROUGH:**
The youth section of DIG has only just been
formed
**HOW TO CONTACT:**
By letter
**REGIONS SERVICED:**
England and Wales
**SPECIAL NEEDS PROVISION:**
See above
**COSTS/WAITING LISTS:**
Membership fee – £2.50

**YOUNG ENTERPRISE (YE)**
Ewert Place
Summertown
Oxford
OX2 7BZ
Tel: 0865 311180  Fax: 0865 310979

Young Enterprise provides young people with
the opportunity to learn about the world of work
and business by running their own company
while still in full-time education, usually through

school or college. Companies are formed producing a very diverse range of products and services. Most important is the support of volunteer advisers from local business. There is also a voluntary examination which recognises the valuable skills acquired, helpful in job interviews or for college and university entrance. Together with Skill (National Bureau for Students with Disabilities) Young Enterprise has developed 'Team Enterprise', which offers an alternative approach to the Company Programme for students who require greater support.

**REGIONAL ADDRESSES:**
Scotland: see YOUNG ENTERPRISE SCOTLAND
Northern Ireland: c/o NISTRO, University of Ulster, Shore Road, Newtonabbey, County Antrim, BT37 0QB  Tel: 0232 365131 (ext 2682)  Fax: 0232 362804
**AGE RANGE:**
14-19
**NUMBERS PASSING THROUGH:**
30,000
**HOW TO CONTACT:**
Programme arranged through school
**REGIONS SERVICED:**
UK
**SPECIAL NEEDS PROVISION:**
Team Enterprise, the special needs version of the programme, is available

**COSTS/WAITING LISTS:**
Each YE company pays a registration fee usually from company income and the voluntary examination costs about £5 which is often paid by the school

---

## YOUNG ENTERPRISE SCOTLAND (YES)
123 Dysart Road
Kirkaldy KY1 2BB
Tel: 0592 51597 Fax: 0592 55708

YES offers young people between the ages of 15 to 19 the chance to develop their enterprise skills, and assists you in making the difficult transition from school to work or further study. It does this by providing the opportunity for you to set up and run your own company. YES issues a business kit containing advice and all the office records required. You will have the help of some of the 700 advisers from industry who will act as consultants, but you have to make the decisions and tackle the real problems of production, selling, personnel, cash flow etc. There are over 250 YES companies each year and you have the option of taking part in the Examination, Company Competition and training events. YES is a combination of fun, stimulation and learning. Provision is made for those with special needs, usually through the Team Enterprise programme.

**AGE RANGE:**
15-19

**NUMBERS PASSING THROUGH:**
Over 3,500 per annum
**HOW TO CONTACT:**
Letter, telephone, fax
**REGIONS SERVICED:**
All regions in Scotland
**SPECIAL NEEDS PROVISION:**
Available through Team Enterprise

---

### YOUNG EUROPEAN MOVEMENT (YEM)
158 Buckingham Palace Road
London SW1W 9TR
Tel: 071 730 5291  Fax: 071 730 5168

The YEM is an organisation of young people, brought together by a common belief in a united Europe, who wish to understand what is going on and to make the most of the opportunities available. YEM organises seminars, study visits and conferences on political, social and cultural subjects, as well as on career and study opportunities abroad. It publishes a newsletter three times a year, together with information about events all over Europe which its members can attend. It is also part of the international Jeunesse Europeene Federaliste (JEF), so that everyone who joins YEM also becomes part of a youth organisation with members in over 20 countries throughout Europe.

**REGIONAL ADDRESSES:**
Scotland: Glasgow University YEM, c/o

Glasgow University Union, 32 University Avenue, Glasgow

Wales: Mudiad Ieuenctid Ewrop, c/o Student Union, St David's University College, Lampeter, Dyfed SA48 7ED

**AGE RANGE:**

16-35

**NUMBERS PASSING THROUGH:**

c 2,000 members

**HOW TO CONTACT:**

Telephone, letter or fax to London office for leaflets and further information as appropriate

**REGIONS SERVICED:**

UK

**SPECIAL NEEDS PROVISION:**

No special provision at this time

**COSTS/WAITING LISTS:**

Membership is £5 pa. Study visits cost about £100, summer schools about £50 and an international seminar about £200. Some travel subsidies are available and business sponsorship can help towards covering costs

---

**YOUNG EXPLORERS' TRUST (YET)**
c/o The Royal Geographical Society
1 Kensington Gore
London SW7 2AR
Tel: 0623 861027

YET is an advisory body concerned with youth expeditions. It provides advice and contacts for groups and individuals planning expeditions, mainly abroad. Whilst YET does not plan expeditions itself, it can put individuals in touch with those who do. YET also runs an approval and grant aid scheme for youth expeditions (groups not individuals) to remote areas overseas.

**REGIONAL ADDRESSES:**
Extensive network of local contacts but initial contact should be made through main office above

**AGE RANGE:**
The lower age limit is 14 and the majority of expedition members should be under 20 although there is some flexibility

**NUMBERS PASSING THROUGH:**
Over 1,000 enquiries

**HOW TO CONTACT:**
By letter to the London office or by phoning the number above for general advice and information as well as personal contacts with local expertise where appropriate

**REGIONS SERVICED:**
UK

**SPECIAL NEEDS PROVISION:**
Advice and contacts available

**COSTS/WAITING LISTS:**
There are no costs for using YET services

## YOUNG FRIENDS CENTRAL COMMITTEE
### (Young Quakers)

The Basement
Quaker International Centre
1 Byng Place
London WC1E 7JH
Tel: 071 387 4820

YFCC is the co-ordinating body of British Young Friends. It endeavours to represent Young Friends' interests and concerns both inside and outside the Society of Friends. It meets in February, May and October in different parts of the country and in September it has a national gathering on one theme (e.g. Lifestyle Choice, in 1992). It sends representatives to many other Quaker committees and other youth groups.

**REGIONAL ADDRESSES:**
For local groups contact the Outreach Group, c/o YFCC at the above address

**AGE RANGE:**
17-30

**NUMBERS PASSING THROUGH:**
100-200 at conferences, about 500 on national address list

**HOW TO CONTACT:**
By letter or telephone to the above address

**REGIONS SERVICED:**
England, Scotland and Wales

**SPECIAL NEEDS PROVISION:**
Disabilities and special dietary requirements can usually be accomodated with prior notice

**COSTS/WAITING LISTS:**
Weekend conferences cost between £6-£10.
Costs vary for other weekend discussions and
trips, and for overseas opportunities for
mixing with other young Quakers. Numbers
are somtimes limited, but this is rare

## YOUNG HUMANISTS (YH)
14 Lamb's Conduit Passage
London WC1R 4RH
Tel: 071 430 0908  Fax: 071 430 1271

Young Humanists is a network of young people
committed to the Humanist idea of 'doing it
without God' – exploring ideas and ethics,
supporting ethical projects and working towards
a free, open society without religious dogma.
As well as working to protect and promote
Humanist values, YH have frequent local and
national social meetings and events and produce
a newsletter *Share*. The YH are part of the
International Humanist and Ethical Youth
Organisation (IHEYO), and all YH members
receive the IHEYO newsletter. As well as an
annual week-long international conference,
IHEYO organises many international exchange
visits where members stay in the homes of local
Humanists who arrange sightseeing and social
events.

**REGIONAL ADDRESSES:**
Contact through Head Office

**AGE RANGE:**
30 and under
**NUMBERS PASSING THROUGH:**
c 100
**HOW TO CONTACT:**
By letter (with SAE) or telephone to Head
Office for general information, leaflets etc.
and a sample newsletter
**REGIONS SERVICED:**
UK
**SPECIAL NEEDS PROVISION:**
Enquiries welcome
**COSTS/WAITING LISTS:**
Annual subscription fee is £1 for under 18s,
£2 for 18 and over

---

## YOUNG MEN'S CHRISTIAN ASSOCIATION (YMCA)
National Council of YMCAs
640 Forest Road
London E17 3DZ

The YMCA provides a range of services and
activities, including vocational training,
recreation, sporting activities, drug and alcohol
counselling and advice, and much more. There
are over 250 YMCAs across the UK and they are
open to people of any religious faith.

**AGE RANGE:**
The emphasis is on young people but anyone
is welcome

**NUMBERS PASSING THROUGH:**
26 million worldwide
**HOW TO CONTACT:**
Check telephone directory or contact Head
Office for your nearest centre and contact
direct for details of services available
**REGIONS SERVICED:**
UK and worldwide
**SPECIAL NEEDS PROVISION:**
Contact your local centre for details
**COSTS/WAITING LISTS:**
Small charge for some activities

---

### YOUNG NADFAS (NATIONAL ASSOCIATION OF DECORATIVE AND FINE ARTS SOCIETIES)
8a Lower Grosvenor Place
London SW1W 0EN
Tel: 071 233 5433

Young NADFAS is the only national movement
specifically catering for young people interested
in fine arts. Its aims are to increase awareness,
and to stimulate interest and care for the Arts,
and to work to preserve our heritage and the
countryside. It is a membership organisation.
Members are introduced to as many aspects as
possible of the visual and performing arts. A
wide variety of activities are offered – craft days,
town trails, visits to houses, castles, galleries,
museums, churches and theatres. All activities
are fully supervised and take place during school

holidays. The parent body of Young NADFAS – NADFAS – assembles small groups of volunteers country-wide to become involved in a wide variety of projects such as book-refurbishing, cataloguing and archival listing, textile preservation, cleaning of armour, ceramics, metals and statuary, house and garden guiding and stewarding.

**AGE RANGE:**
8-18
**HOW TO CONTACT:**
Letter only to above address
**REGIONS SERVICED:**
UK

---

## YOUNG ORNITHOLOGISTS' CLUB (YOC)
c/o RSPB
The Lodge
Sandy
Bedfordshire SG19 2DL
Tel: 0767 680551  Fax: 0767 692365

Bi-monthly colour magazines; competitions with exciting prizes; projects which help the RSPB protect wildlife; over 15,000 local groups in schools and the community; exciting one-day activities at over 200 centres; a touring team which brings activities to many towns in Britain each year; over 50 holidays both in the UK and abroad. Advice is available on careers in conservation.

**REGIONAL ADDRESSES:**
Scotland: 17 Regent Terrace, Edinburgh, EH7 5BN  Tel: 031 556 5624/9042
North: Brookfoot House, Brookfoot Mills, Eland Road, Brighouse, West Yorks
**AGE RANGE:**
5-18
**NUMBERS PASSING THROUGH:**
120,000 members
**HOW TO CONTACT:**
Write to Head Office for information and membership details
**REGIONS SERVICED:**
UK
**SPECIAL NEEDS PROVISION:**
Participation in both residential and non-residential activities is encouraged
**COSTS/WAITING LISTS:**
£6 annual subscription, £2 for careers advice booklet

---

## YOUNG PEOPLE'S TRUST FOR THE ENVIRONMENT AND NATURE CONSERVATION (YPTE)
95 Woodridge Road
Guildford
Surrey GU1 4PY
Tel: 0483 39600  Fax: 0483 301992

The YPTE provides an information service on endangered species, environmental and conservation matters and will answer specific questions on any of these topics. They also provide a school lecture service, one-day field trips and residential 'environmental discovery' courses for schools and individuals.

**REGIONAL ADDRESSES:**
Contact through Guildford office
**AGE RANGE:**
Up to 18
**NUMBERS PASSING THROUGH:**
YPTE reached about 90,000 young people in 1990 through its various services
**HOW TO CONTACT:**
By letter (with SAE) to above address
**REGIONS SERVICED:**
UK
**SPECIAL NEEDS PROVISION:**
No special provision
**COSTS/WAITING LISTS:**
Residential field courses cost about £138 per week. Funding is usually from schools or parents

---

**YOUNG SCOT (publication)**
Scottish Community Education Council
(SCEC)
West Coates House
90 Haymarket Terrace
Edinburgh EH12 5LQ
Tel: 031 313 2488  Fax: 031 313 2477

*Young Scot* has now been going ten years. An

annual subscription of £6 entitles you to: 1) the *Young Scot Information Handbook* which is packed with essential and useful information on life after school and beyond; 2) the Young Scot Euro Under 26 Card which entitles you to savings on travel, eating out, theatre, fashion, music, driving lessons, bikes, hairdressers, insurance, cars, sports gear etc at over 3,000 outlets in Scotland and a further 100,000 across Europe; 3) the Young Scot 24-hour Helpline which offers you access to a team of qualified and friendly lawyers at any time of the year, and any time of the day or night; 4) the *Young Scot* magazine – sent to your home address at least four times a year – giving you up-to-date and topical information on areas such as travel, health, the arts, music, fashion, sport etc, and 5) the Young Scot Action Fund from which members can receive small grants of up to £50 to help turn their ideas into action.

**AGE RANGE:**
Under 26
**HOW TO CONTACT:**
Letter, telephone, fax to SCEC
**REGIONS SERVICED:**
Scotland
**COSTS/WAITING LISTS:**
£6 annual subscription

## YOUNG VISITORS (publications)
c/o ERYICA
101 Quai Branly
75740 Paris

The *Young Visitors* series are pocket guides giving up-to-date information for young people living, studying, on holiday or working in another country. They are published by ERYICA, the European Youth Information and Counselling Association, and are available from the Central Bureau. Guides are available for Britain, France, Germany, Hungary, Ireland, Italy, Luxembourg, Netherlands, Portugal and Spain and provide information on travel, accommodation, leisure activities, welfare, passports, visas, insurance and other topics relevant to young travellers. Some are more comprehensive than others so it is advisable to look for the one you need in your local library before ordering.

## YOUNG WILDLIFE PHOTOGRAPHER OF THE YEAR COMPETITION
c/o BBC Wildlife Magazine
Broadcasting House
Whiteladies Road
Bristol BS8 2LR
Tel: 0272 238166  Fax: 0272 467075

Young Wildlife Photographer of the Year is the junior section of the international Wildlife

Photographer of the Year competition, and is open to people aged 17 years and under. The competition is judged in three age categories and all entries must be photographs of wild animals or wild places. The main competition includes the Eric Hosking Award for the best portfolio of wildlife photographs by a photographer aged 26 years or under. The Award includes a holiday for two people to an exotic location. The winning entries from the junior and main competition are published in the BBC *Wildlife* magazine and are included in an exhibition at the Natural History Museum, London and on tour around the UK and overseas.

**AGE RANGE:**
17 and under, 26 and under for the Eric Hosking Award
**HOW TO CONTACT:**
Telephone, fax, letter to above address for application forms and further information about the current competition
**REGIONS SERVICED:**
UK
**SPECIAL NEEDS PROVISION:**
Enquiries welcome
**COSTS/WAITING LISTS:**
None for entering

## YOUNG WOMEN'S CHRISTIAN
## ASSOCIATION (YWCA)

Clarendon House
52 Cornmarket Street
Oxford OX1 3EJ
Tel: 0865 726110  Fax: 0865 204805

The YWCA runs clubs and community centres
and provides affordable, safe, non-dormitory
accommodation.   Youth participation is
encouraged in management of all Houses and
Youth Centres. Many further education courses
are available through the YWCA as well as
special provision such as drug counselling,
support for single parents etc. – contact YWCA
for further details.

**REGIONAL ADDRESSES:**
Scotland: 7 Randolph Crescent, Edinburgh
EH3 7TH  Tel: 031 225 7592
Wales: 7 Tyrfran Ave, Llanelli, Dyfed SA15
3LW  Tel: 0554 758644
London and Southern England: 16-22 Great
Russell Street, London WC1B 3lR
Tel: 071 580 4827
North East: Jesmond House, Clayton Road,
Jesmond, Newcastle-upon-Tyne
Tel: 0632 815466
North West, West, Midlands and Yorkshire:
via Oxford address above
**AGE RANGE:**
Any

**NUMBERS PASSING THROUGH:**
c 35,000 under 25
**HOW TO CONTACT:**
By letter to Head Office, or in person to your
nearest centre
**REGIONS SERVICED:**
UK
**SPECIAL NEEDS PROVISION:**
Special accommodation units (although most
centres consider applications). Some special
club provisions
**COSTS/WAITING LISTS:**
Annual membership is £6. Accommodation
is subsidised and therefore cheaper than
equivalent in the private sector. Charges for
courses are often met by employers

### YOUTH ADVENTURE
c/o Thanet Youth Club
Malden Hall
Herbert Street
London NW5 4HD
Tel: 071 267 3286/2215

Youth Adventure can give you a grant to help
make your ideas come to life. You may want to
take up a new sport, outdoor or arts activity, or
do something for your community – you decide.
Anyone aged 13-21 and living in the UK can
apply but you must make the application
yourself. First decide what you want to do and
when you want to do it. Then work out the cost

and what you need to do to make your adventure happen.

**AGE RANGE:**
13-21

**HOW TO CONTACT:**
Write to the above address for an application form

**REGIONS SERVICED:**
UK

**SPECIAL NEEDS PROVISION:**
Young people with disabilities and special needs will be given particular consideration

**COSTS/WAITING LISTS:**
A Grants Meeting is held every two months, so you should have a response to your application within 10 weeks

---

**YOUTH AND MUSIC**
28 Charing Cross Road
London WC2H 0DB
Tel: 071 379 6722  Fax: 071 497 0345

Youth and Music run a nationwide ticket concessionary scheme, Stage Pass, which can enable you to get up to 50% off tickets to performances at venues all round the country, details of which are contained in a monthly magazine sent to all members. Youth and Music are also the British section of the Federation Internationale des Jeunesses Musicales and are responsible for recruitment of British musicians and singers for the Federation's worldwide activities including the World Orchestra and World Choir. They also promote their own concerts targeted for young audiences new to music, and are in the process of developing an educational programme.

**REGIONAL ADDRESSES:**
Youth and Music – North East, Dance City, Peel Lane off Waterloo Street, Newcastle NE1 4DW  Tel: 091 230 1130
Yorkshire Youth and Music, Dean Clough Industrial Park, Halifax HX3 5AX
Tel: 0422 345631  Fax: 0422 321823
**AGE RANGE:**
14-30
**NUMBERS PASSING THROUGH:**
15,000 members
**HOW TO CONTACT:**
For advice on musical careers etc. contact the London office by letter, telephone or fax.  For all other matters contact either London or regional offices
**REGIONS SERVICED:**
UK
**SPECIAL NEEDS PROVISION:**
Access depends on individual venues
**COSTS/WAITING LISTS:**
Stage Pass costs: £14 for London and Home Counties, £7.50 outside this area. Stage Pass entitles you to buy two discounted tickets

### YOUTH ARTS DIRECTORY (publication)
Sales Department
National Youth Agency
17-23 Albion Street
Leicester LE1 6GD
Tel: 0533 471200  Fax: 0533 471043

Want to know who is doing what in your locality? Want to know who is doing dance, drama, or video, in your or any other part of the country? The *Youth Arts Directory* gives details of over 250 projects in England and Wales, covering some 30 art forms. The entries are indexed by art form, and arranged geographically.
ISBN 0 86155 136 2. Available through libraries, or direct from the above address (price £5.50 post free) .

### YOUTH CAMPAIGN FOR NUCLEAR DISARMAMENT (YCND)
162 Holloway Road
London N7 8DQ
Tel: 071 700 2393  Fax: 071 700 2357

Youth CND is an organisation run by young people for young people. Members receive a copy of the magazine *CND Today* four times per year, as well as Youth CND publications and campaign materials (posters, stickers etc.). They also run a popular School Speaking Service with a government-funded group called 'Peace through NATO', as well as producing education packs useful for school projects.

**REGIONAL ADDRESSES:**
Scottish CND: 420 Sauchiehall Street, Glasgow G2 3JD  Tel: 041 331 2878
CND Cymru: Bryn Elltyd, Tan Y Grisiau, Blaenau Ffestiniog, Gwynedd LL41 3TW  Tel: 0766 831356
Both of these are national offices rather than regional contacts and should be the first point of contact in Scotland and Wales

**AGE RANGE:**
22 and under

**NUMBERS PASSING THROUGH:**
c 4,000-5,000

**HOW TO CONTACT:**
By telephone, letter or fax to the National Office for information pack, advice and campaign materials

**REGIONS SERVICED:**
UK, but see Scottish and Welsh offices above

**SPECIAL NEEDS PROVISION:**
No special provision

**COSTS/WAITING LISTS:**
Membership is approx £5 per year

---

**YOUTH EXCHANGE CENTRE (YEC)**
The British Council
10 Spring Gardens
London SW1H 9PE
Tel: 071 389 4030  Fax: 071 389 4033

The YEC, a department of the British Council, promotes international youth exchanges through the provision of advice, information, training and grants. The YEC is the UK National Agency for the European Community-funded programme Youth for Europe, which promotes youth exchanges between the EC Member States. Priority is given to groups of young people who would not normally have the opportunity for such an international experience. The YEC provides grant aid to groups of young people aged 15-25. Support is available for exchanges with EC Member States, the rest of Europe, Central and East European countries, the USA and Japan. All groups of young people are eligible for support, provided they meet the YEC's basic criteria. To support its work, the YEC produces a series of *Information Kits*, setting out the step-by-step organisation of a youth exchange, *Help!? Guidelines on International Youth Exchanges*, a handbook for exchange organisers, and a quarterly newsletter *Youth Exchange News*.

**REGIONAL ADDRESSES:**
12 regional committees – details available from above
**AGE RANGE:**
15-25
**NUMBERS PASSING THROUGH:**
Nearly 20,000 took part in youth exchanges in 91/92

**HOW TO CONTACT:**
Telephone or letter to Head Office or regional
contacts for advice/information pack
**REGIONS SERVICED:**
UK
**SPECIAL NEEDS PROVISION:**
Special consideration given to groups
containing young people with special needs
**COSTS/WAITING LISTS:**
There are no costs for using the services of
the YEC

---

**YOUTH EXCHANGE PROGRAMME (YEP)**
Central Bureau for Educational Visits and
Exchanges
Seymour Mews House
Seymour Mews
London W1H 9PE
Tel: 071 486 5101

The Youth Exchange Programme aims to
promote out-of-school exchanges to all young
people, no matter what their occupation. The
programme promotes short cultural exchanges
between groups in two or more EC countries.
You would have to find a similar group in one
or more other EC countries, perhaps through a
twin town. You would need to plan a series
of exchange activities which have a clear
European dimension. Normally, each group
must visit the other, within a two year period, for
between one to three weeks. The groups must

be independent of, say, school, college, sporting or political activities.

**AGE RANGE:**
15-25
**HOW TO CONTACT:**
Letter, telephone to above address for more information
**REGIONS SERVICED:**
UK

## YOUTH HOSTELS ASSOCIATION (England and Wales) (YHA)
Trevelyan House
8 St Stephens Hill
St Albans
Herts AL1 2DY
Tel: 0727 55215  Fax: 0727 44126

YHA is a registered charity. Its aim is 'to help all, especially young people of limited means, to a greater knowledge, love and care of the countryside particularly by providing hostels or other simple accommodation for them in their travels, and thus promote their health, rest and education'. YHA has over 250 Youth Hostels throughout England and Wales and over 5,000 worldwide. 'Great Escape' activity holidays are of particular interest to young people and include walking, cycling, riding and mountain sports and take place at home or abroad.

**REGIONAL ADDRESSES:**

North and Midlands: PO Box 11, Matlock, Derbyshire, DE4 2XA  Tel 0629 825850

South: 11b York Street, Salisbury, Wilts SP2 7AP  Tel: 0722 337515

Wales: 1 Cathedral Road, Cardiff CF1 9HA Tel: 0222 396766

**AGE RANGE:**

Any

**NUMBERS PASSING THROUGH:**

320,000

**HOW TO CONTACT:**

By telephone to the Information Department (tel: 0727 55215/45047) for general information, leaflets and advice

**REGIONS SERVICED:**

UK

**SPECIAL NEEDS PROVISION:**

Many hostels are accessible by wheelchair. Activity holidays can be attended by anyone

**COSTS/WAITING LISTS:**

Membership costs: Under 18 – £3; Over 18 – £9; Family £18; Life membership £120. Overnight fees range from £3.40 up to £15 per night depending on the grade of Youth Hostel.  There are no waiting lists but all accommodation is subject to availability and booking in advance is recommended especially during the busy summer months

## YOUTH INFORMATION SHOPS
c/o National Youth Agency
17-23 Albion Street
Leicester LE1 6GD
Tel: 0533 471200  Fax: 0533 471043

Youth Information Shops are a new development introduced by the National Youth Agency. They are High Street shops where young people are able to get information about all sorts of topics (from accommodation to re-cycling) and in all sorts of forms (from individual counselling to computer print-outs). At present there are two shops up and running – in Bradford and Nottingham - with plans well advanced for many more throughout the country – Rochdale, Liverpool, Coventry, Gloucester, Mansfield, Sheffield, Horsham, Chatham, Huddersfield, Accrington etc. To find out more about the Information Shops, and to find out when there may be one opening in your area (perhaps you could help set one up?) contact the National Youth Agency at the above address.

## YOUTH TRAINING (YT)

Youth Training is an alternative to full-time education and offers you the chance to undertake some form of work-based training as the first stage in a particular job or career or even as the first step towards a university or college course. Young people under 18 not in a job or full-time education are guaranteed an offer of a suitable training place but you can still apply if you are over 18. You can also apply if you have a job – training can be done in your own time through open learning etc. or it is possible your employer will include some form of training as part of your work. Training is available in almost any type of job or career and is structured to your specific needs. Participants have the opportunity to gain vocational qualifications which are recognised by employers nationally and can lead to further training and improve career prospects. Your local Careers Office or Jobcentre can give you more information about the opportunities available in your area.

---

**YOUTHACTION NORTHERN IRELAND**
Hampton
Glenmachan Park
Belfast BT4 2PJ
Tel: 0232 760067  Fax: 0232 768799

Youthaction run various events and activities in sport, competitions and a wide range of personal development programmes in Hampton, a residential and conference centre or in Encounter, a cottage in the Mournes. They run training courses in youth and community work as well as conferences, seminars and workshops on issues of interest to young people and much more. Any enquiries from young people are welcome.

**AGE RANGE:**
No specific age range, mainly 17-25
**NUMBERS PASSING THROUGH:**
40,000 through affiliated groups
**HOW TO CONTACT:**
Letter, telephone or fax for advice and information
**REGIONS SERVICED:**
Northern Ireland
**SPECIAL NEEDS PROVISION:**
Enquiries welcome
**COSTS/WAITING LISTS:**
Examples of costs are 25p per member of an affiliated youth club; £15 for young adult conference (all costs included – food, travel etc.); £2 entry to certain competitions.  Places may be limited on individual programmes

---

**YOUTHAID**
409 Brixton Road
London SW9 7DQ
Tel: 071 737 8068

Information about rights and opportunities for young people in training, education and employment.

**Part Three**

# WHAT TO
# GO FOR
# AND
# HOW TO
# APPLY

# Introduction

This section is designed to introduce CVs, application forms, job search and interview techniques. The information is aimed at giving **you** the edge in today's job market. Although careers are mentioned throughout this section, the techniques described are equally valid for college, university, and vocational training schemes.

Before looking for work it is essential that you 'know yourself' so that you can decide on the type of job and the industry that you want to work in. The next few pages encourage self-assessment aimed at helping you focus your thoughts more clearly on what you want out of life and from your future career.

# Skills Check

## What's a skills check?

Your skills check will help you focus your thoughts more clearly when thinking about your future career and what direction you want to take. It looks at what you have done and what you feel are your strengths.

Put a tick against all the things that you can do to what ever degree – remember to tick things that you have experienced outside work as well as at work. Also put a tick against the things that you feel particularly good at (don't be shy!).

## What are my skills?

|  | What can I do? | What am I good at? |
|---|---|---|
| *Verbal Communication* | ☐ | ☐ |
| Selling | ☐ | ☐ |
| Public speaking | ☐ | ☐ |
| Telephone | ☐ | ☐ |
| Answering queries | ☐ | ☐ |
| Teaching | ☐ | ☐ |
| | | |
| *Written Communication* | | |
| Writing letters or reports | ☐ | ☐ |
| Understanding written reports | ☐ | ☐ |
| Minute or note taking | ☐ | ☐ |
| Correcting mistakes | ☐ | ☐ |

|  | What can I do? | What am I good at? |
|---|---|---|

*Technical*

| | | |
|---|---|---|
| Machine operating | ❏ | ❏ |
| Fault finding | ❏ | ❏ |
| Maintenance | ❏ | ❏ |
| Repairs | ❏ | ❏ |

*Practical*

| | | |
|---|---|---|
| Building | ❏ | ❏ |
| Woodwork | ❏ | ❏ |
| Decorating | ❏ | ❏ |
| Making things | ❏ | ❏ |

*Administration*

| | | |
|---|---|---|
| Keeping files | ❏ | ❏ |
| Organising systems | ❏ | ❏ |
| Organising people | ❏ | ❏ |
| Dealing with letters | ❏ | ❏ |

*Numeracy*

| | | |
|---|---|---|
| Accounts | ❏ | ❏ |
| Cash handling | ❏ | ❏ |
| Using maths | ❏ | ❏ |
| Working out measurements or quantities | ❏ | ❏ |

*Mental Ability*

| | | |
|---|---|---|
| Problem solving | ❏ | ❏ |
| Thinking of new ideas | ❏ | ❏ |
| Figures | ❏ | ❏ |

*Other*
Write down any other skills you feel you have
that are not covered by these.

## What's next?

Look over what you've ticked. It shows the areas
and skills that you already have that will be
useful to future employers. It also shows areas
that you may want to get involved in or improve.

For any job or area of work that you are interested
in try to identify the skills that you think may be
needed. Write them down and see how they
compare with what you have already

> Try it in your spare time
> Do it on a voluntary basis
> Start to get training

then:-

Write action plans to get information from:

> Your local reference library
> Your careers office/job centre
> Talking to people you know

## Work Style

### What's my work style?

Everybody has their own opinion of what gives job satisfaction. For example, some people prefer security – although this often means comparatively low pay. Others prefer higher risk types of work, where there isn't as much security and where pay can be much higher. Most of us tend to choose a compromise between the two.

If you can find out as much about what you want from work as possible, it will help you identify what areas of yourself and your career to work on.

### What do I want from work?

Answer all the following questions using the following key:-

   **Y** (for yes) if this is what you do want
or  **N** (for no) if you do not mind.

Remember, be honest with yourself – there aren't any right or wrong answers.

| PAY | YES | NO |
|---|---|---|
| Enough to live on | Y | N |
| High wages | Y | N |
| Paid by performance | Y | N |
| Regular wages | Y | N |

| **HOURS** | **YES** | **NO** |
|---|---|---|
| Fixed hours | Y | N |
| Overtime | Y | N |
| Flexible hours | Y | N |
| **PROSPECTS** | | |
| Promotion Chances | Y | N |
| Security | Y | N |
| **LOCATION** | | |
| Work near home | Y | N |
| Work anywhere | Y | N |
| Based near home but working away | Y | N |
| Travelling long distances | Y | N |
| **CONDITIONS** | | |
| Hot | Y | N |
| Cool | Y | N |
| Outdoors | Y | N |
| Clean work place | Y | N |
| **OTHER PEOPLE** | | |
| Prefer working alone | Y | N |
| Prefer working in a group | Y | N |
| Like dealing with the public | Y | N |
| **MANAGEMENT** | | |
| Use own initiative | Y | N |
| Be supervised | Y | N |
| Manager available if needed | Y | N |
| **DEPTH OF INVOLVEMENT** | | |
| Like to develop your abilities | Y | N |
| See end result | Y | N |
| **OTHER THINGS YOU MAY WANT** | | |
| Status | Y | N |
| To help others | Y | N |
| To get recognition from others | Y | N |

**Forming a picture of your working style**

Look over the question sheet again. Start to ask yourself questions about some of the answers you have given.

> How do your work style answers reflect your life at the moment?
> How do they match the areas of work you may be interested in?
> What sort of changes in work style would you make to get the right job?
> What would you not change at all no matter what the job?
> Why would you be unprepared to change these?

## The next steps

Having given careful consideration to the previous pages you should now have a clearer idea of what you can offer an employer and also what you want.

Now identify the type of work that you want to research in more depth and compare what you **can** do with what you **want** to do.

Using the information you have recorded about yourself, ask yourself the following:-

- What are my current skills?
- Which new skills could I learn?
- Qualifications/training I have or could obtain
- What are my physical attributes?
- What physical conditions do I want to avoid?
- What situations am I comfortable in/wish to avoid?
- What do I want from my job?
- Any personal interests I would like my job to incorporate

Having researched the job you think you would like, ask yourself the following and compare with your personal requirements:-

- Which skills does the job require?
- Which skills would need to be learned?
- Which qualifications/training will be required?
- Which physical qualities are required?
- What does the job give me?
- Which of my interests are incorporated?

# Job Search

No one can just walk out and get a job. You need to know yourself so that you can choose the right type of job and industry to suit you. You need to have researched that job so that you can develop the skills necessary. Finally you need to be **committed** to finding a job.

Do not just react to advertised vacancies as everybody else will also be applying. Try and be productive and create your own vacancy by using the speculative approach or personal contacts.

## Finding a vacancy

The first step to getting a job is finding a vacancy, below are listed a few methods of finding vacancies:-

### 1. Personal contact
Many vacancies found like this will not have been advertised so there is less competition.

### 2. Speculative
Again these vacancies will not have been advertised. 10% chance of being interviewed using this approach.

### 3. Agencies
Check agency is experienced in your type of

work and that they usually have vacancies not advertised elsewhere.

### 4. Newspapers
Local newspapers usually have a specific day for job vacancies.

National newspapers – check with your team adviser or employment co-ordinator for the best newspapers for your type of work.

### 5. Specialist magazines
Many national publications. Often locally published recruiting newspapers/magazines.

### 6. Job Centres
Vary from area to area.

## Correct tools

Finding a job is a job in itself and must be approached as such.

You will need the correct tools:-

- A quiet place to work
- Relevant notes from this course
- A copy of your CV
- Scrap paper
- Good quality paper
- Envelopes
- Stamps

- Pens
- A ruler
- A dictionary

Put time aside and send a set number of applications each week. Sending the odd application and waiting for a reply is wasting time.

If you hear nothing after one week telephone to ensure your application has been received. Keep a record of all employers contacted.

# Doing my application form

## The first contact

The application form is usually your first contact with an employer so, to make the most of every opportunity, you'll want to create a good impression. Here's a checklist of some of the things you should do:

## Before starting

- Carefully read **all** the instructions
- If there is anything you aren't sure of – **ask someone**

## Completing the form

- Do a test version on a photocopy or blank piece of paper
- Use a good, black pen
- Write clearly and neatly
- Make sure the spelling is correct
- If you do make a mistake on the final version, use Tippex rather than crossing out (wait for it to dry as well)
- Keep your answers short and relevant
- Decide what skills the employer is looking for and reflect those skills on the form

## After completing it

- Check it carefully
- Make sure dates are correct and that they make sense
- Is it clear which job you are applying for?
- Make a copy of the form – you will need to read it before your interview
- Don't cram the form into a small envelope
- Post the form as soon as possible

**REMEMBER:** Many people do not complete their forms properly. Because of this they are not selected for interview. There is no need for you to be in that position – give yourself the best chance by taking time and trouble over it.

## How do I request an application form?

If an advertisement asks you to write for an application form, do that and no more.

## Example to request an application form

```
The Personnel Manager          27 Squat View Terrace
Pearson Perambulators          Stickleback
Nirvana Industrial Complex     Near Troutville
Guppy                          Surrey SM99 4BU
Essex  GU5 1XB                 Tel: 0324 123456
(their address)                (your address)

                               1st January 1992


Reference Number
(if given in advert)


Dear Sirs,

                    Sales Assistant

Please forward an application form for the above position as
advertised in The Chronicle on 28th December 1992 and, if
possible, a job description.


Yours faithfully

Your Signature

S Snurd
(print your name underneath)
```

## Telephone Techniques

### Checklist for telephone usage

* **Smile**

* Give all your attention to the call

* Use the person's name

* Prepare a script of your main points

* **Listen** to what the other person says

* Vary the tone and emphasis of your voice

* Be clear and concise

* Do not be frightened of pausing

**Dial a smile – don't phone a groan!**

Notes On Your Technique

# Interview Techniques

## Preparation

**Arrive on time**
- Check how long the journey takes
- Make sure you know what department to go to

**Do your homework**
- Know as much as possible about the organisation
- Find out as much as possible about the job

**Know yourself**
- Can you outline your life and career clearly?
- Think of examples of your successes and achievements
- Show a positive attitude towards previous employers

**What do you want from the interview**
- List the information that you want to know

## The interview

**Initial impressions**
- Dress smartly and conventionally
- Find out the interviewers name from the receptionist
- When entering the room smile, bid them good day and use the interviewers name
- Do **not** smoke unless the interviewer does

**Conversation**
- A good interview is a two way conversation

- Be normal
- Concentrate on what the interviewer is saying

## Using the interview to your advantage

- Use every opportunity to speak positively about your past and current work/training
- You should be talking for 60% of the time
- Never answer just 'yes' or 'no' Expand your answers
- Be clear and precise
- Be positive

## After the interview

- If you have heard nothing after one week, telephone
- If unsuccessful try to find out why
- All unsuccessful interviews are practice for the next one – you will eventually be successful

## REMEMBER
Enthusiasm
Energy
Experience relevant to the job
Knowledge of the company

## Responding to interview questions:

### a) What did you do in your last job?

Explain what your last job involved and include
the following points:-

- Duties that are relevant to the job you are
  applying for
- Skills used in the job
- Types of people you dealt with
- Reasons for any promotion
- Areas of responsibility
- Machines and equipment used

### b) Why did you leave your last job?

Mention only the reasons that make you look
good. If your health was a factor then do not
discuss in depth but stress that you are now fit
and able to do everything required by the new
job.

Many reasons are acceptable to an employer,
such as:-

- The job was temporary or seasonal
- Part-time
- Deciding to change direction
- Low pay
- Redundancy
- Too much travel
- Unsociable hours

### c) Have you ever done this type of work?

Always try to answer positively and explain any experience that shows knowledge and ability. If you have limited or no experience then tell the interviewer about anything else that demonstrates how quickly you can learn. Stress how keen you are to learn.

### d) What machines/equipment can you use?

This question applies to all jobs. Mention the following:–

–   All equipment and experience that would be used in the job applied for. Be precise and use the name and type of equipment if possible

–   Experience of any other machines that may be relevant. Again be precise

–   Any relevant machinery used for your hobbies

### e) What wage/salary are you looking for?

You will usually be informed of the salary offered. However, this is sometimes negotiable, which can be awkward. If you ask too high a figure you may 'price yourself out', too low and you could be 'underselling yourself'. Here are some ideas on how to respond:–

- Do not specify a figure
- Be a little vague, i.e. a fair day's pay for a fair day's work; standard rate for the job is fine; the company has a good reputation so I'm sure the wage/salary will be suitable

If possible, after the interview find out what other workers doing the same job are paid. If you are then offered the job you at least have an idea and will be able to negotiate.

### f) Why do you want to work for this company

You must give positive reasons which suggest you will be loyal to the company. It also provides the opportunity for you to demonstrate that you have researched well prior to the interview – impressive.

### g) Did you have much time off during your last job?

If you had very little time off then state that fact in a positive way. If you had a lot of time off then explain the reasons and state why it would not happen in this job.

### h) Why should we take you on?

Answer quickly and positively. List your positive attributes, even if this means repeating yourself. Make sure you demonstrate that you are reliable, loyal, efficient, hard working and capable of doing the job.

### i) Do you have good health?

The interviewer is looking for two things here – your fitness for the particular job and your general health.

Try and set his/her mind at rest on both issues:–

- If you are in good health, then say so positively

- If you have entered any health information on your application form discuss this but assure it will have no detrimental effect on the job applied for and that your general health is good

- Refer to examples that demonstrate you have overcome any disability

### j) What are your strengths?

Yet another chance to list your positive qualities. Cover the following:–

- Skills
- Pride in doing a good job
- Enthusiasm for the job
- Experience
- Ability to get on well with others
- Interest

- Reliability
- Efficiency

### k) What are your weaknesses?

Never admit to any weaknesses. It is possible to respond as follows:–

- I have none that prevent me from being a good worker
- None in relation to this job

### l) Tell me more about yourself.

This gives you a chance to expand aspects of your personal life. You should demonstrate that you have outside interests; have links between these interests and the job; have normal domestic circumstances.

Mention the following:–

- Hobbies/leisure activities
- Clubs of which you are a member
- Position held in any club, etc.
- Past job experience
- Your family
- Brief personal history

### m) What did your last employer think of you?

Give a positive answer, mentioning jobs for which you received praise. Stress your efficiency, reliability, punctuality, etc. if you have an open reference from your last employer, then show that. Never criticise previous employers as this give the impression you may criticise this employer in the future.

**n) How old are you?**

If you are asked this question then the employer may be worried you are too young or too old for the job. Don't just give your age but point out the advantages and discuss any disadvantages.

## Example of CV

**PERSONAL DETAILS:**

NAME: Andrew Craddock

DATE OF BIRTH: 5 June 1971

ADDRESS:    12,  Keats Ave.,
            Anytown
            AT1 2BU

MARITAL STATUS:
Married with one child aged 2.

TELEPHONE: (0728)  97532

GENERAL HEALTH: Good

---

**EDUCATION:**

*Sept. 1982 – May 1987*

St. Mary's Comprehensive School,  Anytown.

**TRAINING:**

*July 1987 – June 1989*

2 years apprenticeship in Engineering with A. Grease & Co. Ltd. Attended Lastown Technical College on day release and evening classes.

Gained part 1 of City & Guilds Mechanical Engineering. Awarded Technical College prize for Best Project 1988.

**WORK HISTORY:**

*July 1987 – June 1988*

Apprentice Engineer, A. Grease & Co. Ltd., Lastown.

*Duties*

Working on all aspects of Mechanical Engineering in a large contract toolroom.

*Equipment Used*

Centre Lathe, Capstan, Jig Borer, Hand Press.

*July 1989 – Jan. 1990*

Unemployed as a result of moving to a new area.

*Feb. 1990 – Sept. 1990*

Capstan Setter Operator, Blank Engineering Co., Anytown.

*Duties:*

Setting and operating C.N.C. machines.

*Oct. 1990 – Feb. 1991*

Unemployed due to redundancy.

*Feb. 1991 – Oct. 1991*

Waiter, Rose Garden Tea Rooms, Anytown.

*Duties:*

Reception of diners, taking orders, waiting on table, dealing with complaints, accepting payment for meals.

*Oct. 1991 – Mar. 1991*

Participant on a Drive For Youth Programme devised to test and develop through a series of difficult scenarios.

Showed a particular ability to get on with others and persuade them to undertake tasks with the minimum of friction.

**SPARE TIME ACTIVITIES:**

Member of Anytown 5-a-side football team.

Volunteer youth worker at Leasowes Youth Club.

Hill walking.

**ADDITIONAL INFORMATION:**

Clean driving licence

**REFERENCES:**

Mr. K. Fu,
Supervisor,
A. Grease & Co. Ltd.
China Street,
Lastown, LT1 2TL

Tel: (0428) 87654

Mr. V. Young,
Youth & Community Worker,
Leasowes Youth Club,
Leasowes Ave.,
Anytown, AT1 2BZ

Tel: (0728) 25791

Miss A. Trouble,
Minister,
56, Vicarage Way,
Anytown, AT1 4ZB

Tel: (0728) 665598

## Covering Letters

### To cover a CV

Your Ref: UT 168

FAO: Personnel Manager

13 North Street,
Newbridge,
Essex. OD2 9PZ

Tel 0968 446966

15th October 1992

Dear Sir

ASSISTANT UNDERTAKER'S POST

I was very interested to see your advertisement in the Sunday Times.

I feel positive that my previous work experience and training make me a suitable candidate for the position currently offered. During my five months training on the Drive For Youth Development Programme I have worked hard with a team making me more aware of the needs and sensitivities of others. I have also developed my organisational and planning abilities.

The full breadth of my training and experience is shown in the enclosed CV.

I would be grateful for an interview at your earliest opportunity.

Thank you for your time and attention.

Yours faithfully,

J Jones

## When applying without any previous advertisement.

13 North Street,
Newbridge,
Essex.
OD2 9PZ

The Personnel Manager          Tel 0968 446966

15th April 1992

Dear Sir

### TRAINEE EMBALMER

I am applying for any vacancies in your embalming department.

During the past five months I have been on the Drive For Youth Development Training Programme. Over this period I have been improving my team work, planning, organisation and communication skills. I am very enthusiastic and keen about my work and I believe I have a very approachable character with my work colleagues. I am also very tactful and sensitive to the needs of others which I feel could be useful when dealing with customers at a time of their bereavement.

I enclose my CV and look forward to your reply regarding any current or future vacancies that you feel I may be suited for.

Thank you for your time and attention.

Yours faithfully,

J Jones

## To cover an application form

Your Ref: UT 168/SMB/jh     13 North Street,
Newbridge,
Mr C J Jameson,     Essex.
Personnel Manager     OD2 9PZ

Tel 0968 446966

15th April 1992

Dear Mr Jameson,

     ASSISTANT UNDERTAKER'S POST

Please find enclosed my completed application form for the above position as advertised in the Sunday Times.

I am very interested in this position and I am confident that I have the necessary drive and self-motivating approach to my work that you are looking for. I have been developing my interpersonal and organisational skills during my training over the last five months and I am keen and enthusiastic to learn new approaches and develop my abilities.

I am looking forward to meeting you at any interview you may arrange.

Thank you for your time and attention.

Yours sincerely,

J Jones

**Part Four**

# HELP!

**AL-ANON & AL-ATEEN**
61 Great Dover St
London SE1 4YF
Tel: 071 403 0888  (N.Ireland 0232 243489)

Help for relatives and close friends of people
with drinking problems. (Al-Ateen provides
support for young people aged 12-20 who have
a relative with a drinking problem). Check
telephone directory under 'Alcoholics', or
contact above for a local group.

Alcohol Concern, 305 Gray's Inn Road,
London WC1X 8QF  Tel: 071 833 3471
Scotland:137/145 Sauchiehall Street,
Glasgow G2 3EW  Tel: 041 333 9677
Wales: PO Box 2010, Cardiff  Tel: 0222
398791
Northern Ireland Council on Alcohol, 40
Elmwood Avenue, Belfast BT9 6AZ  Tel: 0232
664434

All these addresses can put you in touch with a
local contact for advice if you think you or
someone you know is drinking too much.

**BRITISH PREGNANCY ADVISORY SERVICE
(BPAS)**
7 Belgrave Road
London SW1V 1QB
Tel: 071 222 0985

Counselling and advice on contraception, pregnancy and abortion.

### BROOK ADVISORY CENTRES
153a East Street
London SE17 2SD
Tel: 071 708 1234

Counselling and advice on contraception, pregnancy and abortion. Centres based around the country - contact above for nearest one.

### CARELINE
England - Tel: 071 226 2033
Wales - Tel: 0222 229461
Scotland - Tel: 041 221 6722
N.Ireland - Tel: 0232 238800

Counselling helpline for children, young people and families.

### CHILDLINE
Freepost 1111
London EC4B 4BB
Tel: 0800 1111

Free 24-hour service for children and young people in danger or in trouble.

## CITIZENS ADVICE BUREAUX

Can provide help and advice on a wide range of issues such as housing, benefits, debt, the law, employment rights etc.

Check telephone book under 'C' for your nearest CAB or contact: National Association of Citizens Advice Bureaux (NACAB), 115 Pentonville Road, London, N1 9LZ  Tel: 071 833 2181

## COMMISSION FOR RACIAL EQUALITY
Elliot House
10-12 Allingham Street
London SW1E 5EH
Tel: 071 828 7022

Help and advice in cases of racial discrimination.

## EATING DISORDERS ASSOCIATION
11 Priory Road
High Wycombe
Bucks HP13 6SL
Tel: 0494 21431

Support for anyone with anorexia and bulimia. Can put you in contact with a local group.

### EQUAL OPPORTUNITIES COMMISSION
Overseas House
Quay Street
Manchester M3 3HN
Tel: 061 833 9244

### FAMILY PLANNING ASSOCIATION
27-35 Mortimer Street
London W1N 7RJ
Tel: 071 636 7866

Free contraceptive advice. Check telephone directory under 'Family' for nearest clinic or contact above.

### FREELINE SOCIAL SECURITY
England, Scotland and Wales –
Tel: 0800 666555
N. Ireland – Tel: 0800 616757

Free telephone enquiry service offering information on all aspects of welfare benefits.

**Other languages:**
Tel: 0800 289188 (Urdu)
Tel: 0800 521360 (Punjabi)
Tel: 0800 252451 (Chinese)
Tel: 0800 289011 (Welsh)
**Disability Information:**
Tel: 0800 882200 (voice)
Tel: 0800 243355 (minicom)

## GAMBLERS ANONYMOUS
Tel: 081 741 4181

24-hour helpline for for people with problems with gambling.

## GLAD - LESBIAN AND GAY LEGAL ADVICE
Tel: 071 253 2043
Monday to Friday 7pm-10pm.

## LAW CENTRES

Can provide free legal help and advice. Details of your nearest centre in telephone directory under 'Law Centres' or contact: Law Centres Federation, Duchess House, Warren Street, London W1P 5DA Tel: 071 387 8570.

## MESSAGE HOME

Anyone who has left home can record a confidential message for their family. Lines are open 24 hours.

**Regional numbers:**
London - Tel: 071 799 7662
Scotland - Tel: 0968 76161
Birmingham - Tel: 021 426 3396
Liverpool - Tel: 051 709 7598
Leeds - Tel: 0532 454544
Wales - Tel: 0633 271834

Bristol - Tel: 0272 504717
Portsmouth - Tel: 0705 733899

---

### MIND
22 Harley Street
London W1N 2ED
Tel: 071 637 0741

Information and advice on all aspects of mental
health. Referral to local groups.

---

### NATIONAL AIDS HELPLINE
Tel: 0800 567123
Minicom: 0800 521361

24-hour free and confidential helpline

**Other languages:**
Asian languages - Tel: 0800 282445
Cantonese - Tel: 0800 282446
Arabic - Tel: 0800 282447

---

### NATIONAL ASSOCIATION OF YOUNG
### PEOPLES' COUNSELLING AND ADVISORY
### SERVICE
Magazine Business Centre
11 Newarke Street
Leicester LE1 5SS
Tel: 0533 554553

Confidential counselling service for young
people. Contact above for details of your nearest
service.

## NATIONAL DEBTLINE
Tel: 021 359 8501
10am-4pm Monday and Thursday,
2pm-7pm Tuesday and Wednesday

Helpline for people with debt problems.

## NETWORK FOR THE HANDICAPPED
16 Princeton Street
London WC1R 4BB
Tel: 071 831 8031/7740

Provide legal advice and assistance to people
with disabilities.

## RAPE CRISIS CENTRES
PO Box 69
London WC1X 9NJ
Tel: 071 837 1600

Offer free counselling for women and girls who
have been raped or sexually assaulted in any
way. Check telephone directory under 'R' for
the nearest centre or ring 071 837 1600 - line
open 24 hours.

**RELEASE**
388 Old Street
London EC1V 9LT
Tel: 071 729 9904
(Advice line, Monday to Friday 10am-6pm)
Tel: 071 603 8654
(Emergency line)

Information, advice and counselling on drug use and legal problems.

**SAMARITANS**

24-hour confidential helpline. Check telephone directory under 'S' for local number or ask the operator (dial 100) to put you through directly.

**SHELTER - National Campaign for the Homeless**
88 Old Street
London EC1V 9HU
Tel: 071 253 0202

Campaigns for the homeless and has a national network of advice centres.

## SURVIVORS
38 Mount Pleasant
London WC1X 0AN
Tel: 071 833 3737
7pm - 10pm, Tuesday and Thursday

Helpline for any man or boy who has been sexually assaulted by another man.

## UNITED RESPONSE
162/164 Upper Richmond Road
Putney
London SW15 2SL
Tel: 081 780 9686  Fax: 081 780 9538

United Response is a national charity helping an increasing number of young people with learning disabilities and/or mental health problems. It specialises in support for people who live at home, and the development of a network of residential and day services in the community.

## VICTIM SUPPORT
Cranmer House
39 Brixton Road
London SW9 6DD
Tel: 071 735 9166

Help and support for victims of crime. Can put you in touch with a local group.

# INDEX

# NOTE

This index can be used as a supplement to the main categories in Part One. If you are unable to identify your interests with any of the categories listed on page 18, you may find what you are looking for by browsing through this index. You will also find here a listing for every organisation or publication with an entry in Parts Two and Four and a reference to many other organisations, activities and publications mentioned in those entries.

# Additional copies of *Go for it!*

If you would like to order more copies of this book for whatever reason, whether you are a private individual, a school, college or any other organisation or business, please contact the address below by letter or by phone. If you prefer you can complete the order form on this page or copy the information required onto a postcard or letter.

Please send me ..... copy/copies of
*Go for it!* at £7.99  (postage included)
Name .........................................................
Address ......................................................
.................................................................
.................................................................
I wish to pay by Access(Mastercard)/Visa/
cheque the total amount of  £.............
Card no ☐☐☐☐☐☐☐☐☐☐☐☐☐☐☐☐
Card expiry date ........................................
Cardholder's signature .............................
All cheques payable to Lennard Associates
Telephone credit card orders accepted
on 0582 715866.
Send orders to: Lennard Associates Ltd,
Windmill Cottage, Mackerye End,
Harpenden, Herts AL5 5DR